To Charles Baker, without whose long companionship this work could not have been imagined. And to my children, Brook and Clea, who have been most patient with the twists and turns in my career. And to my parents, whose talents are responsible for what talent I have to bring to the work.

And to everyone at Riverdog Fine Arts Foundry, in both its incarnations, and to the crew at Walla Walla Foundry and to the many here on the island who have assisted me in this truly collaborative effort. My lifelong thanks.

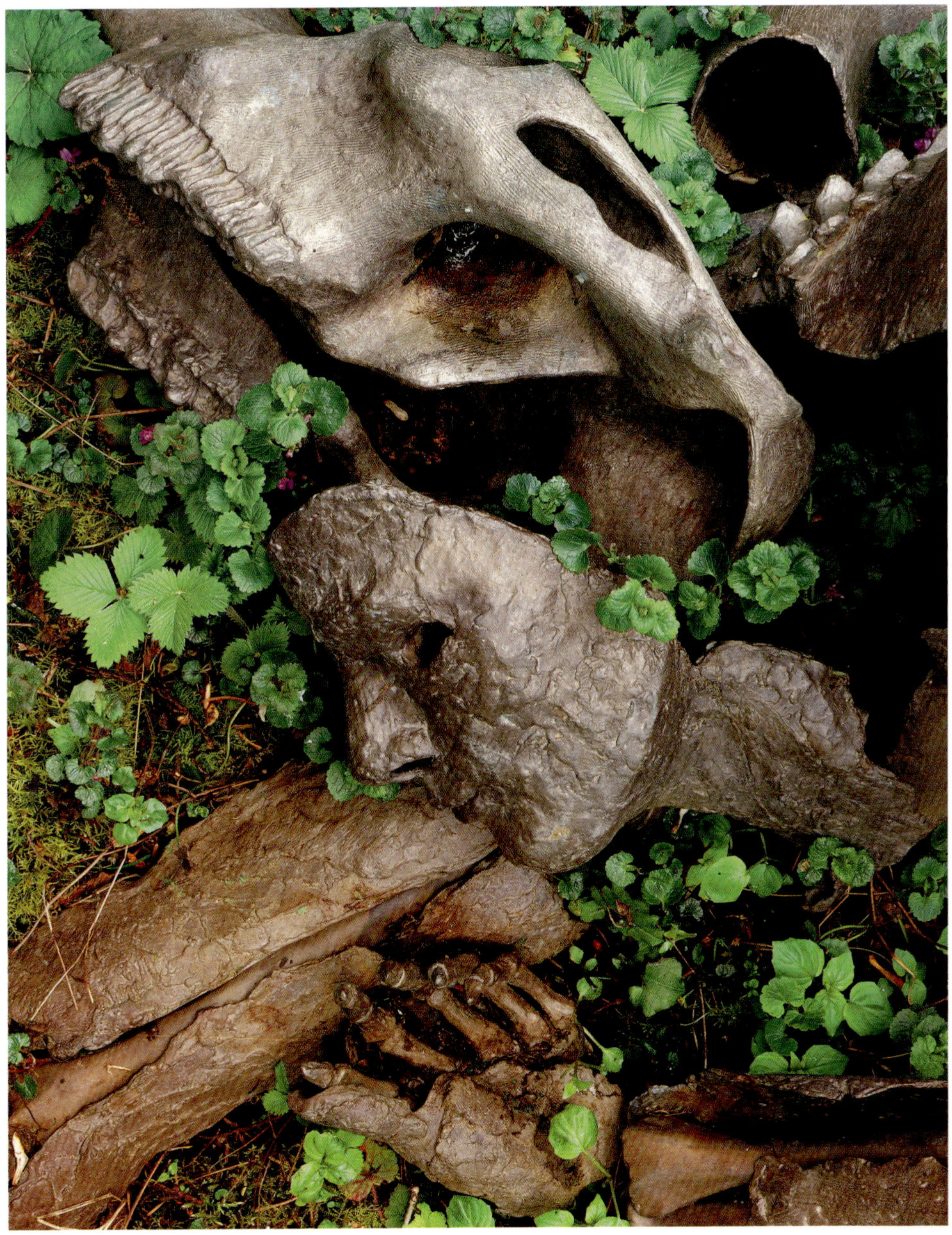

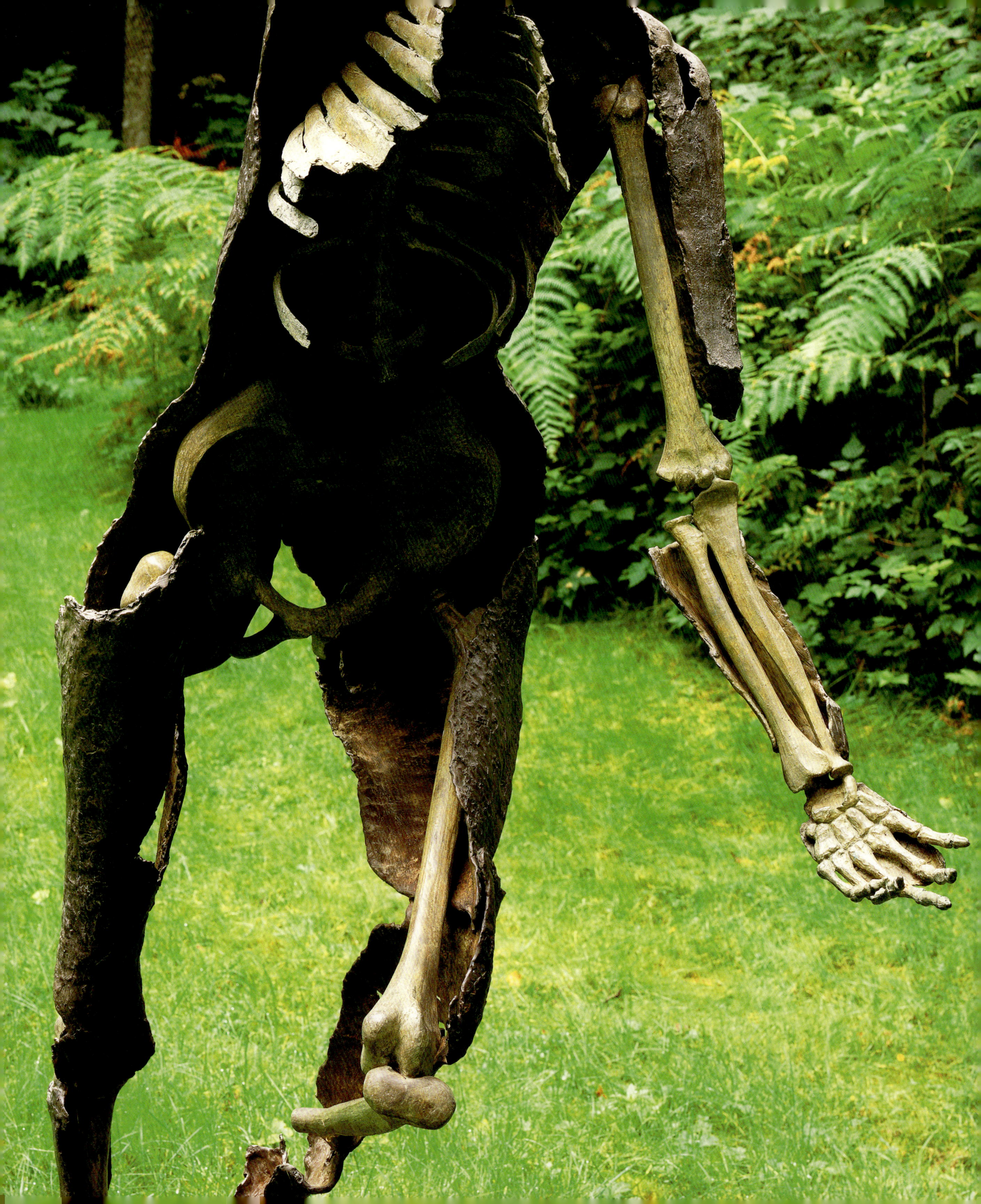

Ted Lindberg
Jake Seniuk

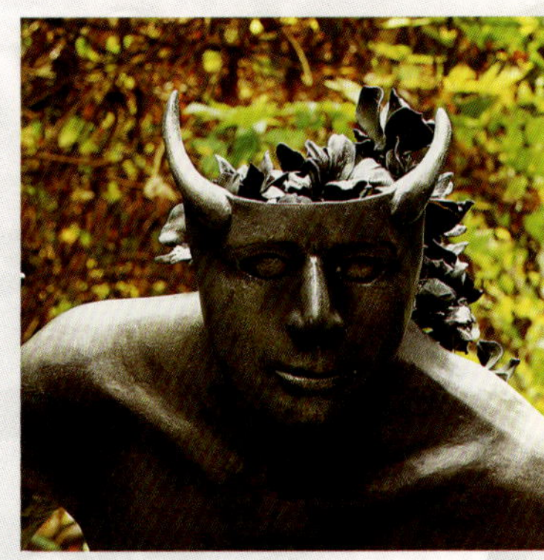

Sculpture Woods

Studio Grounds of Ann Morris

Museum of Northwest Art
La Conner, Washington

CONTENTS

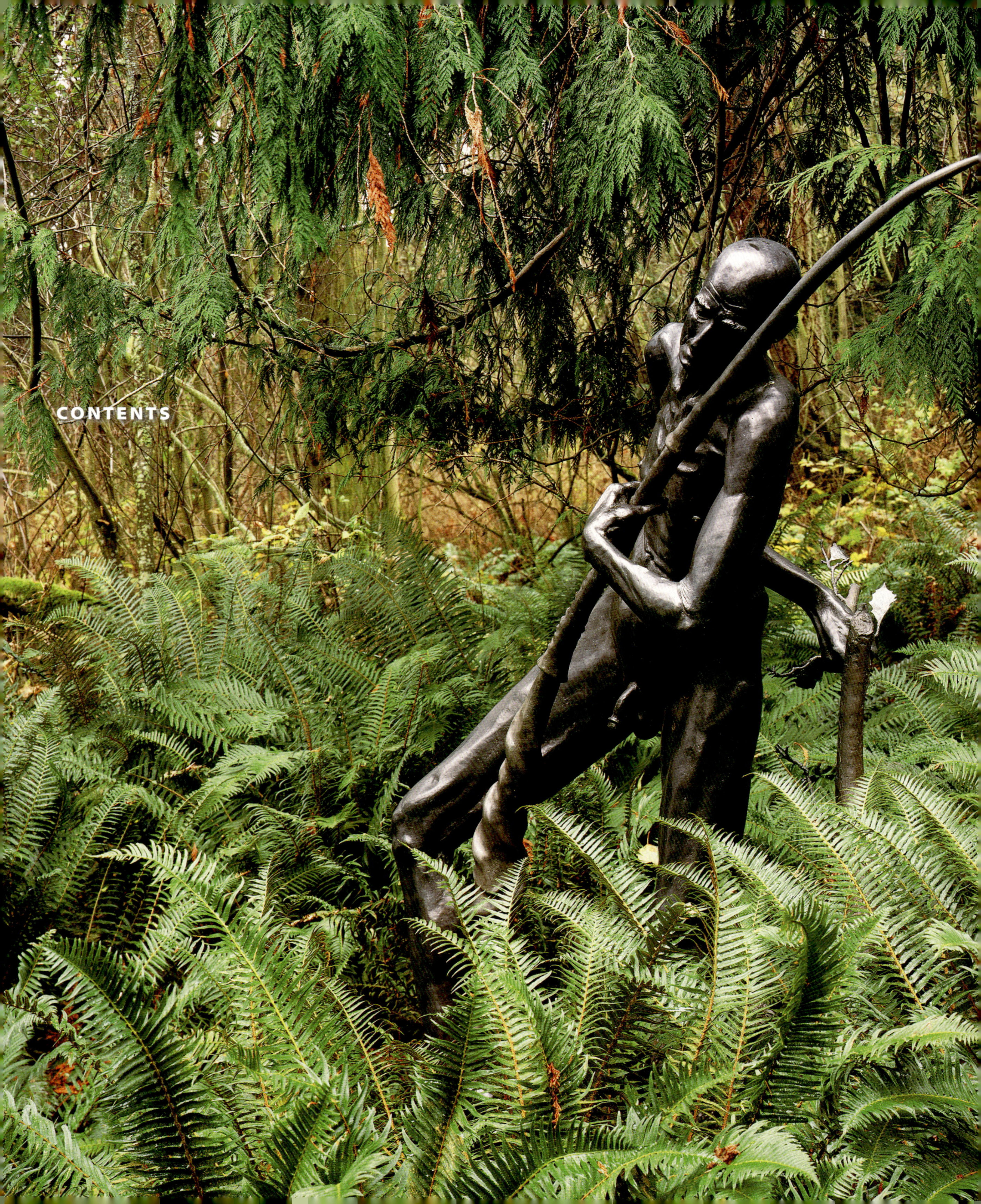

FOREWORD

Ann Morris creates her own paths—in the Sculpture Woods she has shaped on a fifteen-acre wooded plot on Lummi Island in western Washington State, and in her passion to manifest her inner thoughts and philosophy in tangible form.

From her early career as a printmaker, through the evolutions of her sculpture, the force of her intentions has driven Morris. When she wanted to learn silkscreen printing, she sought out a master, Guy Williams at Pasadena Art Museum. When the figure attracted her interest, she studied anatomy with noted Bellingham artist Tom Sherwood. When it was time to cast her work in a permanent form, she looked to Tom Jay at Riverdog Fine Arts Foundry in Chimacum.

"I am not a linear person," Morris said in 2001, "I see outlines, shapes, and color. With silkscreen, I had a medium in which to develop a [visual] language of my own."[1] By the 1970s, her visual vocabulary had expanded and for the next twenty years the figure became her focus for an ambitious exploration of personal creation myths. *Life/Death/Life* (1994) exemplifies her attempts to articulate the human spirit in relation to the cycles of nature. The bronze, larger-than-life female form, protected by oversized antlers, reclines into a grassy knoll. While parts of the figure are "fleshed out," other areas are skeletal. She seems to be both settling into the earth and rising up from it, a representation of both mortality and regeneration.

The bones and the animal structures that played a part in the allegorical figurative works of the 1990s have now assumed a role of their own as Morris explores what may be her most fruitful and successful work to date. "The figure seems to have left my mind, and bowls and bones are the images I am working with now."[2] In the series *Bone Journey,* Morris combines her fascination with bones (which, she writes, "are given form by the forces of each individual life and support it, but [whose] beauty is invisible until after death"[3]) with vessels or boats or pods to represent symbolically the human journey through nature and time.

More recently still, the bones themselves, often enlarged to monumental proportions, have become subject matter for Morris. These outsized renderings from actual bones have an almost confrontational presence that at once commands attention to their structure and beauty.

Whatever the path of Morris's journey, the lush landscape of the Pacific Northwest, its old-growth forests, its water and the natural cycles of life, death, and rebirth, inform the artist's work.

In 2001, many of the works from the Sculpture Woods were featured in the Museum of Northwest Art exhibition *In the Garden of Myth and Logic.* It is a testament to the artist that they retained their integrity when transferred from primal forest to "white cube." The museum is pleased to endorse this publication, which provides the record to date of a memorable career.

Susan Parke
Curator of Collections and Exhibitions
Museum of Northwest Art
(August 2005)

1. Ann Morris to Barbara Starker James, March 2001.
2. Ann Morris to Susan Parke, August 25, 2003.
3. Artist's statement, 2003.

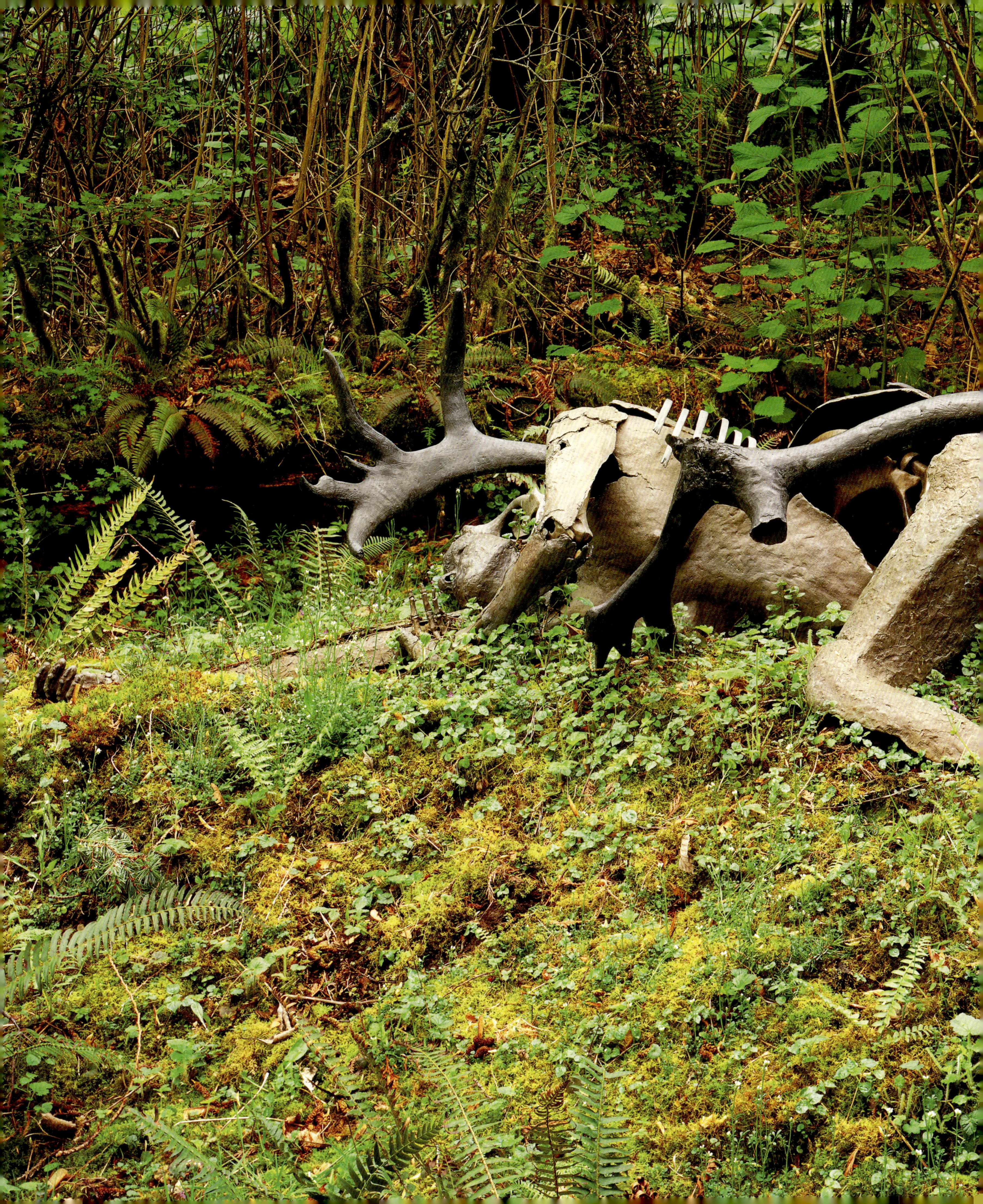

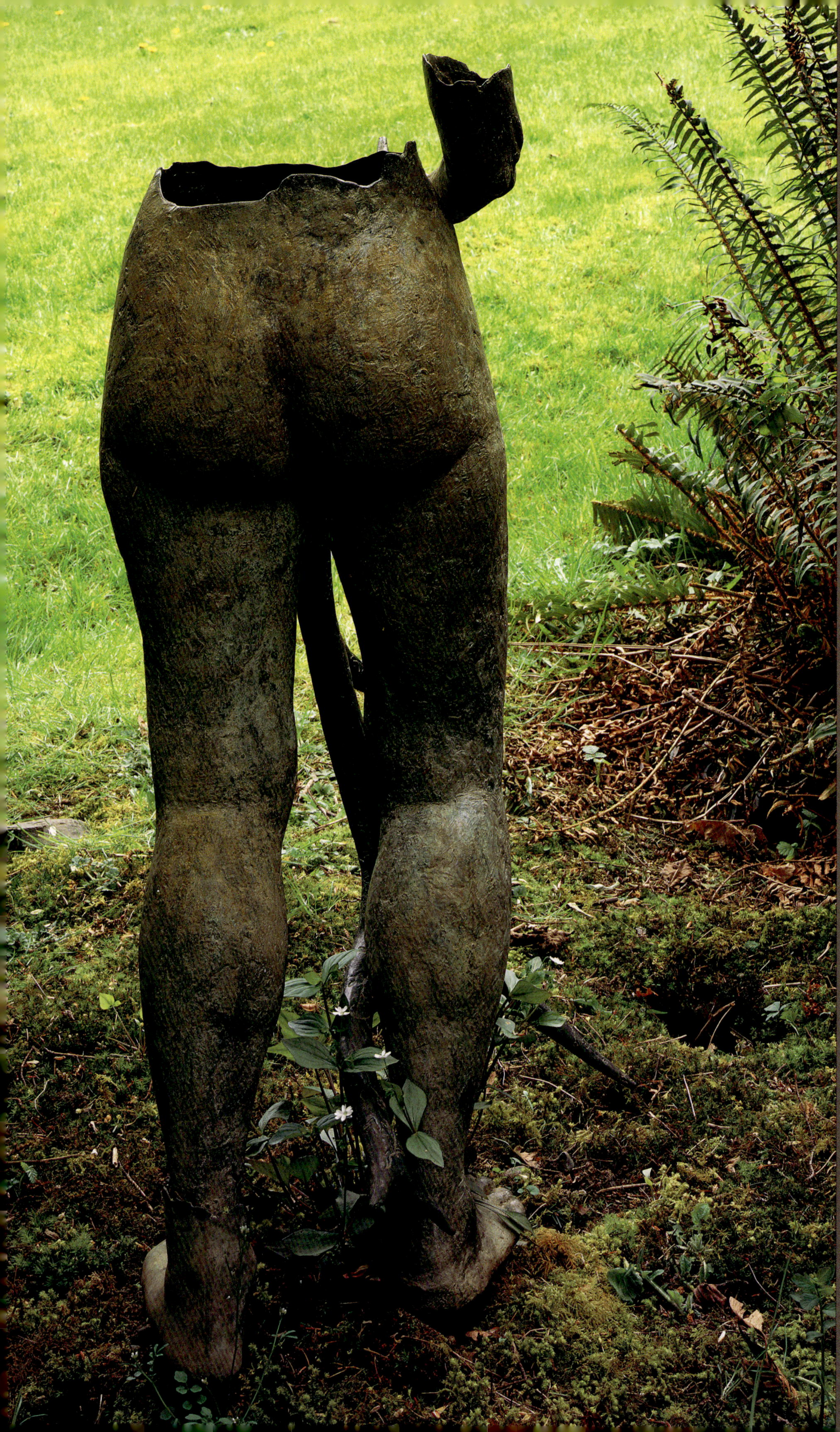

Sculpture Woods

BY TED LINDBERG

ON A FORESTED LUMMI ISLAND SEAFRONT ON PUGET Sound are fifteen acres inhabited by a series of primal and enigmatic cast bronze figures. Human forms—male, female, sometimes both—meld with animal horns or branched configurations, signaling deliberate, arresting transformation. Mythic creatures mingle with the deities of the natural world. The sculptures have become consciously integrated with nature. They share with the trees, ferns and grasses, boulders and moss, the endless cycles of light, weather, birth, death, and renewal. This environmental melding hints at purpose and meaning.

The mysterious bronze figures share the landscape with their creator, Ann Morris, whose home and studio are close by. The sculptures are parables of the artist's profound spiritual and ecological engagement, and constitute a rambling, quasi-narrative installation. Their detailed realism makes them perfectly accessible. Yet compared to more familiar commemorative or decorative sculpture, they are cloaked in mystery and anomaly, as if Morris wants the viewer to go away wondering, because that is how and where transcendental experience begins.

Morris has christened this place Sculpture Woods.

Beginnings

Sculpture Woods is the culmination of Morris's lifelong quest to give form to the difficult concept of "being." A self-described autodidact, Morris has always set her own pace and combined art, philosophy, and mythology. She has sought more than the formal, art-for-art's-sake exploration of methods and materials. She has guarded herself against peer-group conformity and popular or avant-garde movements and has steamed ahead with her own vision.

Ann Morris was born in New York City, but she grew up in tiny Osborn, Ohio, a place small and rural enough for her to walk out of town to the country and wade the creeks to their end. Her father served in the Air Force and worked in nearby Wright Patterson Field, and perhaps more importantly to Morris, he was also an inventor. It is to him Morris attributes her ability to solve problems with her hands. Her mother, a professional watercolorist, she credits with shaping her aesthetic sensibilities.

Morris's grandmother, a poet, an independent woman who lived alone in a cottage above a river in Vermont, influenced her most of all. She would write letters to her granddaughter—in green ink, Morris remembers—describing the doings of the family of muskrats who lived on the bank below her. Morris vividly remembers the gift her grandmother sent for her tenth birthday, a box containing a turtle shell and a pair of grouse wings. How could she have known the gift would kindle Morris's lifelong interest in bones, animal artifacts, and skeletal remnants?

Morris became fascinated with road kill and wildlife misadventure, and like more than a few little girls, assumed the solemn responsibilities of neighborhood priestess and undertaker, burying the departed in shoe boxes topped with flowers. Unlike the other girls, young Ann would wait long enough for disintegration to set in and then dig up the remains to see what had happened. These were her first experiences with life, death, and transformation.

Morris's art maintains the same aura of earnest, childlike wonderment and awe about "things" and animist objects. Her focus, from the beginning, was not on curios such as hunters' trophies and taxidermy but on primal, ultimately beautiful talismanic forms. The child paleontologist.

She read C. S. Lewis, Joseph Campbell, classical Greek, Roman and Celtic mythology, Arthurian legend, with a particular interest in the shape-shifting seer, magus and sorcerer, Merlin. She has been a receptive reader of "The White Goddess," Robert Graves's study of the ancient fertility goddess. She later read Carl Jung, that enthusiastic interpreter of mythology and the originator of male and female "archetypes" and "collective unconscious."

She finished her formal education in Southern California. In a single year, 1956, the year she graduated cum laude from Pomona College with a degree in philosophy, she was studying Plato one moment, the next was married, and the next became pregnant with her first child, a son. These events alone could shape the direction of her prolonged metaphysical journey.

Silkscreens

It was only after her children—she bore a daughter in 1961—started school and her husband had begun a law career that she began a serious study of art, though at the time, it seemed serendipitous. A friend accompanied Morris to learn silkscreen printing. Uncannily, as the process was being explained, Morris felt she knew in advance what the instructor was going to say next. "It felt like coming home," she says. Her only work space was the kitchen table in a small house, so when a class was offered at the Pasadena Art Museum she signed up just to have a place to work. By now it was the mid-sixties and she immersed herself at the Pasadena Art Museum's graphic arts program. It is in Morris's early prints that the issues that have consistently engaged her art first made their appearance.

She encountered difficulty with linear drawing, she says, but found initial achievement with the manipulation of shape and color in the silkscreen printing process. For a time, the process itself was enough. Her prints tended to be carefully designed, landscape-oriented, and atmosphere-evoking expressions, which often conjured up the element of water. There were biomorphic shapes—Morris speaks of them as "promiscuous parts" which suggest the time-space randomness of collage—in pastel color values, transparent washes, rainbows, and amorphous "clouds" held in some kind of restraint. Notably, the cloud shapes may have evinced her inchoate desire to express the ungraspable: the psycho-spiritual issues that accompanied environmental and social change. An early print, *Metaphysics* (1970)—which she has described as "clouds escaping through the silver bars of a box"—illustrates this perfectly.

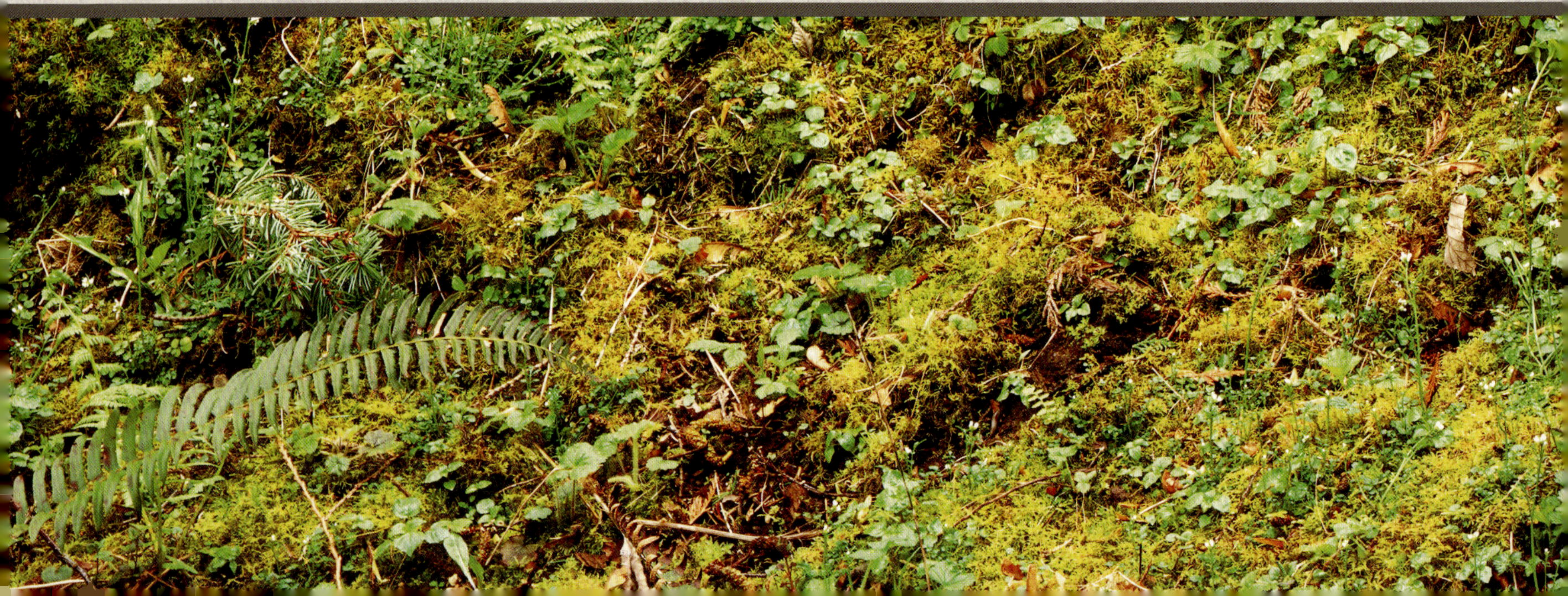

When her teacher, a painter, left the Pasadena Art Museum to teach at Pomona College, he invited Morris to take his place giving printmaking classes, which she did for several years, 1968–1972, thus launching her art career. Morris's portfolio of photographic reproductions and critical reviews from this period reveal a broad progression of experimentation as well as the critical shift from two to three dimensions. The sixties feminist movement opened non-traditional artistic roles to increasing numbers of women, allowing them to seize areas of competence long assumed to be a male terrain. The very boundaries between "art" and "craft" were suddenly in for readjustment and redefinition. Morris began her serious work at this yeasty time.

The increased emphasis on women's art brought to the fore artists such as Judy Chicago, who in 1979 distinguished herself with the highly publicized installation *The Dinner Party,* and whom Morris met at the Women's Building in Los Angeles while she was writing and printing her letterpress version of *Word Dreams, A Creation Myth* (1982).

Word Dreams traveled widely in "artist book" shows and now resides in several library collections. *Word Dreams,* as it turned out, became a kind of graphic and linguistic mandala: a poem accompanied by illustrations of pared-down, circular forms, which defined a Buddhist representation of the universe, the ball, coupled with the Jungian archetype of a circle held to symbolize a striving for unity of self and of completeness. With these, Morris invents a wondrous beginning and ending of it all—a yin and yang of shadow and light spun out in words. A dichotomous universe.

Water Sculpture 1975–1980

Morris's move from two- to three-dimensional work came about inadvertently. To display a water mural she began making envelopes of clear vinyl to protect it, and decided to fill one with actual water.

"Suddenly," she recalls, "all the images I had been struggling with in two dimensions were realized in three dimensions with water as the medium. Clear water naturally conducts color, reflects color, casts shadows and rainbows, [and at the same time] creates volume with strong surfaces and edges. My task was to use the qualities which water naturally possesses and to present them simply. The beauty of water in itself was what I wished the work to express." Photos of the early water sculpture *Homage* (1975) suggest a hanging transparent vinyl frieze of repeated cup-like shapes filled with water. One can easily imagine the play of light, refraction, displacement, and subtle movement around such a phenomenological piece.

These formal statements, columns of contained water arranged in groups against flat white reflective backing, also meant for Morris a step (albeit a temporary one) into complete abstraction. Most significantly, she made the great leap to sculpture, once and for all.

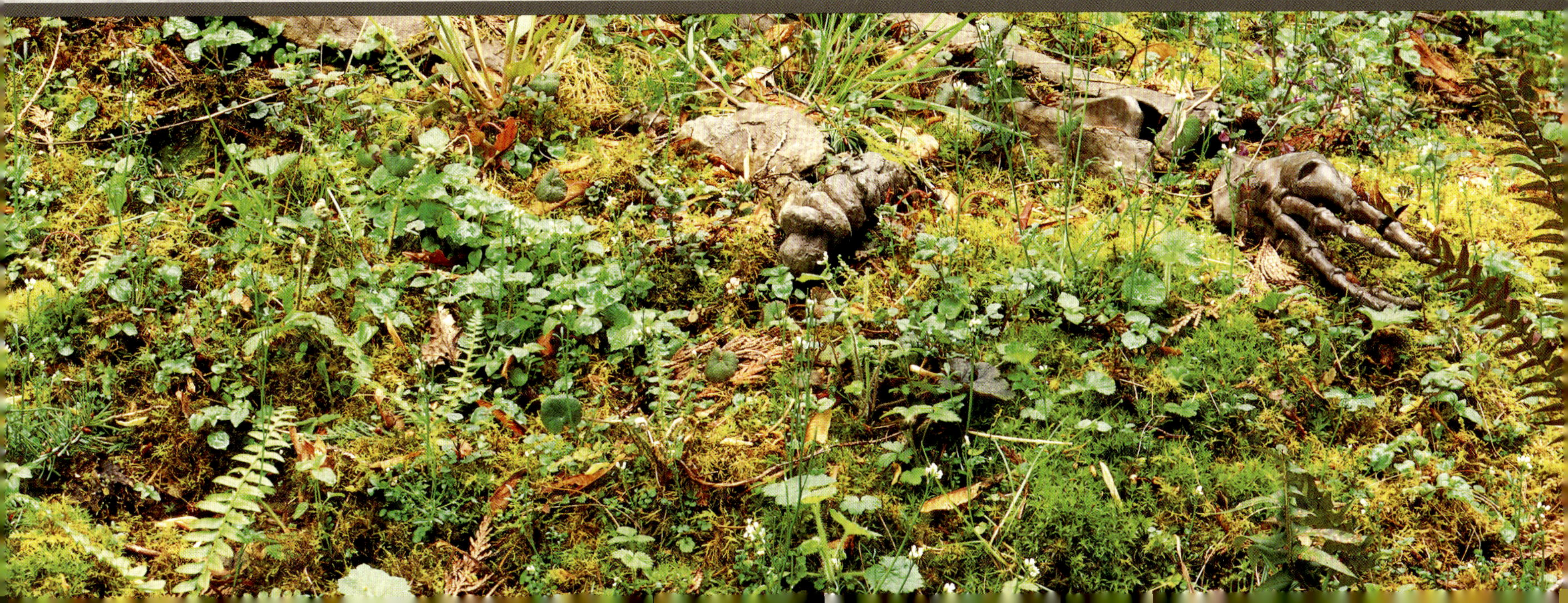

Plaster Works in Assemblage

1980–1990

Morris continued to experiment with new materials and effects. She explored assemblage—the three-dimensional collaging of disparate objects and materials—and she discovered casting with plaster. She could not have foreseen how her forays into plaster and assemblage would come to express her developing and deepest beliefs about selfhood, her identity as a human being, a woman, wife, mother—and her deepening relationship to the natural world and its environmental hazards.

She began by taking impressions from her own body—certainly one way of mirroring selfhood.

True to her autodidactic methods, Morris embarked on this new phase independently of developments in the art world. By this time pop art sculptor George Segal had been creating impressions directly from the human figure by wrapping it with plaster-soaked fiber and cloth originally developed to make casts for broken limbs. Segal had even published a widely distributed paper about the technique. Even so, Morris did not learn of Segal's methods until she had been working with plaster for several years.

While the casting of "life masks" and "death masks" had been practiced historically, the notion of casting body parts and even whole, often clothed, human figures, had heretofore been about carving or welding or accretively building a three-dimensional object, and the modeling of plastic materials such as clay and wax. As well, there was the question of whether or not casting from a characterless mannequin could be considered a work of art. The pop art movement simply asked, "Why not?" Everything was a matter of definition. And definitions themselves were ever changing in the fine art canon.

The decade of the eighties was one of emergence, both technically and philosophically for Morris. As each new concept for a piece came to her, she was faced with fresh technical issues, and forced to find the tools and means to put it together. The early plaster works incorporated castings of faces, arms, and legs. She arranged them in assemblages of found objects, thrift-store furniture, and hat stands. Natural elements—branches, horns, bones, and skulls—found their way into these compositions, almost from the beginning. These were not just handy and available props; they presaged the need for deeper, iconic ingredients in her work. She used what she had collected, giving the objects new functions and meanings.

Plant forms, vines, and leaves surrounded and blanketed recumbent figures closer to the living earth. Morris experimented with coloring and texturing the plaster, moving ever nearer to the qualities she would find most achievable in bronze.

"My body's relation to the world is very important to me," she wrote in an artist's statement in 1983. "It is how I keep in touch with life, how I touch life back. It is the way my energy is released and how my energy is drawn in."

There is a kind of poetry in letting moldy plaster figures crumble and dissolve into the ground, which is what she did in her first work on Lummi Island. In 1985, she made five casts of herself in cement, clay, plaster and wood, plaster and copper. She installed them as supine relics in a cedar grove and allowed them to disintegrate into the land, and let time and weather reclaim them. She felt "their return to the earth was acceptance into her new place."

As Morris became more proficient with the figurative technique, she enlisted friends to lend part or all of their bodies to the casting process. Whereas her early efforts sometimes produced disarticulated combinations of faces and limbs, which resembled

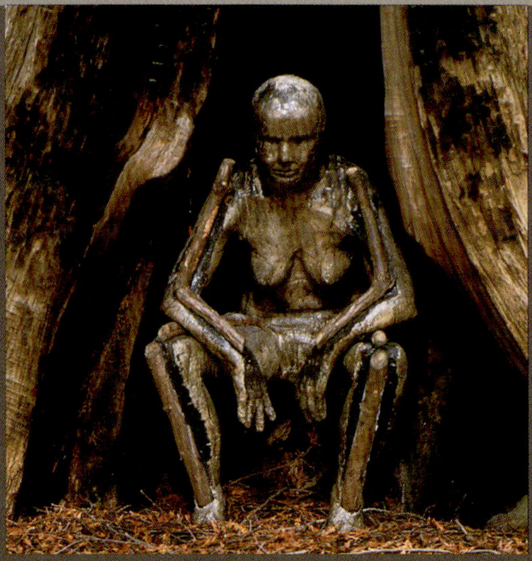

GUARDIAN (PLASTER/WOOD)

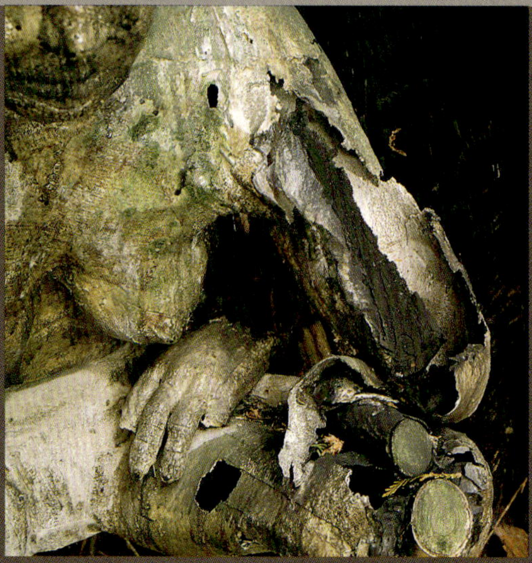

GUARDIAN (DETAIL)

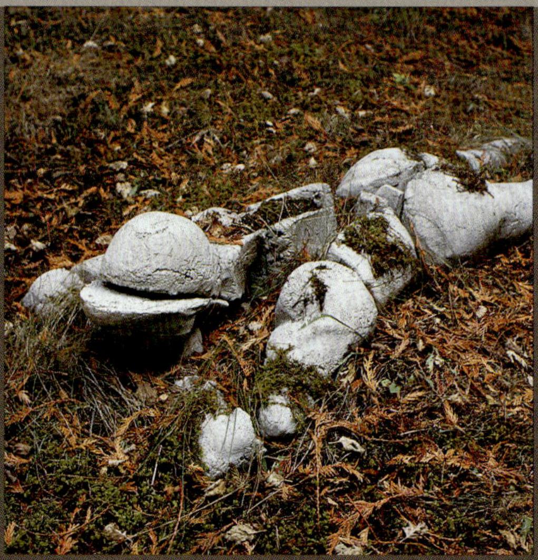

MOSS WOMAN (CONCRETE)

mannequin parts in a store window, Morris shows a growing understanding of anatomy and composition. She found that even disparate parts could be made to flow in invisible lines that the eye could easily follow—like the intervals of silence between musical notes.

In the earliest plaster period, Morris's figures appear stodgy and doughlike. They seem to have been cast from subjects in body stockings, or they evoke the plaster Pompeian body-casts derived from hollowed-out volcanic ash. Gradually though, the figures take on sharper and clearer definition.

Toward the end of these learning experiments, Morris began using male and female figures together and increasingly sought ways to express the meaning of these relationships. "I want to explore the mystery of the interaction between spirits male and female, and to enlarge my own awareness of the Great Spirit which is completely male and completely female," she wrote about her work in 1988. "By casting real bodies, I hope to turn the human being back into myth, exposing the universal male/female duality of the universe which it is our task to discover if we are to be truly human."

While Morris was mastering the very necessary technical skills for the sculptor she aspired to be—the modeling and mold-making subtleties that would lead her to the lost-wax method of bronze casting—a fuller grasp of anatomy permitted her to manipulate plastic sculptural materials directly. She also rehearsed and further defined her spiritual and philosophical agenda.

When Morris was ready, the move from plaster to bronze was a natural one, made on grounds of permanence, weathering qualities, and the sheer nobility of bronze among artists' mediums. Gold and silver signify opulence; bronze denotes, somehow, venerableness. No matter how sealed and protected, plaster objects cannot endure time in the open. Bronze casting would change all this. While there was a sense of justice and rightness in permitting the natural disintegration of the pieces exposed to the elements (as would certainly occur), she wanted more permanent resolutions. Morris wanted to create work that would outlast her own life, that possessed permanence and could bear out and convey her artistic legacy.

Morris wanted to take her work out of doors and into natural surroundings. Her work would no longer be confined inside standard gallery space—an environment sometimes referred to as "the white cube"—with its formal viewing aspects and hygienic white plinths. With growing assurance, she was prepared to create her own pantheon of mythical deities. The figures, drawn from mythology and modern psychology, would exist in an Arcadian surround. They would state a three-dimensional vision of psychic balance and ecology. They would foster ontological and metaphysical issues. They would urge wonderment and provoke questions from the viewer. Perhaps, in unforeseen ways, they would supply answers.

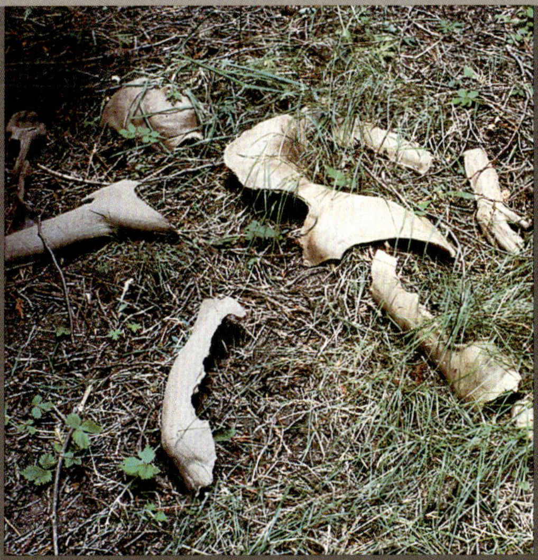

Weed Woman (fired clay)

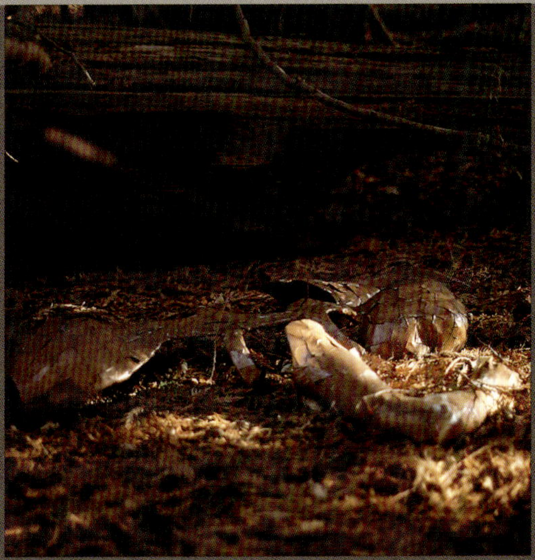

Copper Woman (plaster/copper)

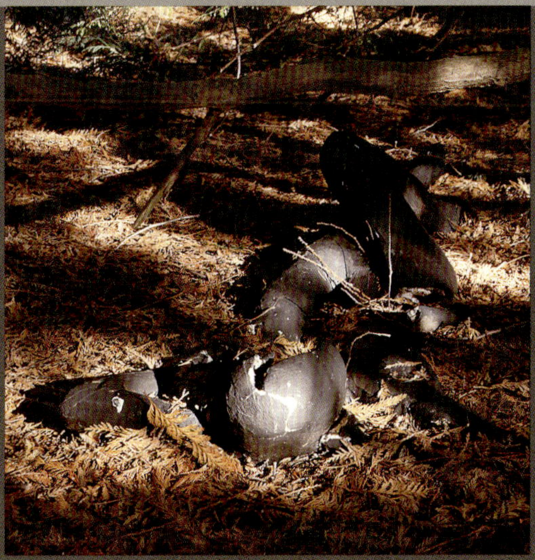

Water Level Woman (plaster/tar)

Bronze Figures 1990–2001

In the 1990s Morris began an ambitious project, a series of sixteen large figures cast in bronze. She calls the series *Figuration of the Human Spirit* and the sculptures are now permanent residents of the land around her studio, sited on the fifteen acres of Sculpture Woods. As with her earlier work, Morris wrote poetic statements of meaning and intent to accompany the visual images.

Morris began her cast-bronze series with *She of the Piece* in 1992, a mixed-media assemblage that is today installed on the deck of her studio building. Fittingly, it "begins at the beginning." That is, the first piece Morris made for this new body of work was an arresting self-portrait, a statement of self-identity and self-actualization.

A female figure stands to her waist in water contained in an enormous bronze vessel with a flared lip. This, in turn, stands on a flattened chunk of native granite. The figure and vessel are bracketed by the longitudinally split, curved trunk of a driftwood beach log that evokes the tusks of an elephant. The figure is "coifed" with the curving horns of a cape buffalo, implying (à la paleontologist Louis Leakey's proto–Earth Mother, Lucy) a primeval Africanness about this bronze, wood, and water tableau. With one hand, the implacable woman tests the sharpness of her horn, which is in direct contrast to the softness of her arched, full breasts. Morris conjures a mythic woman, oblivious of Edenic original sin: the curse of a hapless Eve-kind.

Newsbringer (1992), earlier exhibited and photographed in its plaster incarnation, is a hollowed, lower female torso with a right forearm holding a curved antler spike. The horn not only protects her groin but is inscribed with a ring of Anasazi runes that suggest an integrated masculinity—and perhaps what femininity meant in other times.

In an ironic twist, *Newsbringer* may momentarily bring to mind Percy Bysshe Shelley's "Ozymandias," a cautionary poem about the futility of erecting ostensibly timeless monuments to oneself.

> Two vast and trunkless legs of stone
> Stand in the desert. Near them, on the sand,
> Half sunk, a shattered visage lies, whose frown,
> And wrinkled lip, and sneer of cold command,
> Tell that its sculptor well those passions read,
> Which yet survive, stamped on those lifeless things,
> The hand that mocked them, and the heart that fed . . .

Double Dream (1993) involves four figures: the two larger, a seemingly somnambulant, mature man and woman, bear on their backs the opposed, scaled-down figures of smooth and lush adolescents, male and female. The smiling, youthful figures, oblivious of their bearers, attempt to lock hands as the sober or preoccupied adult figures move laterally apart. Morris recounts that this configuration was originally a dream image; that the adolescents are psychic figures. How can one escape the poignance of Eros being displaced by Thanatos—or perhaps more entrancingly, of two primal male-female instincts perpetually entwined in some universal Unconscious?

Her Cry (1993) presents a pregnant, proudly erect, and defiant female figure, whose head consists of the lower portion of Morris's own face, deeply helmeted in a cow's skull and horns. She, like the *Newsbringer,* girds herself with a bowed rack of caribou horns, symbolic of Nature, evoking a mystical totemic bond with fierce mammalian protective instinct.

As the series progressed, Morris continued her exploration of the feminine, through representations of the ancient mother

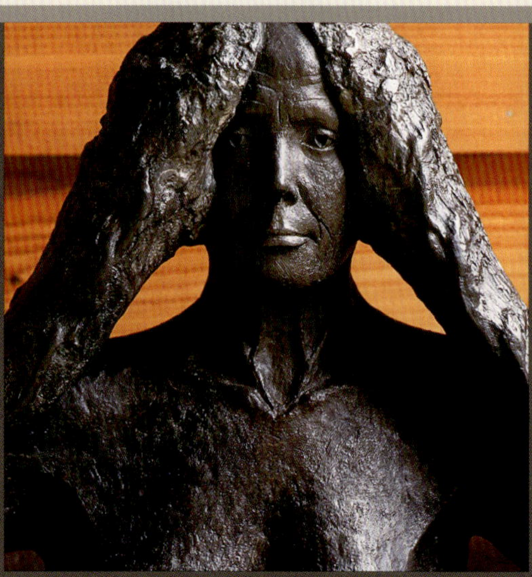

She of the Piece

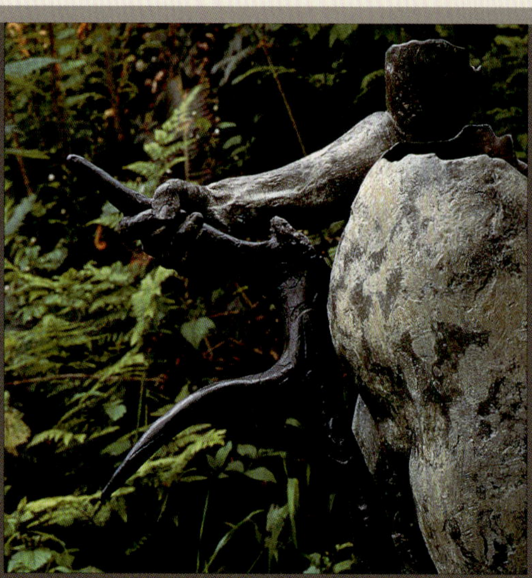

Newsbringer

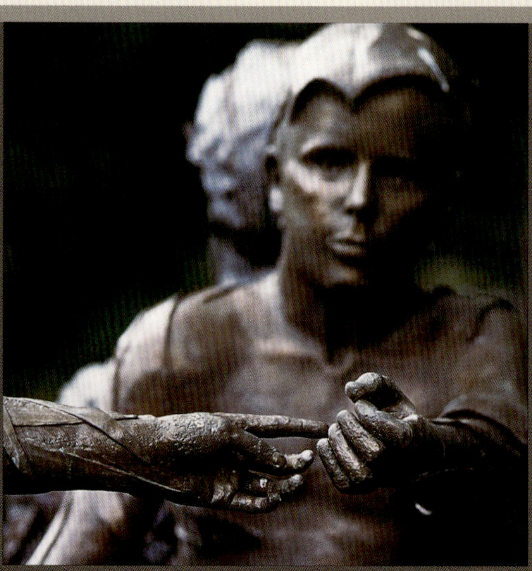

Double Dream

goddess Gaia, goddesses or mythic figures signifying fertility, nature, sexuality. In several of Morris's bronze pieces, female figures are crowned or protect themselves with horns. Representations of horned women date back as early as the Egyptian goddess Hathor, known as protector and nourisher of the living (and later, protector of the dead) in the eighteenth dynasty, 1587 to 1375 B.C.E. Through this personal iconography, Morris endeavors to create a unique definition of "woman," raised once again to the mythic power and grandeur that existed before the Judeo-Christian invention of taboos and patriarchal relegation of the "weaker vessel."

The horned, magisterial female figure kneeling amidst a delicate rack of caribou horns in *Will There Be a Place for Me?* (1994) may initially remind one of Diana, the mythological goddess of the hunt, the moon, and fertility. Behind the masklike face is the verdured Lummi Island forest-surround of the piece—which recalls Dylan Thomas's metaphor for the life force: the "Green Fuse," the source of her special, unerring knowledge.

The iconography that Morris invented as she progressed is actually quite accessible—like any historical religious iconography—once one is made aware of the semiotics and semantics. Morris draws on elements as ancient as cave drawings of the Stone Age shaman—part human, part deer—as unexpectedly credible and strangely beautiful as Nijinski transmuted into a faun; as symbolically assertive as the impulse of elevating the acquiescent Earth Mother into a feminized Minotaur proclaiming the labyrinths of dim, vestigial memory carried in our blood and bones.

Siting is everything. Ann Morris's mythical figures seem to demand outdoor settings, insist on the natural chaos and randomness, fecundity and rot, the seasons and cycles of life and death. The venerable, patinaed bronze surfaces impart the feeling that everything is relic—the dance is stilled, the pantomime frozen—yet in their discovery and recognition, the spirit is lingering and eloquent. Rather than seeking monumentality in her forms, Morris nurtures integration and oneness.

Life/Death/Life (1994) is an allegory of the commonality of all living existence and its eternal cycle of atomic redistribution: a strangely comforting emblem of our collective presence (in one molecular form or another) at the Beginning and the End. This tragic, moldering female figure is embraced by the same caribou horns that *Her Cry* thrusts forward.

The closest thing to a full-blown psychosexual drama is Morris's *Dance of Life* (1995). A female figure joyfully straddling the snout of a Minotaur, the work forcefully proclaims male potency and vigor and simultaneously the illusion of female erotic rapture and transport. Almost as a disclaimer to what is unfolding before [our] eyes, Morris advises (with pure Jungian logic) "women who voluntarily journey into the inner labyrinth will discover, and can release joyous instinctual masculinity." *Dance of Life,* ultimately, reflects not just the pure heterosexual eroticism of, for instance, classical Indian sculptures (such as found in the Ajunta Caves) but suggests something far more sublime: the ultimate androgynous congress.

Ask Gaia (1996) is dramatic and beautifully hermetic, a hair-raising oracular scene out of a Federico Fellini film. All of Morris's sculptures have multiple reference points and interpretations, the mark of a strong universal and transcultural appeal. Aside from the mythical, art-historical and psychological sources of her art already cited, the term that repeatedly comes to mind is "pantheism."

Morris remains adamant about her most salient beliefs. In *Gifting the Giver* (1997), a headless, hermaphroditic figure with a rack of moose antlers on its back offers a vessel to the heavens

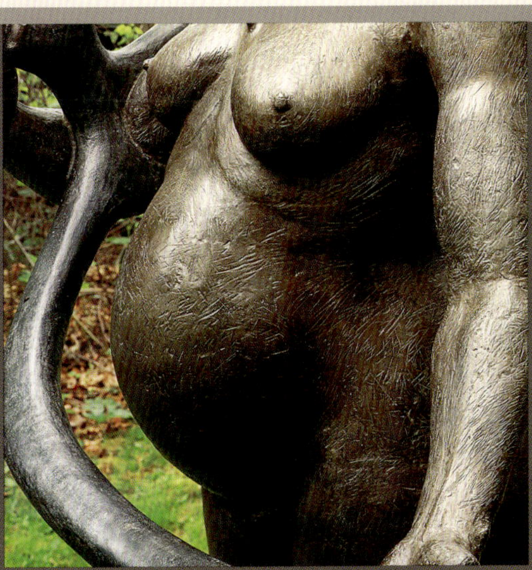

HER CRY

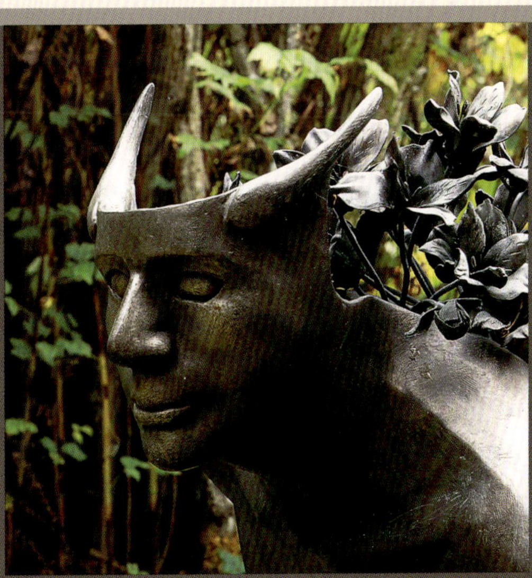

WILL THERE BE A PLACE FOR ME?

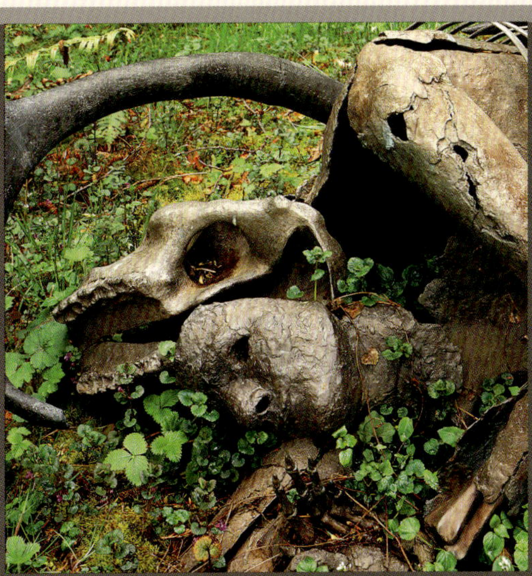

LIFE/DEATH/LIFE

in supplication. In the vessel is the face of the artist. The piece reiterates Morris's desire to balance human male and female principles, to the good of the planet. Exploitation, greed and bellicosity will give way to nurturing; hunting and endless slaughter to agriculture. Women will take on the "masculine" strength to achieve their rightful equality and co-sovereignty.

In the late nineties, Morris concentrated on a highly ambitious three-part installation powerfully imbued with Celtic mythology and Merlin in particular. Morris had by now reached the full extent of her artistic and technical skills, free and competent to imagine a powerful scenario.

King Arthur and Merlin are legendary figures of no historically verifiable domains who engendered stories of mythical lives and deeds on both sides of the pagan and Christian eras in northern Europe and the British Isles. The pre-Christian Celtic Merlin is by far the more colorful and protean character, one who takes on a Druidic priestly guise, and is variously regarded as a magus, sorcerer, and wild man of the woods and at times takes on what is seen as the role of a messianic prophet. The etymological origins of the word *druid* are varied and doubtful enough that the word may be pre-Indo-European. The widespread view is that "druid" derives from the Celtic word for an oak tree (*doire* in Irish Gaelic), a word whose root also meant "wisdom." It is said that the Celtic runes themselves were inspired by the observed crisscrossing and interstices of tree twigs against the sky.

(In a television series some years ago titled "The Body in Question," the British polymath Doctor Jonathan Miller stated that a high percentage of human DNA not only matches that of other vertebrates but that the resemblance of configuration between human DNA and that of an *oak tree* is almost as high.)

Using casts from the bodies of willing friends and neighbors, Morris speculatively imagines the arrival of Merlin to the Pacific Northwest—conjecturally similar to the Church of Latter Day Saints' placing of Jesus in the New World after his death, preaching to the aboriginal people. In *Merlin Wakes!* (1997), a lean, but distinctly muscled bronze man carrying a spiraled, tusklike lance appears to be extricating his leg from a sawn tree stump. Surely Morris's allusion here is the transfer of the male principle from hunter-warrior to one of agriculture and nurturing husbandry—man in cooperation with nature, not using his force to overcome it.

The following year, Morris produced *Becoming Merlin* (1998), in which a youthful, androgynous, apprentice sorcerer conducts himself on a primitive cart. *Not Merlin* (1998), made the same year, suggests the opposite: a contemptuous male nature that refuses to comprehend the imperatives of environmental survival, and is portrayed as a false prophet. In the context of Morris's art and belief system, it is not too far-fetched to see Merlin insinuated into the personification of the New Reconstructed Man. Who, after all, could better aspire to be an authentic consort to Gaia?

Acceptance of Sorrow (1999), because it is less dependent on iconography than other works, is more immediately accessible. A grieving female figure stands in a wide, shallow bowl filled with, Morris writes, "the water of her tears," comforting herself with the caress of fern fronds. Perhaps based on a personal tragedy in Morris's life, it represents a general human condition and the restorative power of an authentic and intimate understanding of nature.

Backbone of the Universe (1999) is a monumental dissertation on our vertebrate brotherhood and infers some subtle and not-so-subtle differences between male and female principles, hunting and agriculture, "aggression management" in pursuit of a longed-for Arcadia, and possibly even vegetarianism versus the

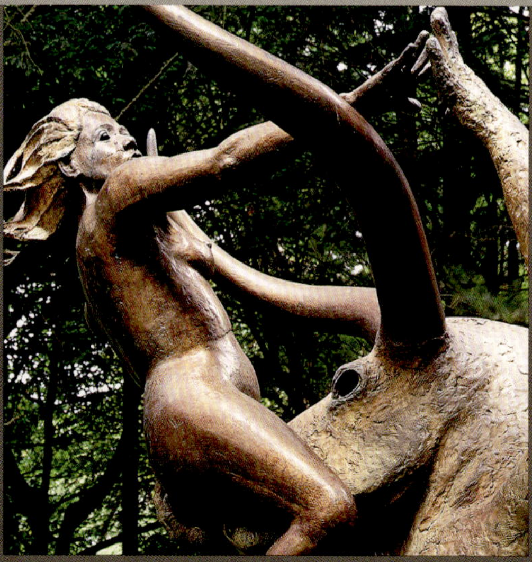

Dance of Life

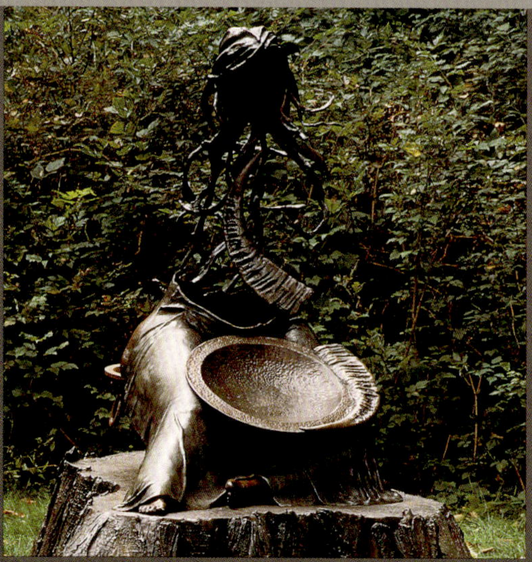

Ask Gaia

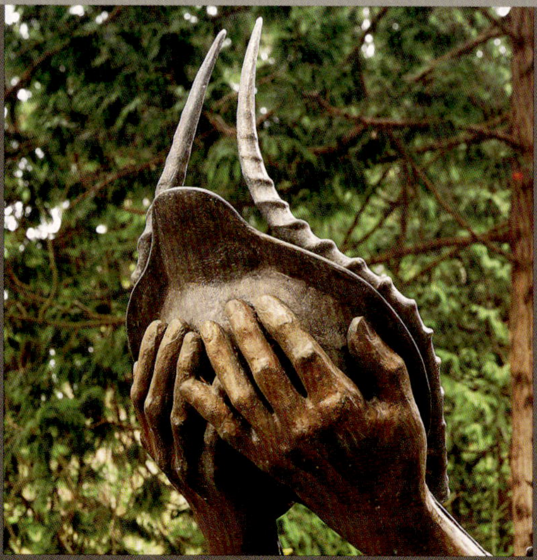

Gifting the Giver

flesh-eating proclivities of the human species. Morris tackles an enormous range of subject matter here, but it is consistent with her lively and wide-reaching ontological interest. In this piece, bone is enlarged in scale for the first time in her work.

In a grassy forest clearing, *Trinity* (2000) represents (once again) one of the artist's greatest attempts to orchestrate a very large and fervid testament of pantheist belief. The skeletons of a plant (an enlarged cholla cactus fragment), an animal (a scaled-up rendering of what she says is "perhaps a fish bone"), and a female human with her skeleton showing are adjusted into somewhat equal scale and presented as a Trinity of Life. *Trinity* is a beautiful tract, an ecological coda to Morris's entire body of cast bronzes standing in her Sculpture Woods. It is the sum and substance of her spiritual, psychological, and environmentalist senses of engagement, which she cannot and will not suppress.

If *She of the Piece* (1992), Morris's first formal bronze self-portrait, performed a new peak of her optimism and powers, the last piece in the *Figuration of the Human Spirit* series, the elegiac *Death's Sister* (2001) could be her vision of an acceptable and ultimate demise: recycling oneself back into the endless cycles of nature. At first sight, *Death's Sister* might produce a reaction of moderate shock. A hollowed, split tree stump contains the seated, desiccated figure of an apparently mummified human being. It is so realistic it might be a horror-film crime scene; or perhaps *National Geographic* magazine photos of the fifth century B.C.E. "Tollund Man"—an apparently strangled felon found in a Danish peat bog in the mid-1950s, preserved quite completely by the tannic acid in the enveloping soil.

Whatever the source, Morris's figure has a demonstrative function. The split tree trunk and skeletal human form equate arboreal and human life. The tree under certain conditions can actually regenerate. Can humans? Do we die so absolutely? In the metaphoric sense, Morris demonstrates a Druidic notion of life's all-embracing continuities.

With the casting of an artist's proof of *Death's Sister,* Morris decided on several radical changes in her direction, both in content and in scale. She concluded a roughly ten-year body of major bronze works that put forth her ontological, ecological, and aesthetic principles. She had sited these works to best advantage, in a natural setting, to commence their weathered surfacing and woodland integration.

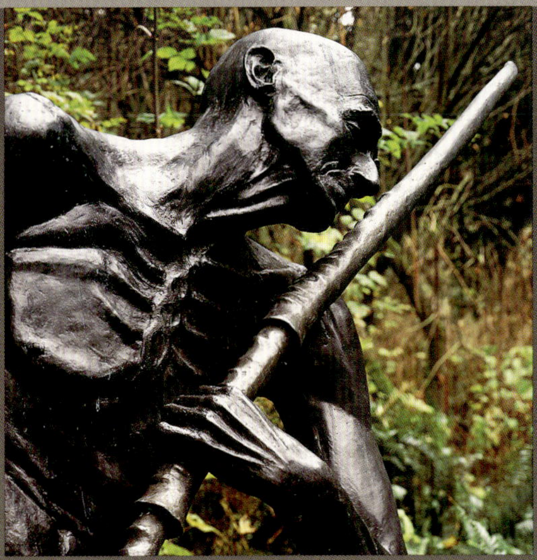

MERLIN WAKES?

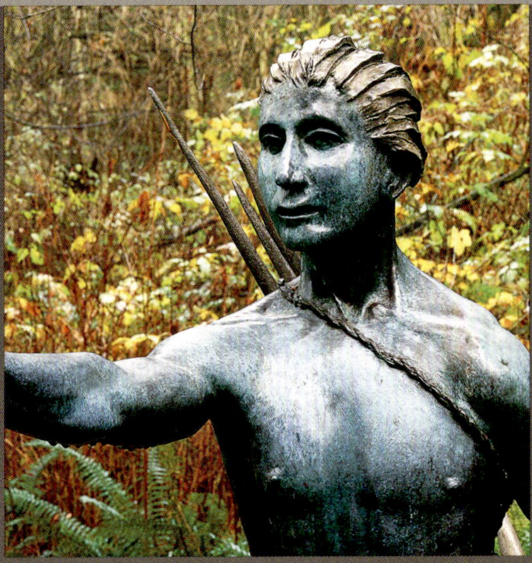

BECOMING MERLIN

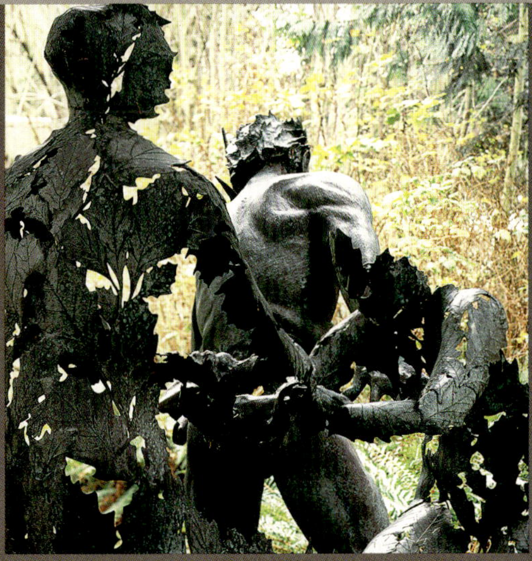

NOT MERLIN

Reliquaries and Vessels **2000–PRESENT**

What one sees in Morris's large-scale bronze works, beginning in the late nineties, is a rationalization for smaller and more readily exhibited and saleable works. Reliquaries (as containers or shrines in which sacred relics are kept) could also, by art-definition, be called assemblage. Morris in this mode seems to have chosen the most personal and intimate icons: icons more distilled and accentuated to graphically demonstrate the most potent ideas.

The Marriage Box (2000) inventively underscores the extreme importance to Morris of Jung's concept of animus and anima, the masculine and feminine components of the unconscious. The reliquary, constructed of distressed cherry-stained wood, contains a double-ended penis/vulva device in cast bronze, conjoined by antique medicine bottles (which originally contained "water and wine"—now dried residues—and the desiccated remnants of miniature flowers). Surrounding the holy box is a brocade ecclesiastical stole, and for "traveling" Morris has fashioned a chamois hammock to support the hermaphroditic effigy. The idealized marriage/union suggested here is the melding of a perfectly balanced androgynous figure—while the other symbols and trappings of "marriage" wither away. On the lid of the box, Morris has inscribed: "Each of us is two / the wedding is in the self / Whoso joins these two / shall be made whole."

The Snout Box (2000), its hinged sides bound up in a band of black-and-white cowhide, is an independent adjunct to her bronze piece *Dance of Life* which zooms in on the sensuous muzzle of the transporting Minotaur. If we have not already discerned the erotic inference of the libidinous animal, Morris makes clear the penile similarity of the snout, the vulvic outlines in the hollow of its throat.

Together with other, more delicate, vertebrate parts, she has brought to the fore another elegant talismanic object which is the archetypal shape of a vessel/leaf/pod/vulva. It is not difficult to recall the use of the term "vessel" with regard to the primary definition of "woman."

In a 2004 artist's statement, Morris writes,

> Vessels or boats are expressive of journey. Their forms are pod-like, suggesting nature's verdant growth. They float. They shape and are shaped by water—life's principal ingredient. Plants and animals are life's most abundant forms and provide us with the nourishment to continue. . . .

The vessel also becomes a kind of reliquary, such as those that contain the hallowed bone fragments of saints. As hand-built receptacles, cast in bronze, they take on the contemplative allure of the ancient Chinese temple bronzes known as "tings," which stressed balance and symmetry of form, and communicated solemnity and ceremony. Like real boats (canoes, punts, kayaks, and gondolas; dories, skiffs, and whaleboats), Morris creates vessels in endless configuration. One may well wonder if each craft is designed for its cargo or the other way around. In each case, the magical combination seems aptly struck.

Life Dugout (2001) is a classic canoe form bearing the rib cage and vertebrae of a lamb. The vessel is reddish bronze, and the rib cage, also cast bronze, is patinaed gray-white to resemble naturally bleached bone. The vessel and its contents are both majestic forms, rife with associational inferences, but very different in nature: simple and complex, man-made and nature-made, smooth and rough. An inventive child might see it as the model for a boat, figuratively propelled through the water by an organically derived bellows machine. It is least of all macabre.

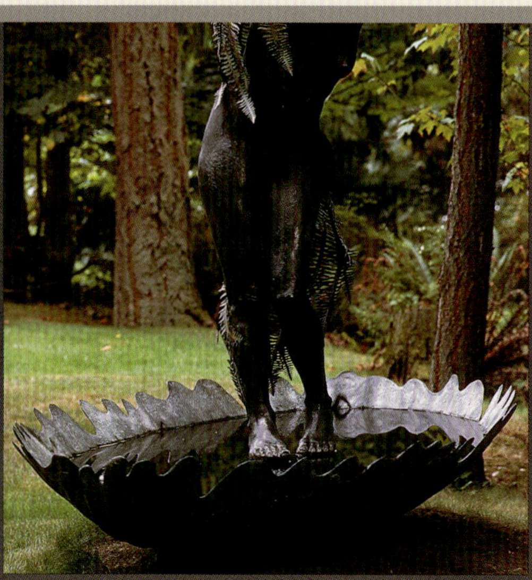

ACCEPTANCE OF SORROW

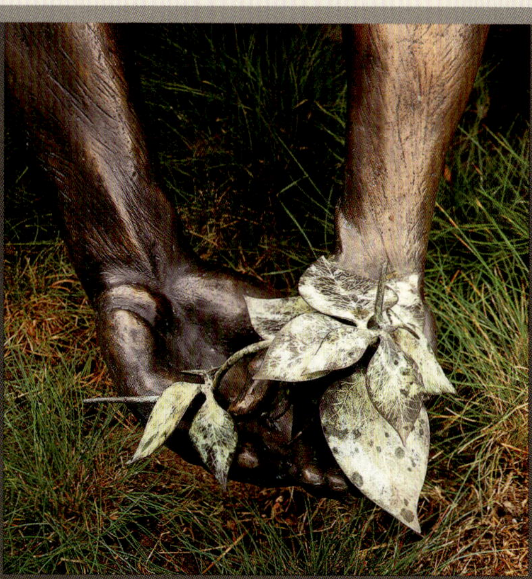

BACKBONE OF THE UNIVERSE

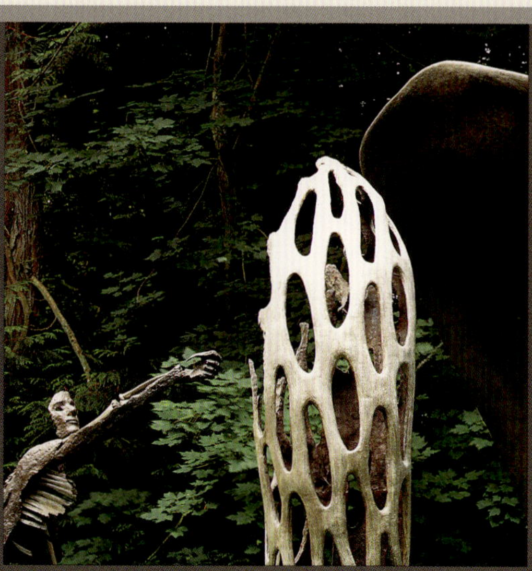

TRINITY

Morris continues along this line of differentially shaped vessels and the arrangements of their contents with a single, curved member (perhaps the one Adam lent to Eve?) in *Rib Boat* (2003). Once the viewer becomes accustomed to Morris's reverence for the sheer beauty of bones, a sense of the poetic is immediately graspable. In many other pieces, Morris employs whole, articulated skeletal portions of a bird, fish, or animal to suggest that the bony structure of the creature can dictate the direction of the shape—as if it is the natural armature of an imaginary, fleshed-out three-dimensional piece. *Heron Bowl* (2004) seems derived entirely from a heron skull and spurs, yet Morris knits its lines into a full, proportional bird shape. She achieves the same wholeness, this time in a vessel shape, in *Frog Bowl* (2005). One thinks of road kill (and Morris's childhood interest in death) and flattened, desiccated frogs brought back to life in a bizarre circular dance.

Pod Drift (2003) is an empty vessel, and perhaps its meaning is inherent in the word "drift": the idea of aimlessness. The interior is a brilliant copper oxide green, so in a sense its cargo is the phenomenon of reflected color, itself. Its lipped transom renders it momentarily fishlike.

Raven Bowl (2003) is a chalice for still another beautiful form, the beak of the raven, inverted to reveal its breathtaking lines, and doubled for a perfect symmetry. In pottery making, the mystique of the vessel is often lauded as the engine of the potter's repeated, untiring quest for the perfect form. Morris's endless variety of containing shapes is no less demonstrative.

As a separate, provocative subplot, which she has dubbed *Bone Journey,* Morris heightened her serious attention to bones and animal parts, seeking to raise them to the level of exotic found objects, and sculpturally rendering them anew in wax and bronze. Enlarging their scale and displaying them as objets d'art, as she had already performed in her cast bronze piece *Backbone of the Universe,* she creates an effect much the same as the underscored presence of a natural piece of river rock, turned just so in a Zen monastery garden. She introduces *Bone Journey* in an artist's statement:

> I have always been fascinated with bones. They are forms that grow. Bones are given form by the forces of each individual life and support it, but their beauty is invisible until after death. They are the synthesis of life's function and form, death's architectural remains.
>
> . . . Combining bones and vessels becomes for me a Bone Journey, a symbol of my own journey through Nature and Time. Each of our journeys is one of life and death. These vessels are its echo.

Of the freestanding and rescaled bone pieces, it is of little artistic importance whether the object is correctly identified as (for instance) a scapula, ilium, or femur. Morris chose the bones and fragments for their appearance as abstract forms. By altering their scale and remodeling their intrinsic shapes, she has further abstracted them away from their animal origins. This distancing from the source gives us a moment to regard the piece purely as form, composition, and effect as sculpture, not as a scientific anatomical display. "Nature is the true sculptor," Morris writes. "My wish is to present these forms at a confrontational scale so that this functioning beauty can be encountered fully."

Morris always supplies titles for her pieces, whether they are monumental scale or miniature vessel-tableaux. The titles can provide specific clues, such as *Crow Boat* (2002), *Halibut Mast* (2003), and *Beak Shelter* (2003), or be poetic and ambiguous—*Used Summer* (2002), *New Spring* (2002), and *Lion* (2002). An

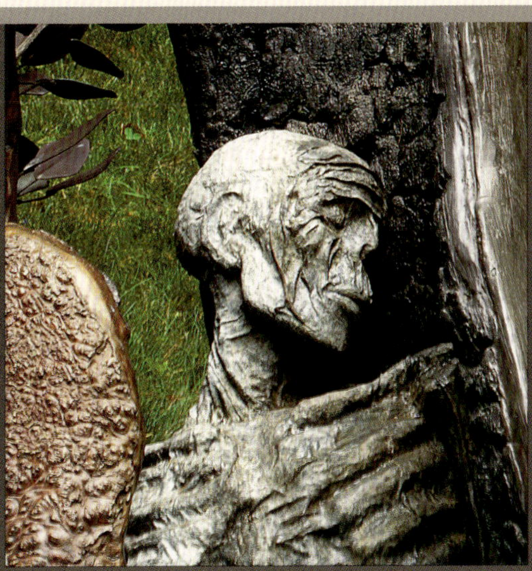

Death's Sister

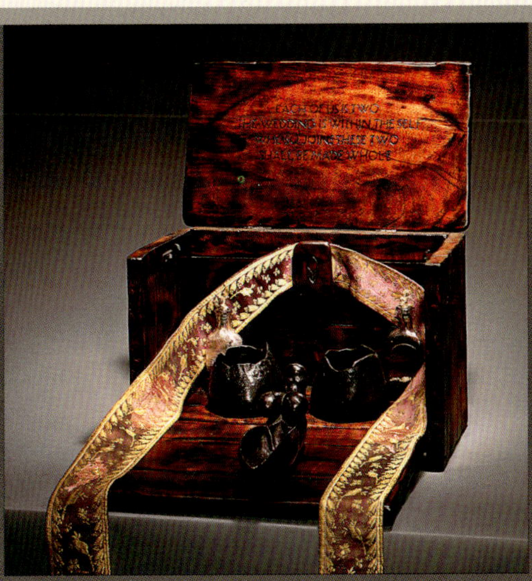

The Marriage Box

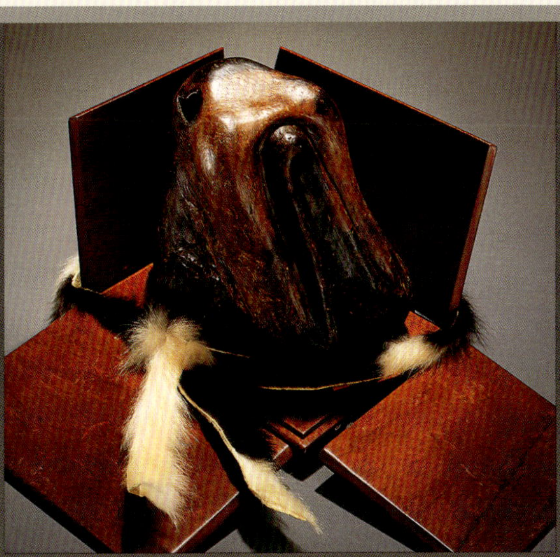

The Snout Box

eight-foot-high work abstracted from a lion's skull, *Lion* bears no resemblance to its source, yet is magisterially beautiful. In *Lion Maquette* (2002) one can see immediately what she has in mind by turning the form a certain way, so that it seems to be pirouetting, toplike, on the tip of a single straightened-out canine tooth. It is no longer a lion: it is a cyclonic tree-form whipped out of molten bronze. Morris has created dozens of these bone and vessel pieces, which as a body of work are wholly separate from her earlier, demonstrably symbolist and iconic pieces.

In 2000, a 45-foot gray whale became stranded and died in the shallows off a Lummi Island beach near Morris's home. While such occurrences can quickly become public health and nuisance issues, Morris, sensing the largest and most important bone-trove of her life, immediately assumed responsibility for its removal and disintegration at a more remote beach. Here, for over a year—with the help of friends and machines—she dismantled the rotting animal, freeing its framework and baleen from its flesh and internal organs, indulging on a grand scale her childhood fascination with decay.

Among the many insights derived from the whale experience is that provided by the retrieval of the rib cage from the leviathan. Morris made one piece from the original bones, arranged on an earthen slope near her studio. The rib-forms have engendered yet another series of sculptural investigations. She relates animal rib structures to those of boats and canoes—one thinks of Viking long boats, voyages, and funeral pyres at sea—and again ties them in with the talismanic vessel form that has so long fascinated her.

Bronze, Bone, and the Talismanic Form

The bits and pieces that comprise this text describing and commenting on the life and work of Ann Morris are, in a sense, like the long and digressive path Morris herself has taken. While her earlier figurative bronze works, and even the reliquaries, carry discrete meaning and are rich in iconographic content, her vessels and bone pieces depend on wordless beauty with formalist interpretations.

The bronze sculptures of Ann Morris give concrete form to ideas, dreams, and emotions. She transfers the formless and internal into configurations that may be universally comprehended, and privately interpreted. She articulates a personal creation myth that effectively reunites the human spirit with nature. This impulse, a reflection of art's most primordial wellsprings, is given shape and form within a modernist tradition that includes both Symbolism and Surrealism. Through a rich vocabulary of accreted, realistic components, Morris palpably deepens and enriches the continued potential of figuration.

Like the Surrealist artist, Morris utilizes the ironic power of "realism" to draw us into her dream. As with the shamanic medium, she applies the conceptual power of dismemberment and renewal, ritual death followed by resurrection, and the promise of spiritual awakening. Consistent with Buddhist and Taoist thought—specifically, the dilemma of the egocentric "illusion of separateness from nature"—she speculates with notions of personal identity, whether male or female, in an immeasurably larger and holistic context.

Even the realization that Morris's completed bronze figures are essentially hollow skins of metal carries a certain symbolic weight: that these are but mirror images—the simulacra—of three-dimensional forms she has laboriously constructed in wax.

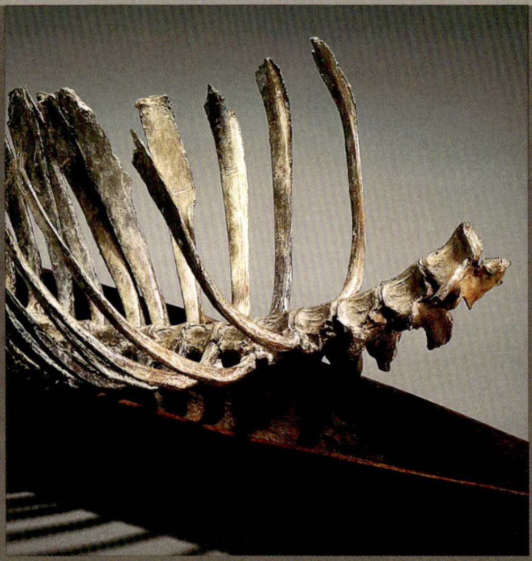

Life Dugout

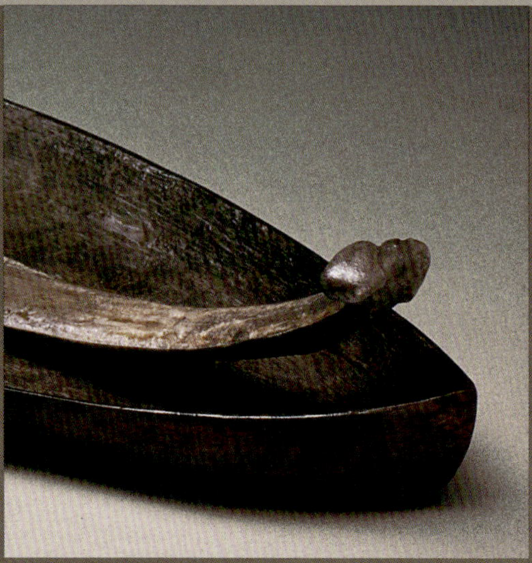

Rib Boat

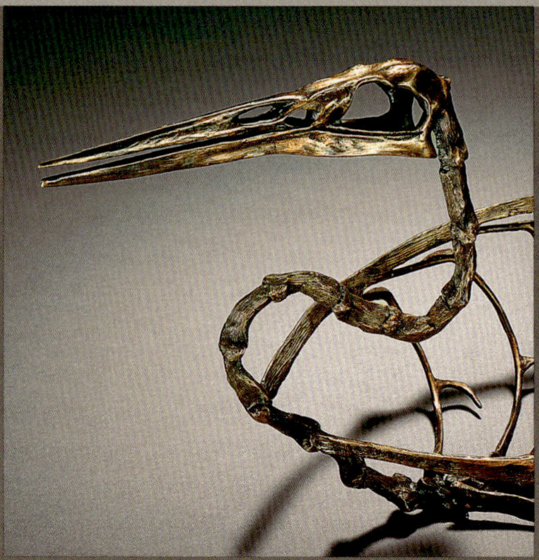

Heron Bowl

Morris demonstrates the mystic paucity of a society that lacks the creation myths of "primitive" peoples. As Picasso and his modernist confreres attempted to exorcise the magical power of primitive art, Morris summons the formidable and oracular power of women warriors, confident (rather than apologetic) of their sexuality and being equal to any test.

In metaphysics, such investigation is known as ontology, which explores the nature and relations of human existence. Morris puts it in simpler layman's terms: she has "always wanted to get to the bottom of things." In her case, these concerns are by no means biased or sullied by anthropocentrism, the belief that humankind is necessarily the center of her universe. Rather, her work inferentially questions the Biblical assertion that mankind has somehow been granted dominion (read *separateness*) "over the fish of the sea, and over the fowl of the air, and over the cattle, and over all the earth, and over every creeping thing. . . ."

Morris has sought to express a concept of wholeness, a unity with humankind and nature, which at moments is dependent on many other creation myths, sagas, and dreams. She boldly breasts the perplexing weight and diversity of evolution and mythology. She has hewn a poetic ensemble of figures, relics, and talismanic objects that metaphorically suggest her own alternative woodland demigods.

The eminent scholar and comparative mythologist Joseph Campbell has stated that artists are the mythmakers of our time. In Morris's case, we see the compounding of her strengths: as an artist and as a keen observer of our mythical and pantheist heritage.

Morris has reached the height of her artistic powers and moral seriousness. Assembled around her are all the creation myths, belief systems, poetic insights, and ontological schemata sufficient to fuel several more careers.

She could, among other things, be truly deemed a "magic realist," which, although ordinarily a literary term, fits her perfectly. By definition, magic realism is the capacity to enrich our idea of what is "real" by incorporating all dimensions of the imagination, particularly as expressed in magic, myth, and spirituality.

She has her books and tools and innumerable talismans and relics that will find their way into her continuing body of work. Suddenly, as it must, everything makes sense: Morris, with her Merlinian vision, her goddess guidance, and Arcadian sense of hopeful history—as indeed, a "woman warrior"—brings to mind William Blake's (also Arcadian) vision of "Jerusalem," where he sings,

> Bring me my bow of burning gold:
> Bring me my arrows of desire:
> Bring me my spear: O clouds unfold!
> Bring me my chariot of fire!

Ann Morris testifies her particularized mythical faith, her beliefs, in a grand and glorious manner. In a lifetime body of work, Morris has given literal shape to a metaphysical worldview that constitutes a broad and comprehensive "creation myth," equal and parallel to any that have emerged from the Old and New Worlds, from Arthurian England to Indige-nous America. Ultimately, Morris's work is broadly accessible, deeply affecting, and timeless.

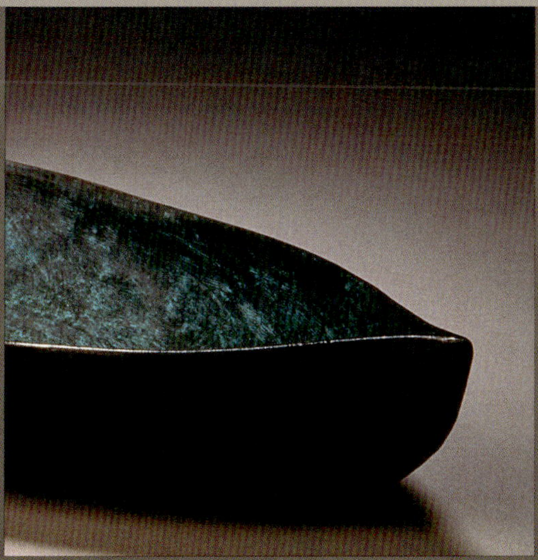

Pod Drift

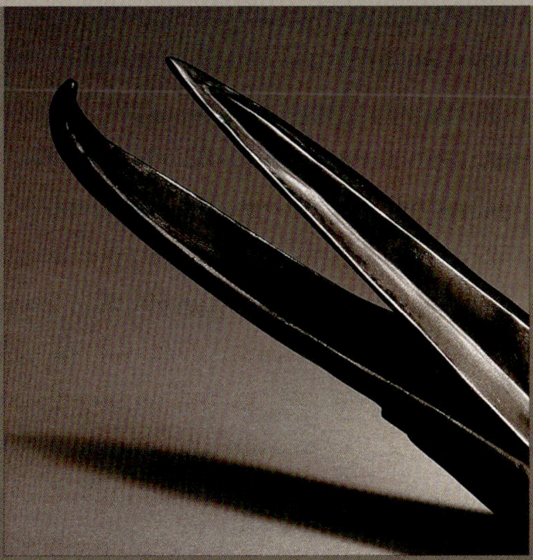

Raven Bowl

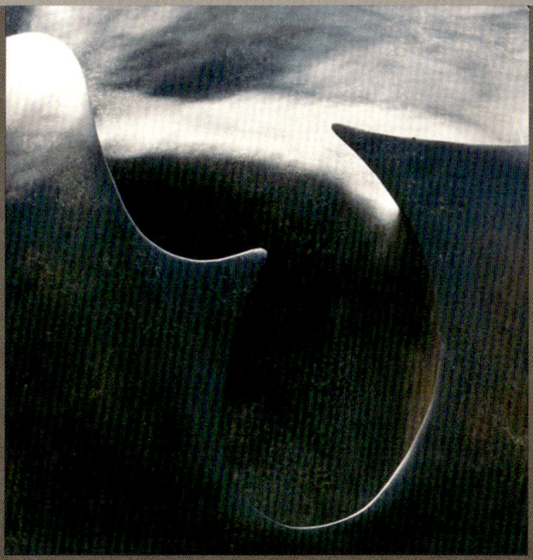

Lion Maquette

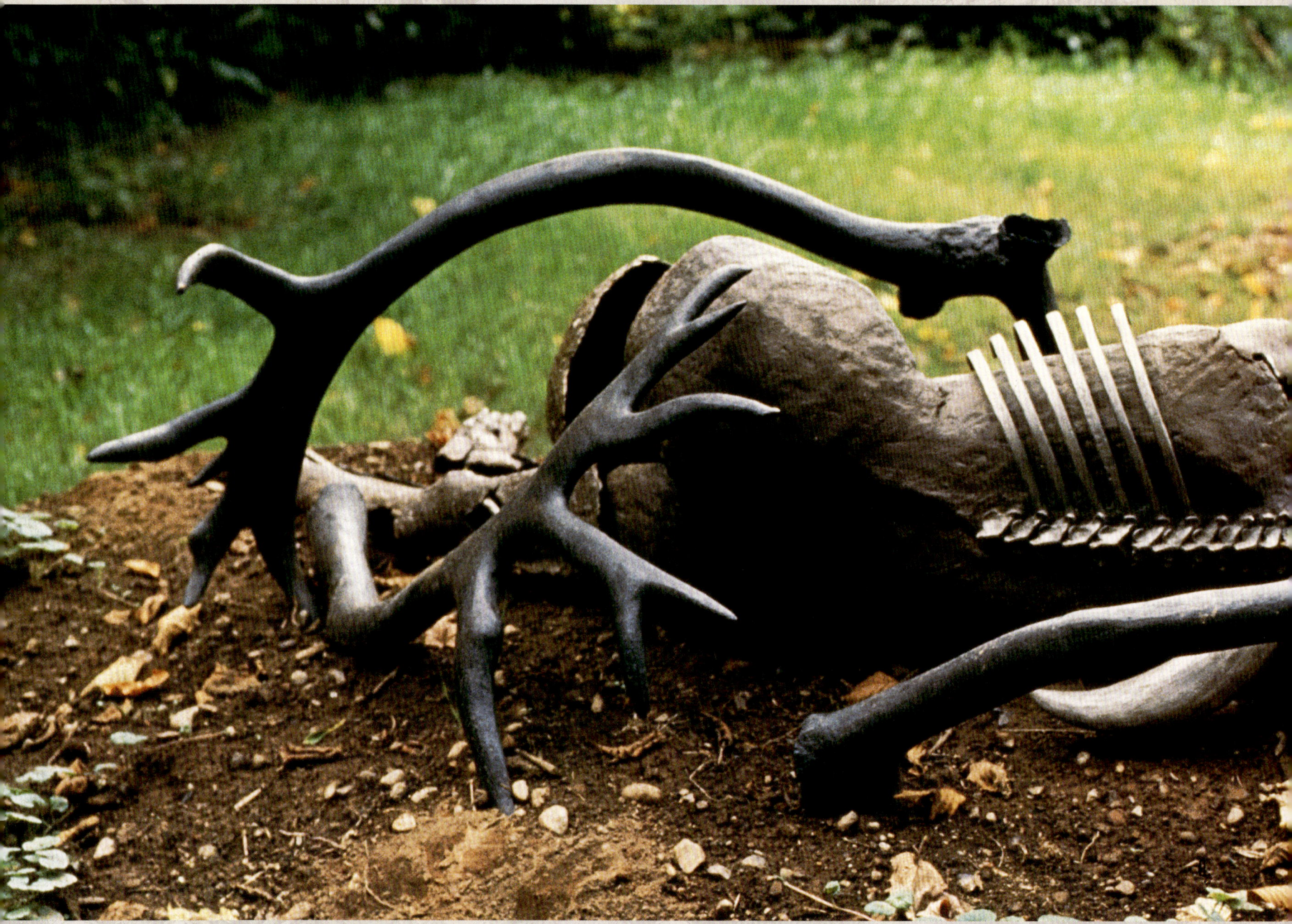

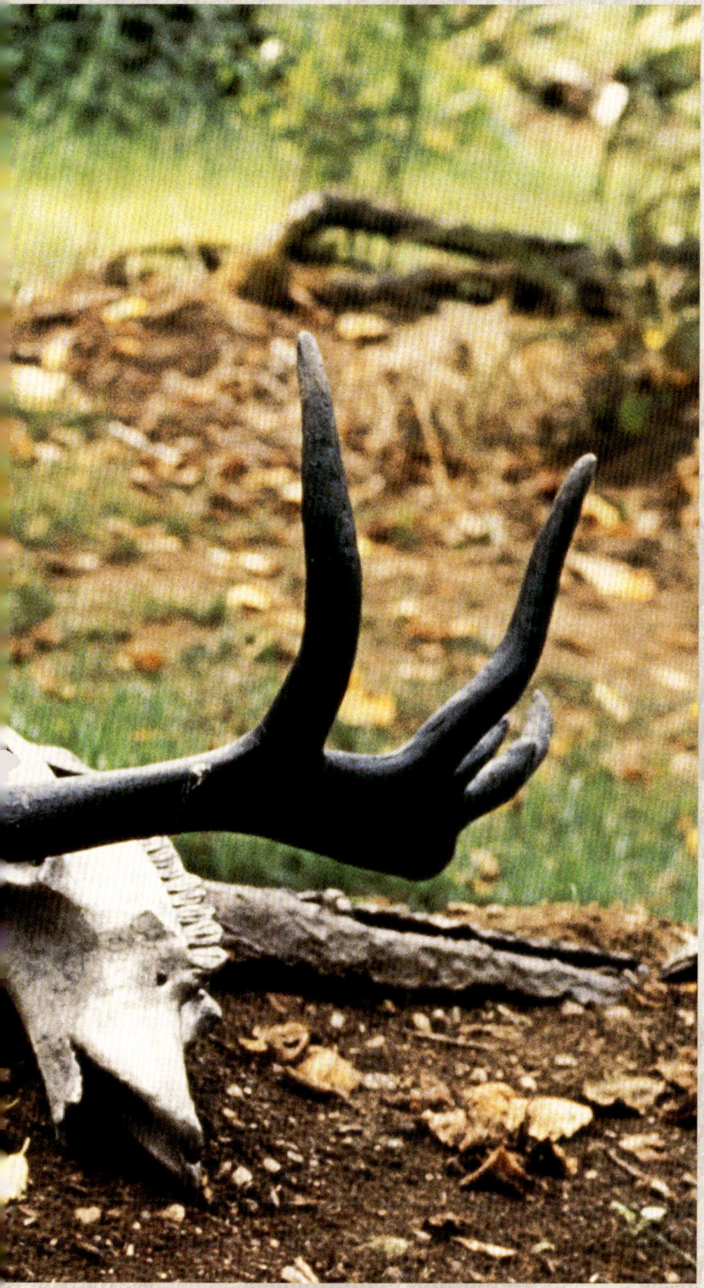

God guard me from those thoughts men think
In the mind alone;
He that sings a lasting song
Thinks in the marrow-bone.

—William Butler Yeats

She of the Piece

She stands contained in the soul-making vessel of consciousness, but she has the strength to enlarge the container at any time. She is Nature's creature—her horns the symbol of that connection and of her power. They serve as antennae with which she, light-fingered, receives news from the Universe. She stands on the rock of her island and is surrounded by bare bones of wood washed up on its shores. She is in command of herself and her powers and reminds us to have the courage to be ourselves.

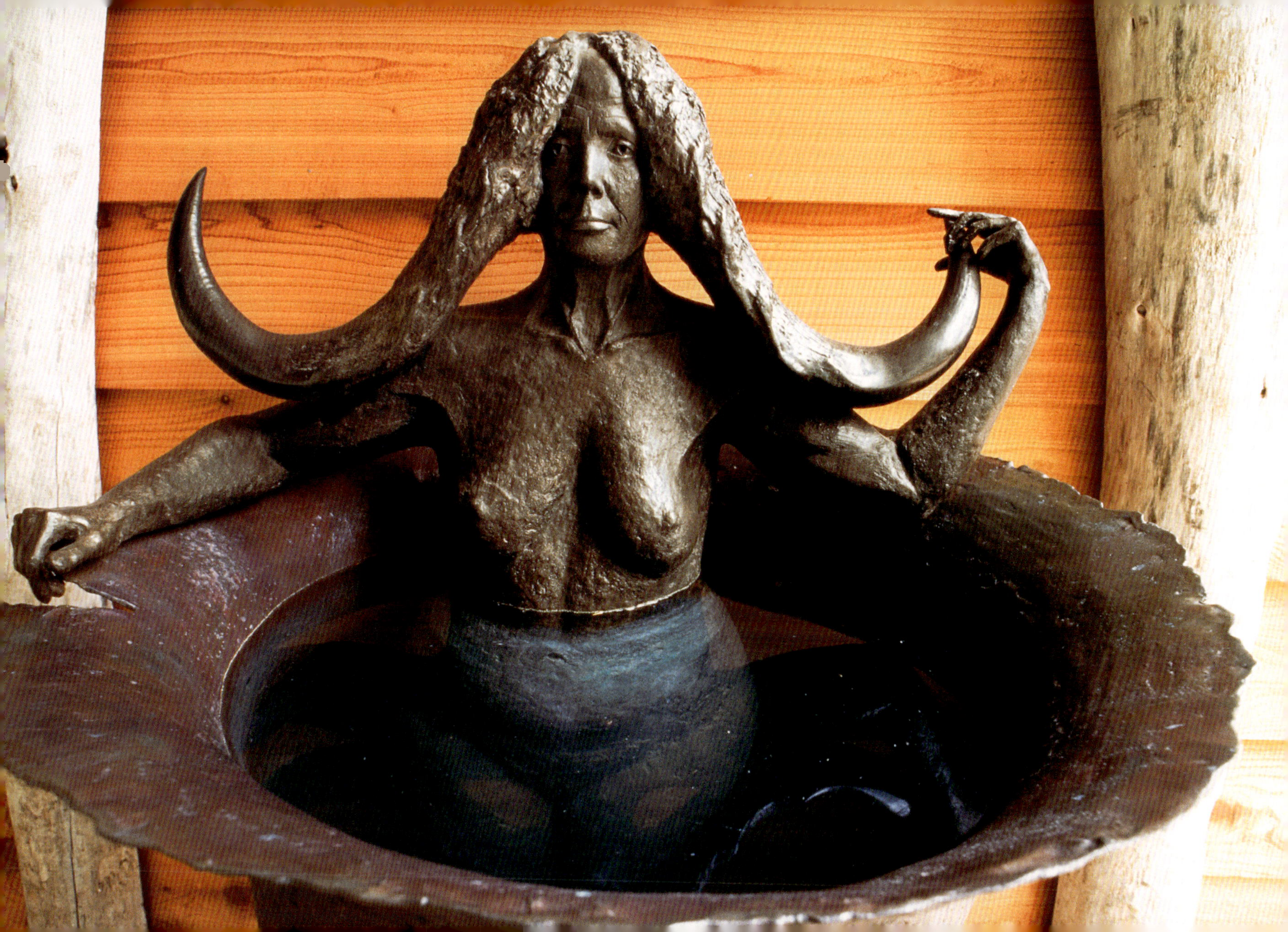

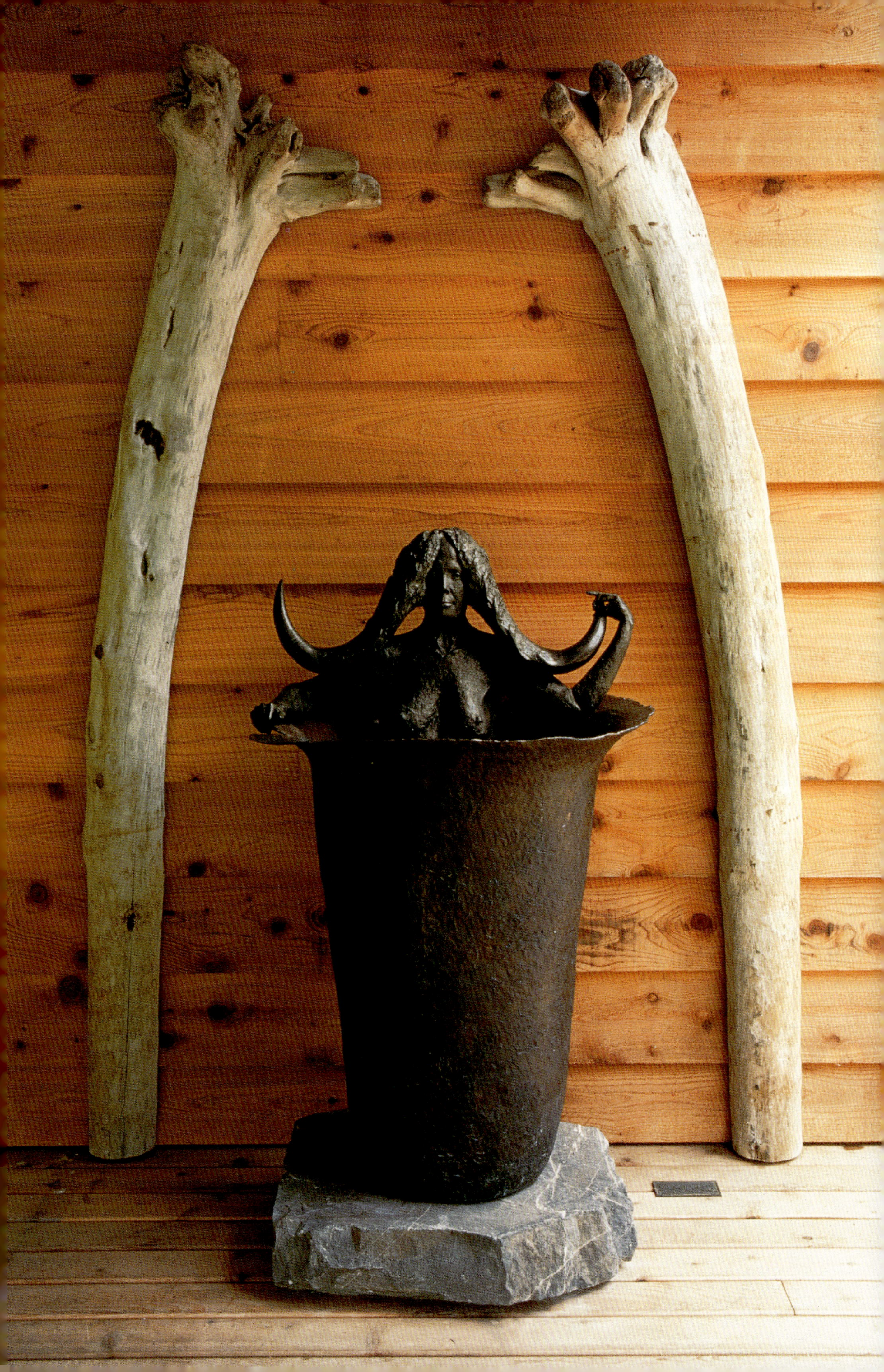

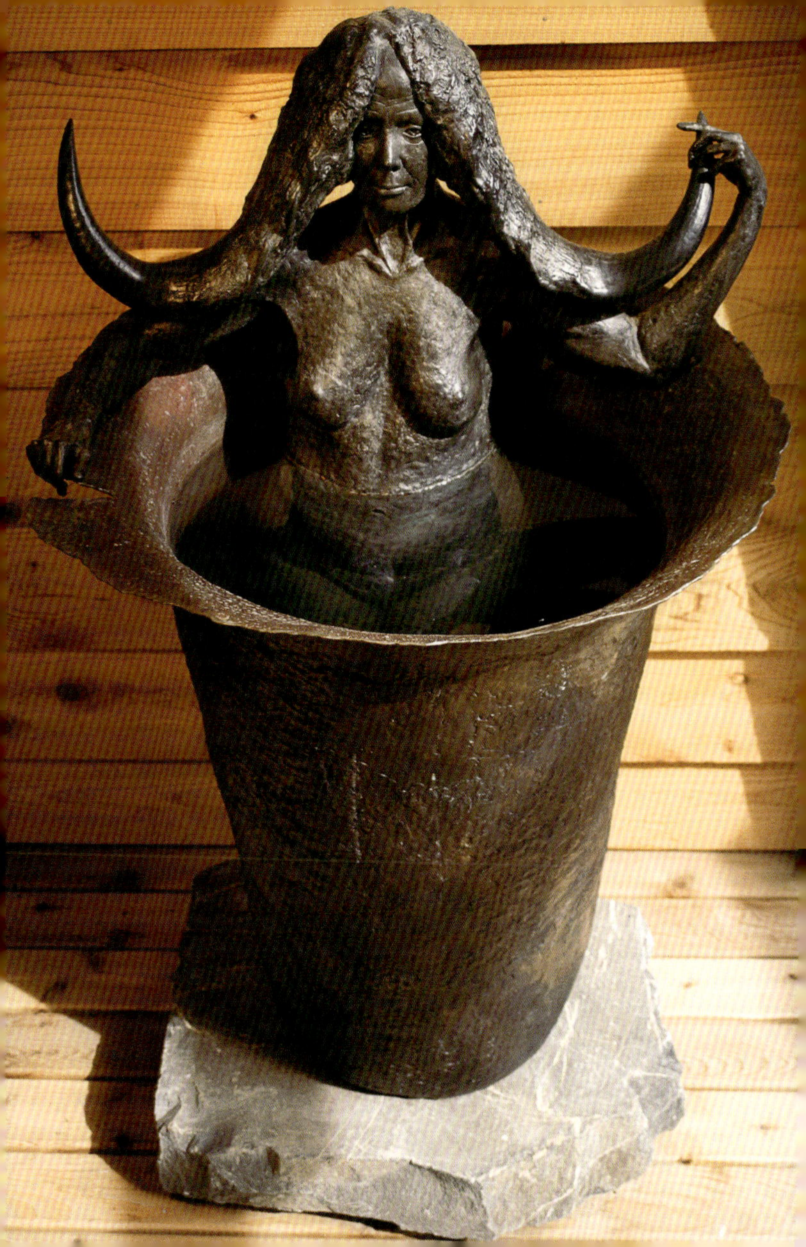

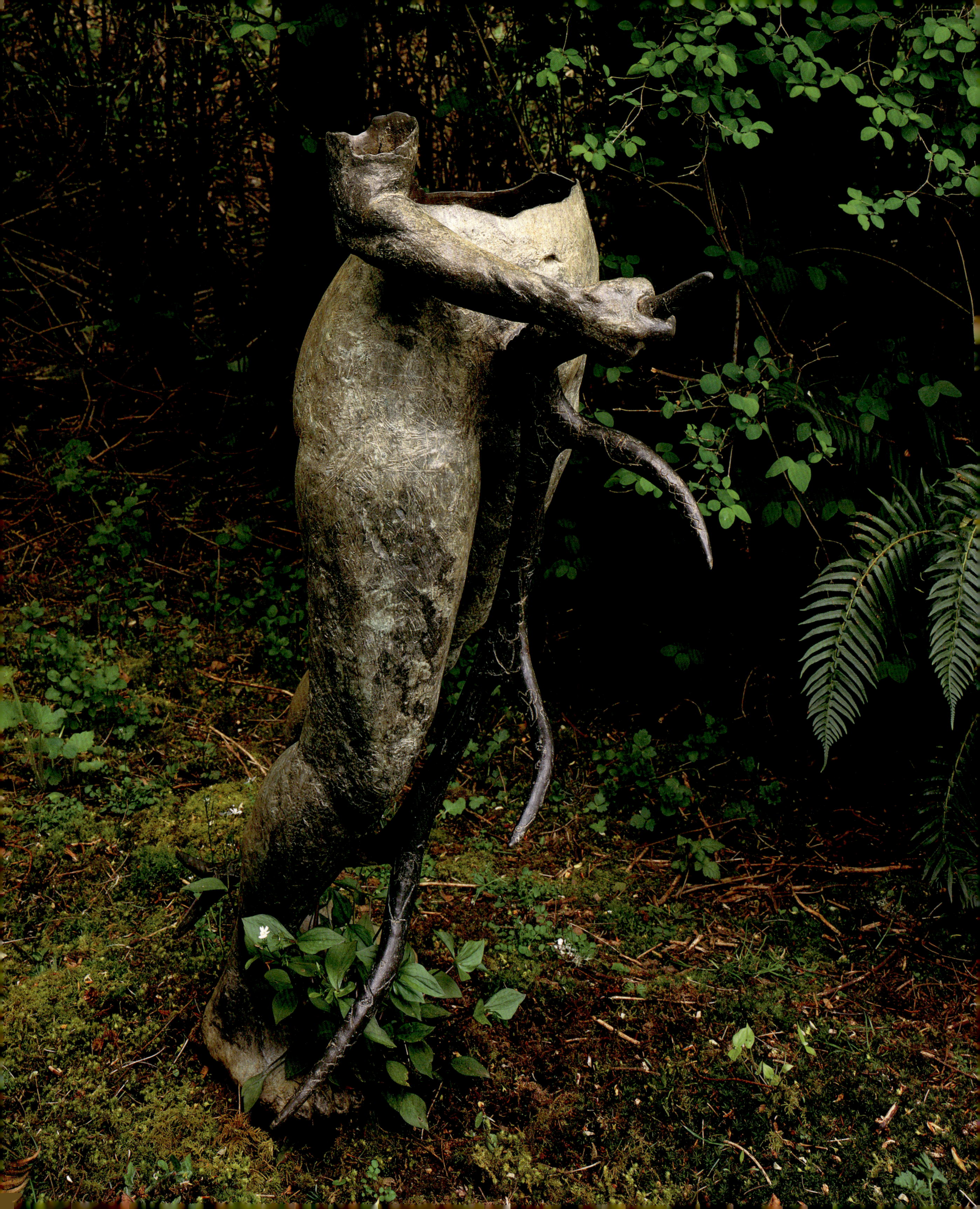

She is instinctual womanhood striding out of the ancient woods, holding her integrated masculinity which bears her news. She reminds us that being female is not her definition of womanhood. Ancient womanhood is related to the male as her internal partner and is wise in the ways of Nature, instinct, and creativity. She brings this news of ancestral motherlines into the 20th century, and because she does so, wears the slipper of the heroine. Her feet are connected to the heart of the earth, and she is open to the winds of the world. It is her body and bone which know. She needs no head; the planet is her heart.

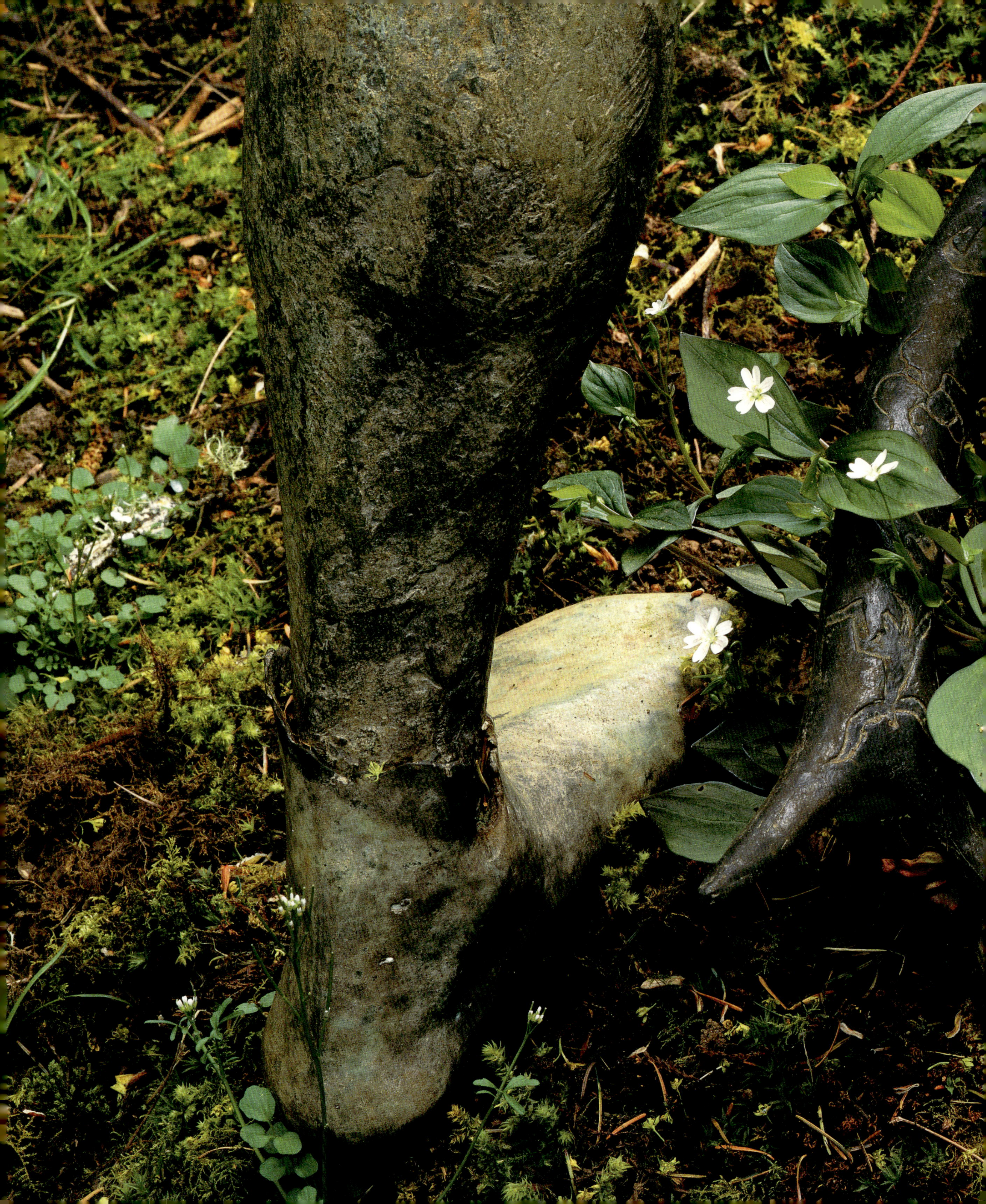

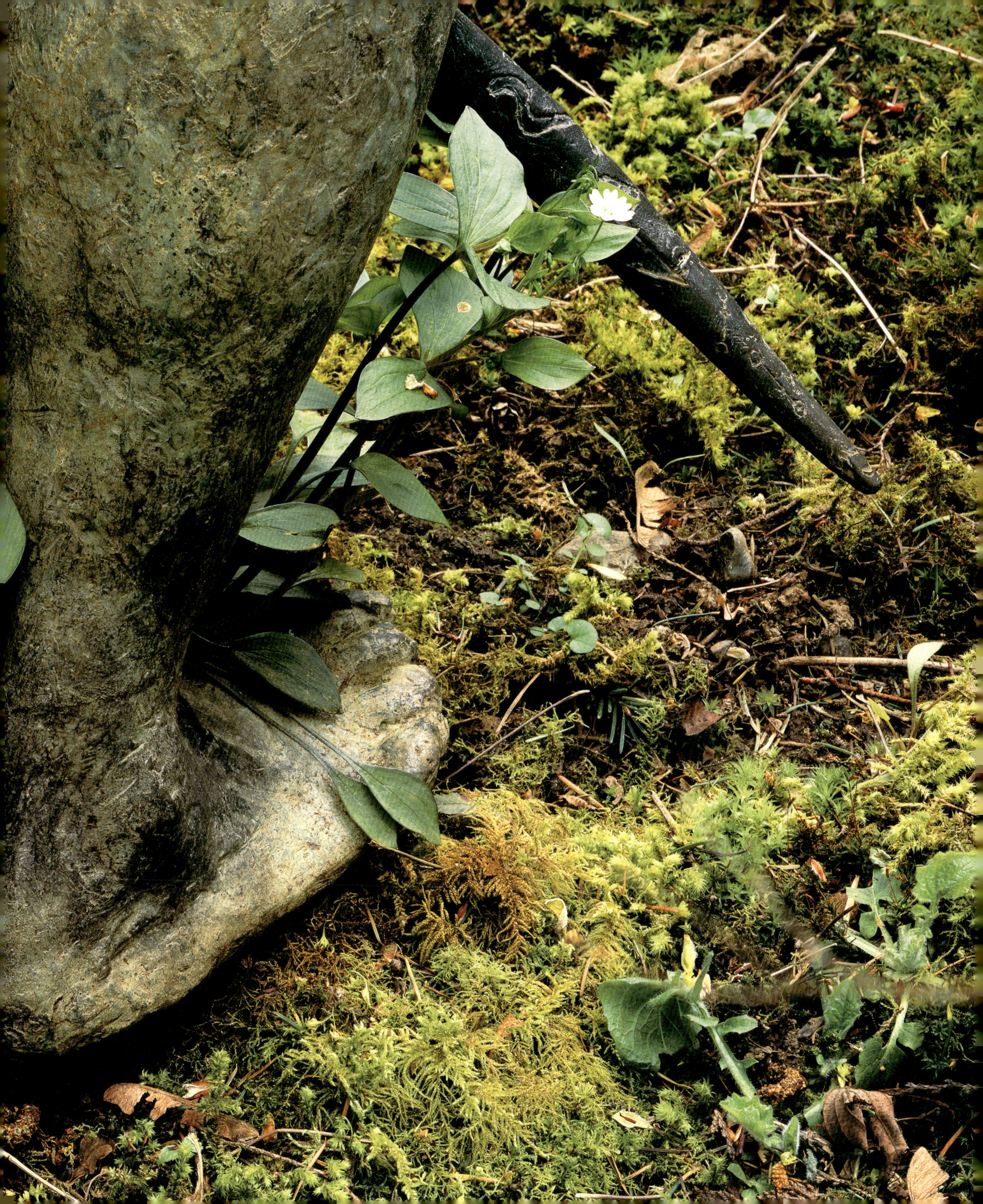

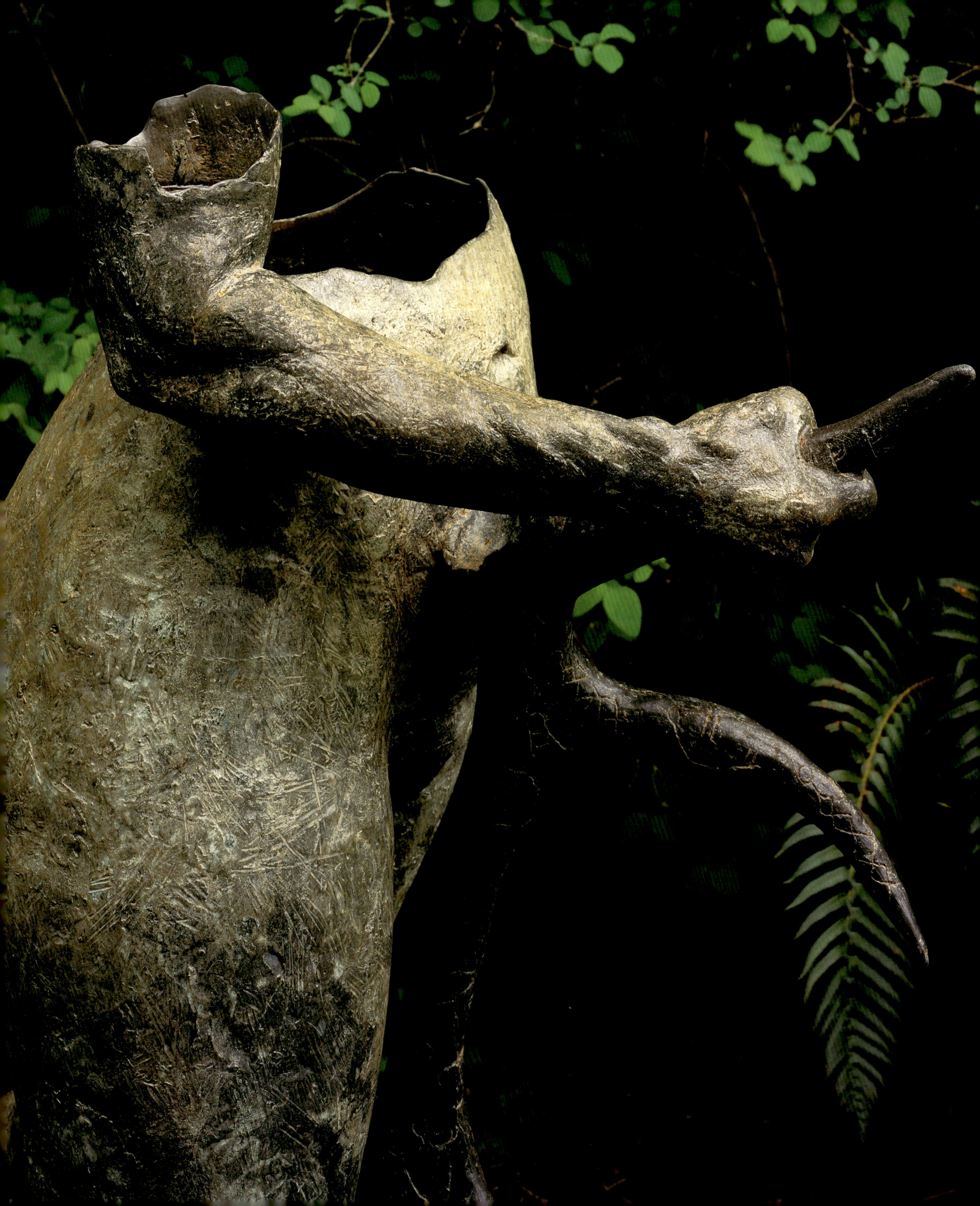

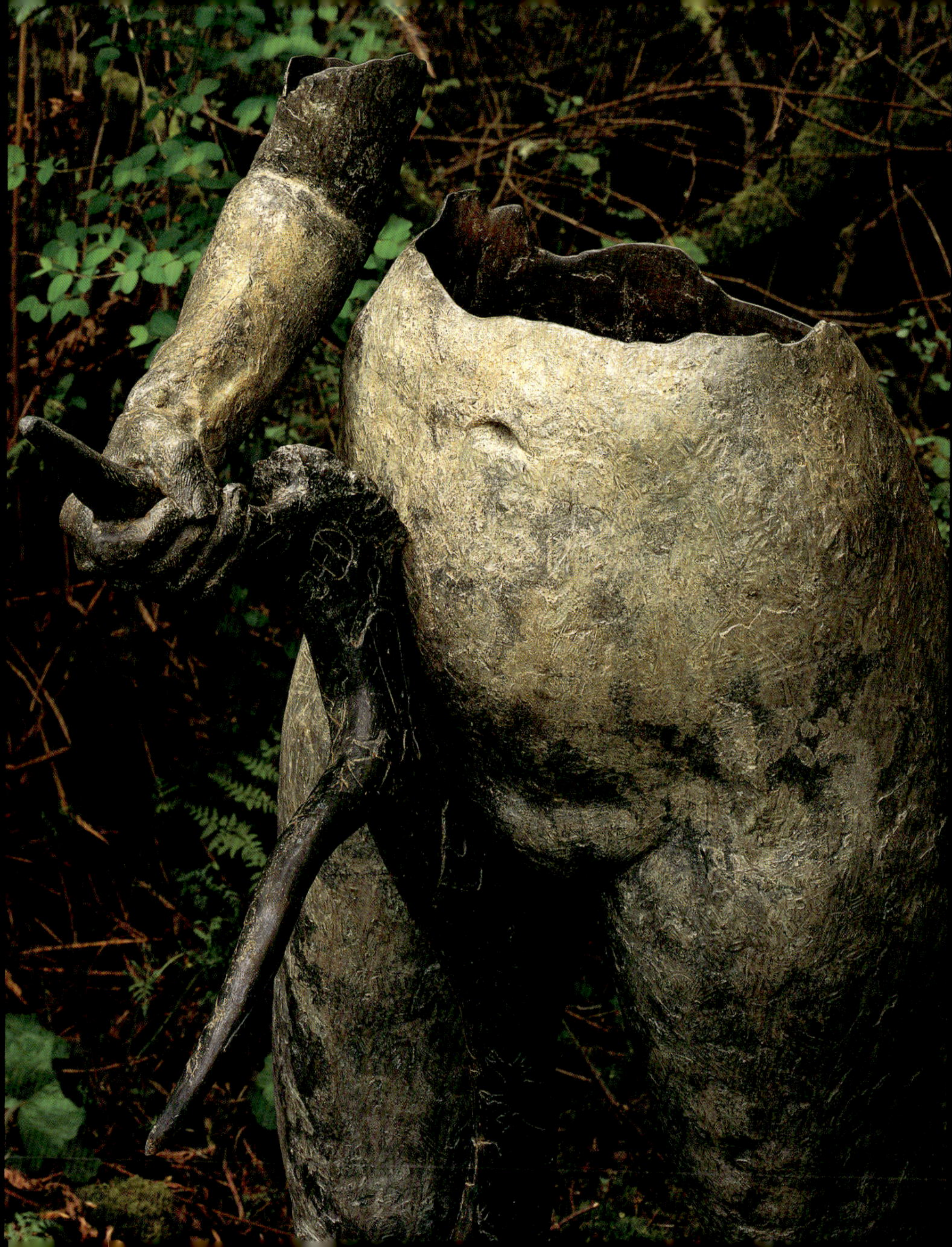

Double Dream

A psychic state in dream time. The young male and female dressed in fresh seaweed and iris leaves are the internal masculine and feminine aspects of the larger figures. It is they who know about soul meeting, whereas the larger figures seem unaware of this internal knowing and walk away. Their leaves and weeds are coarse and withered and cannot be refreshed unless they look back and within. They stand reflected in a pool of consciousness, yet they are unreflecting. Their inner figures know, wait, and reach for one another —a tension unresolved.

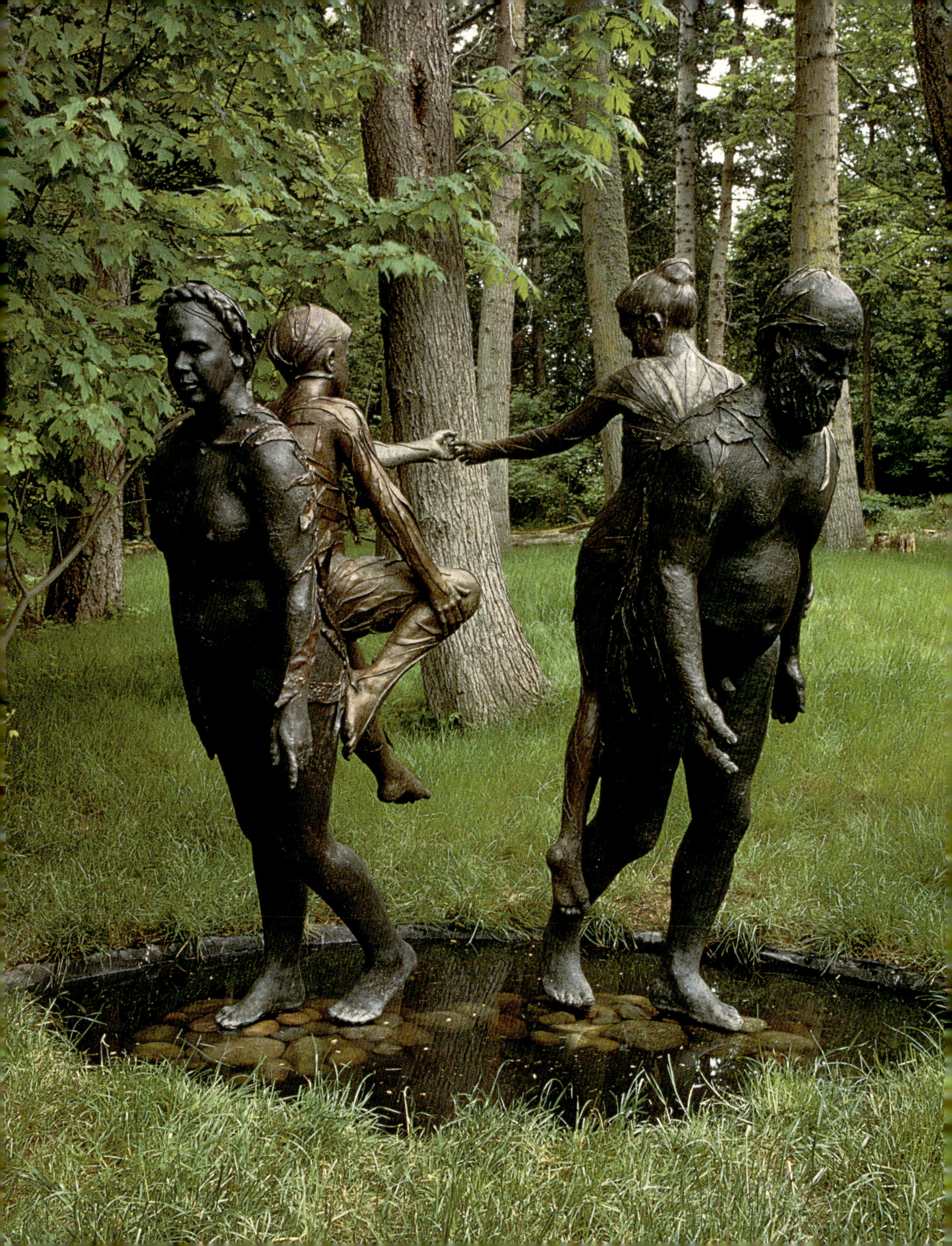

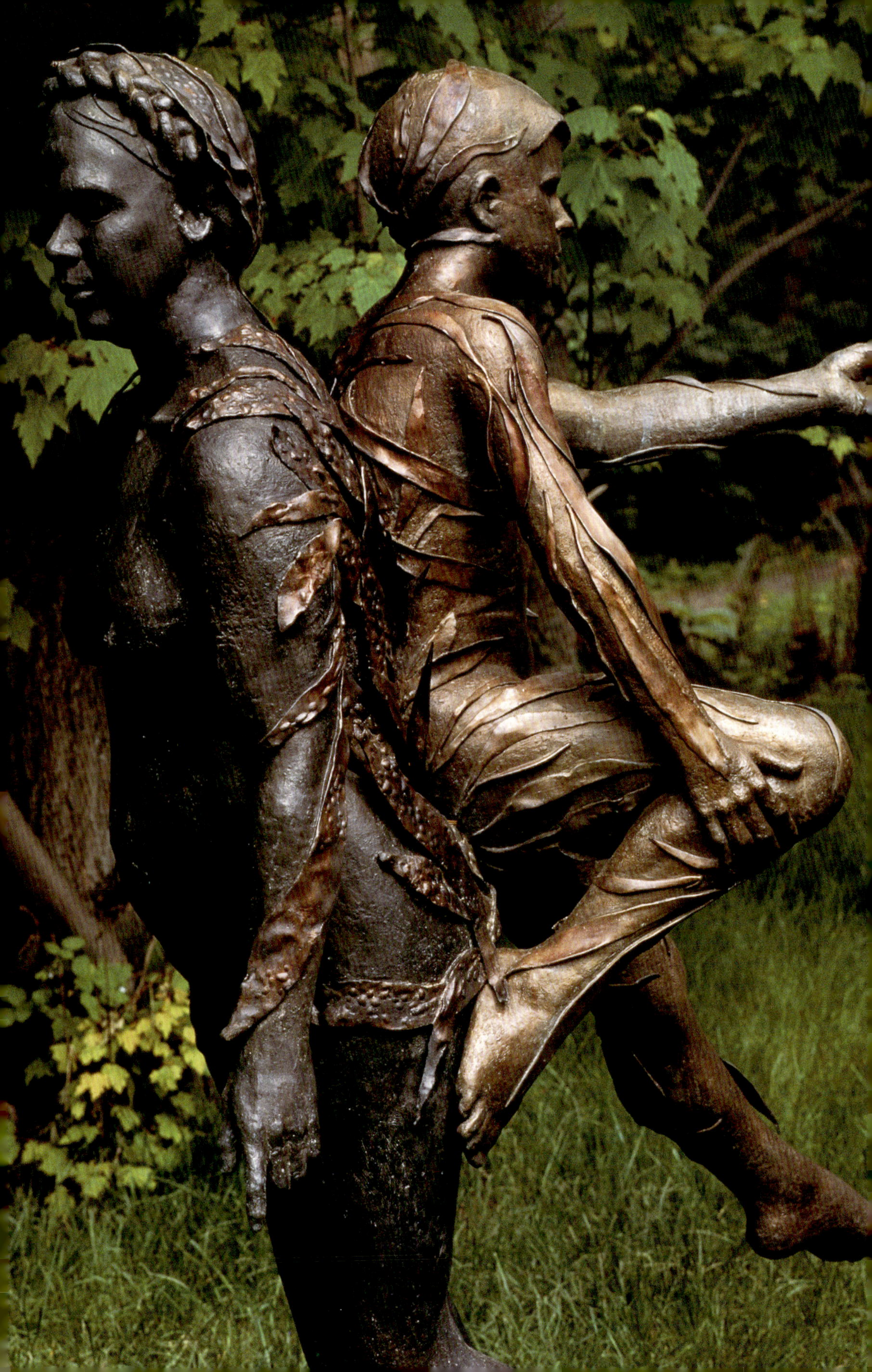

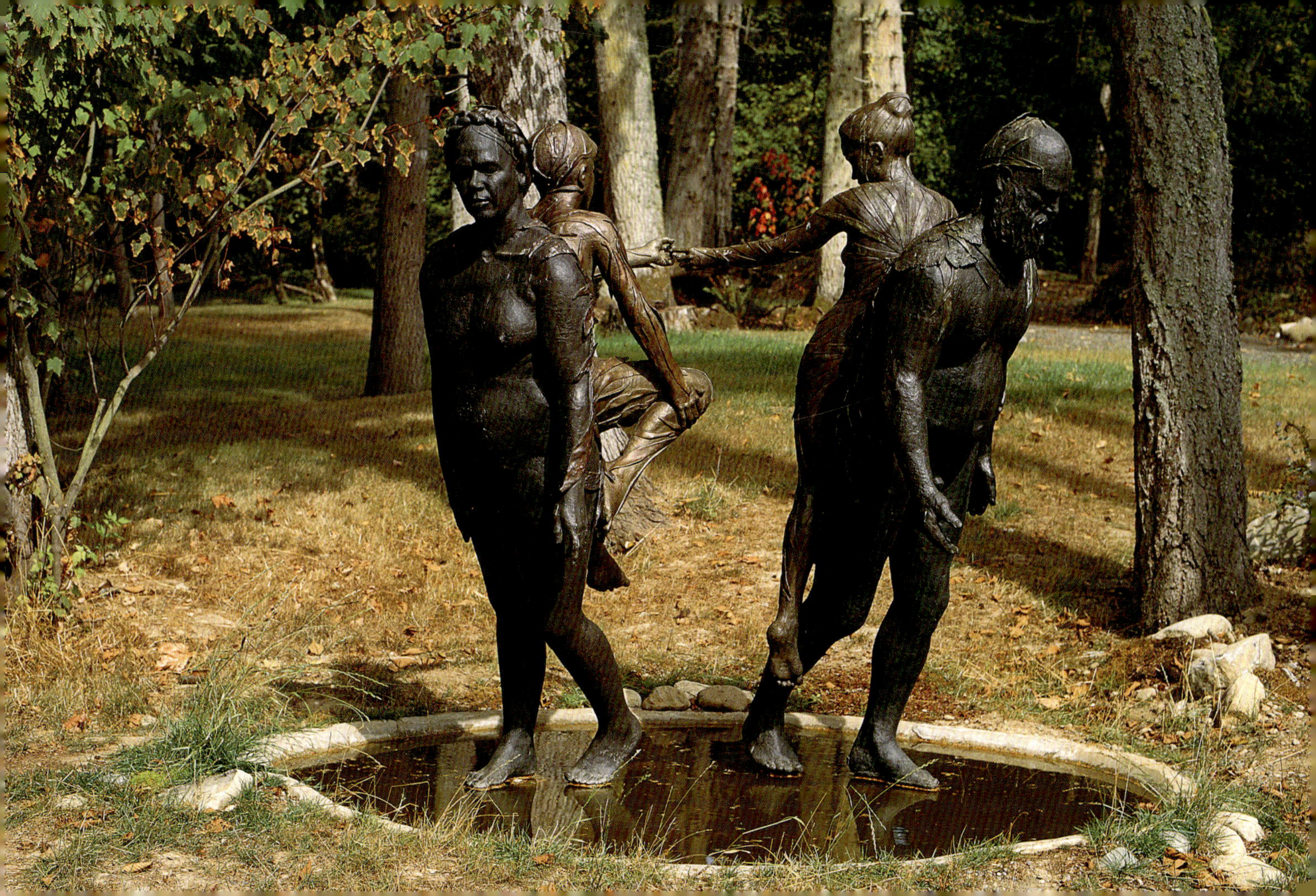

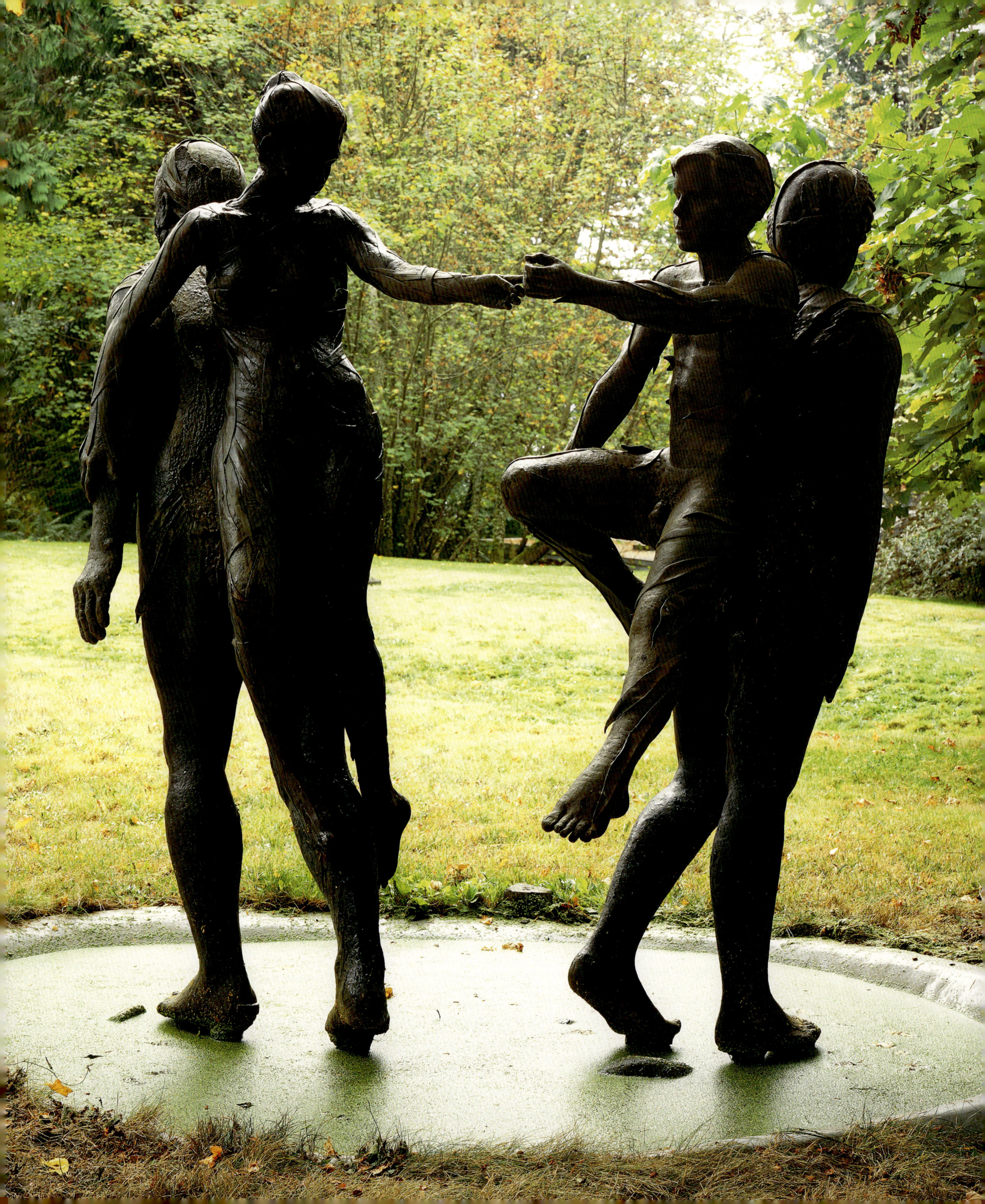

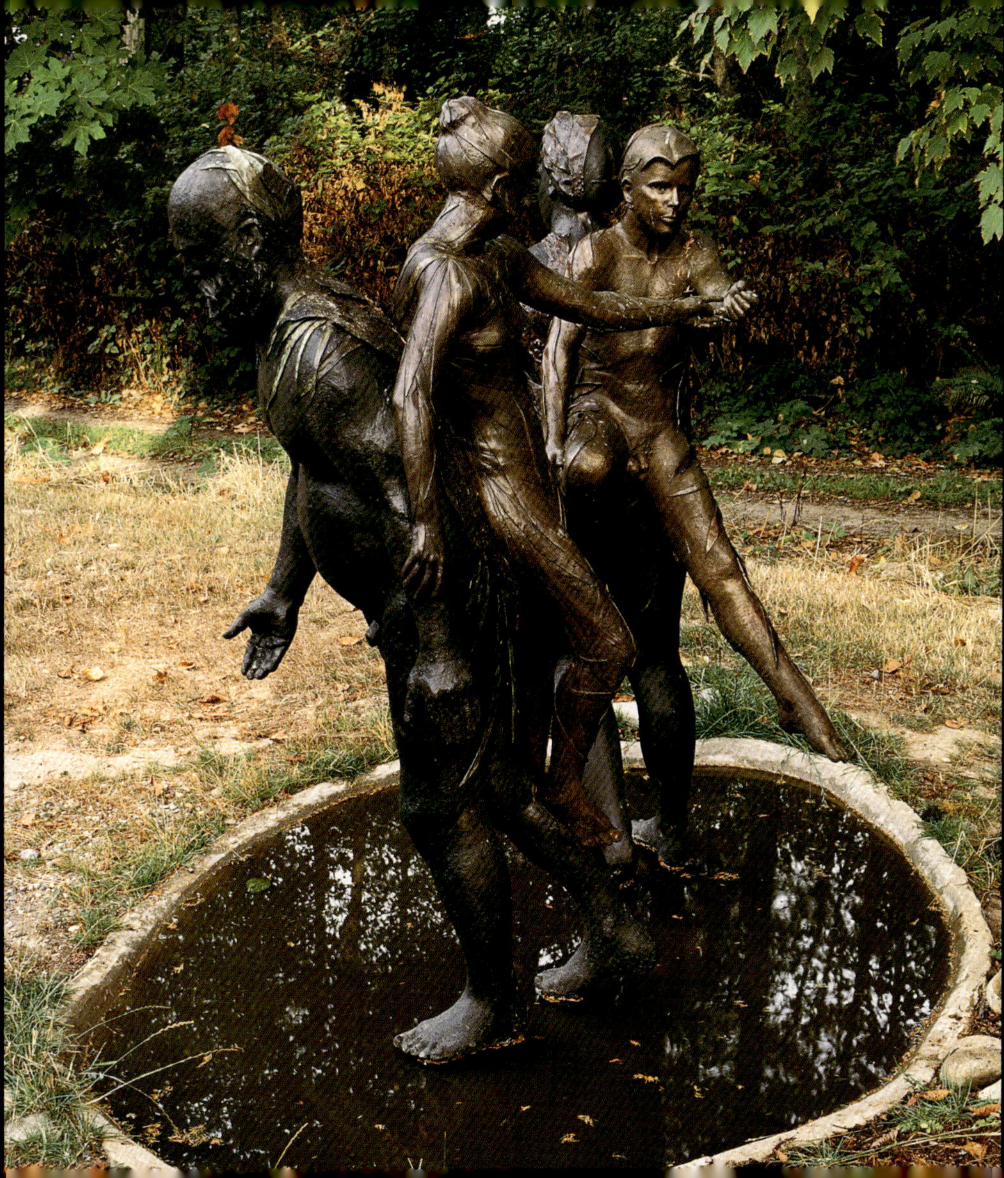

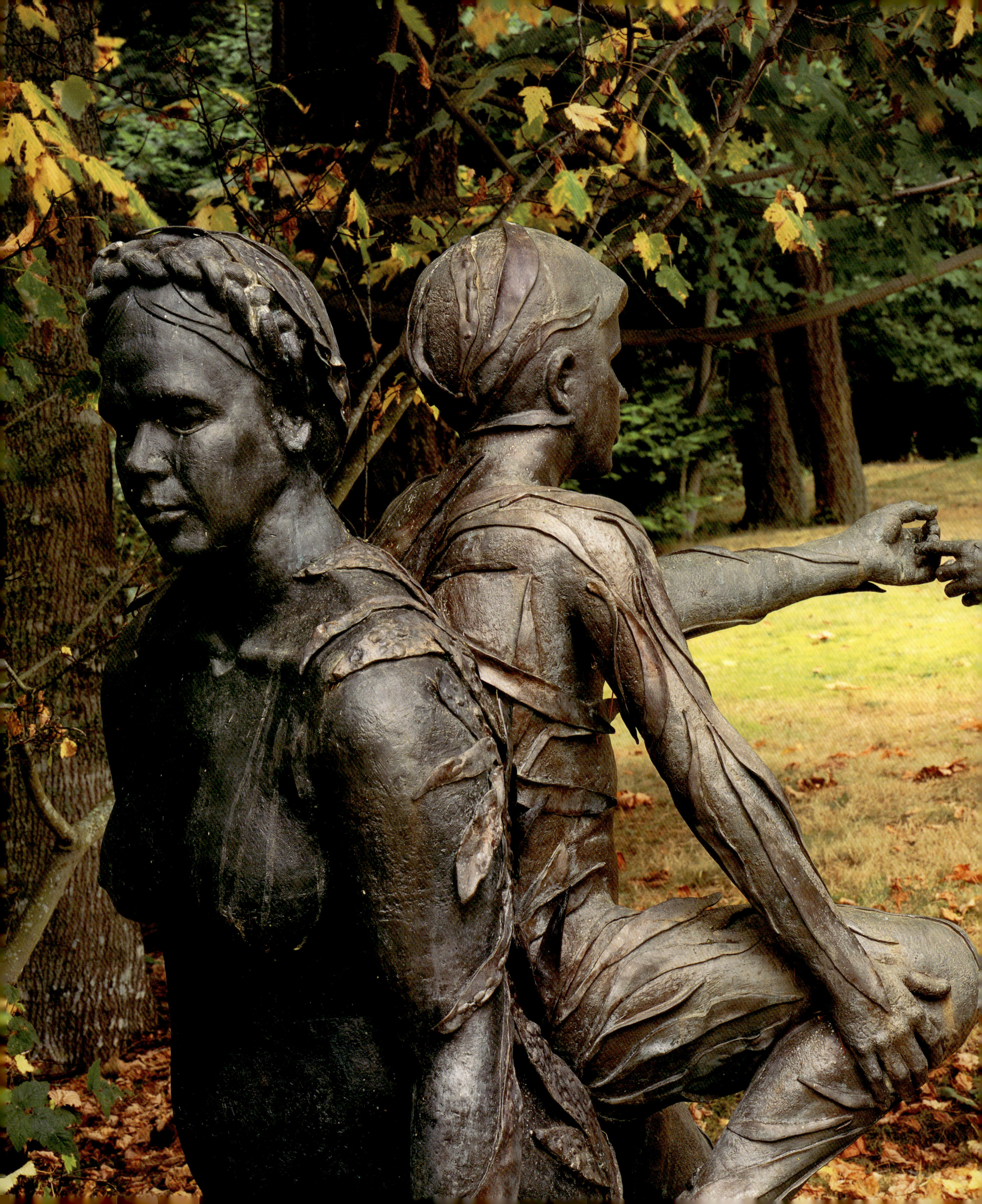

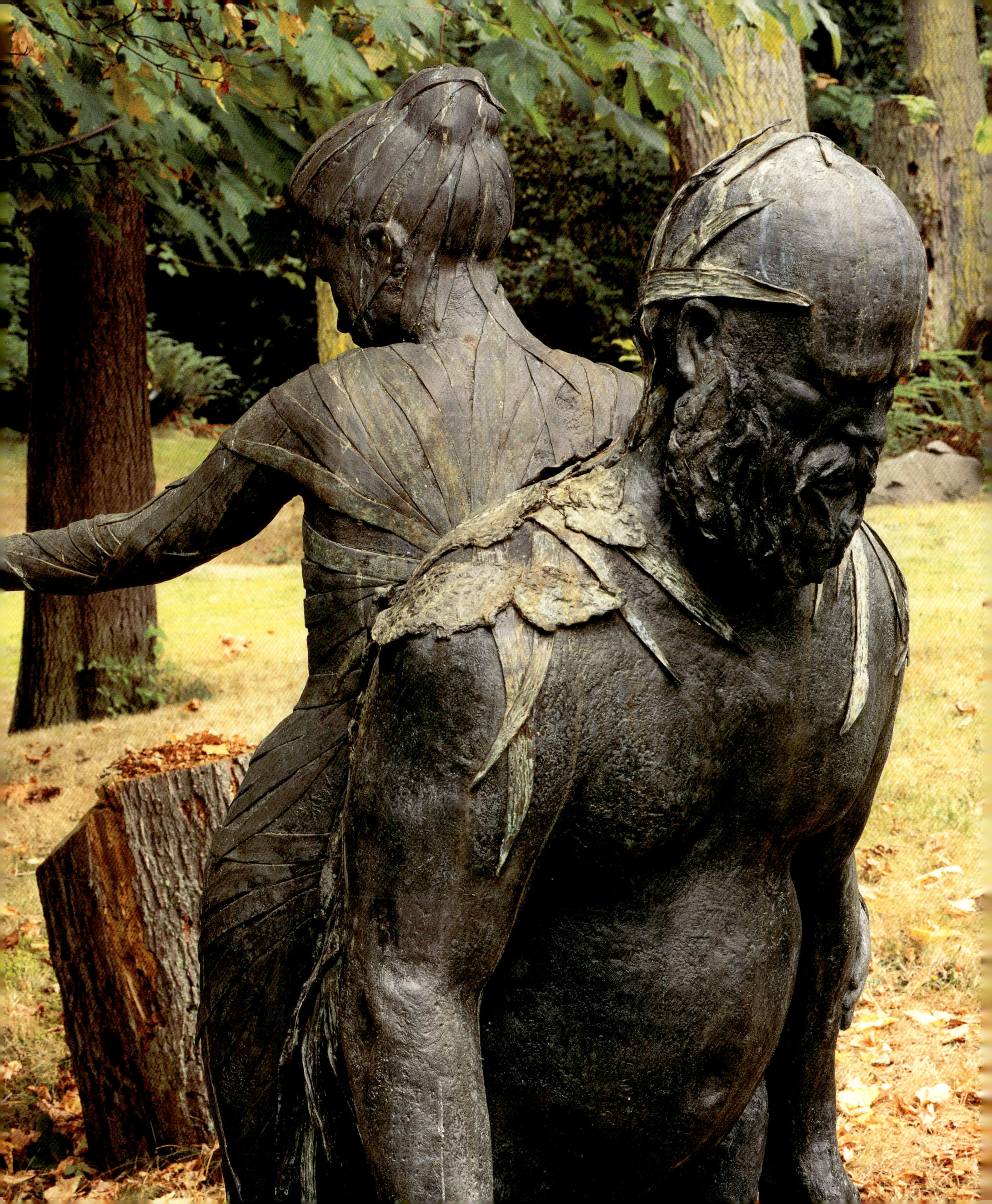

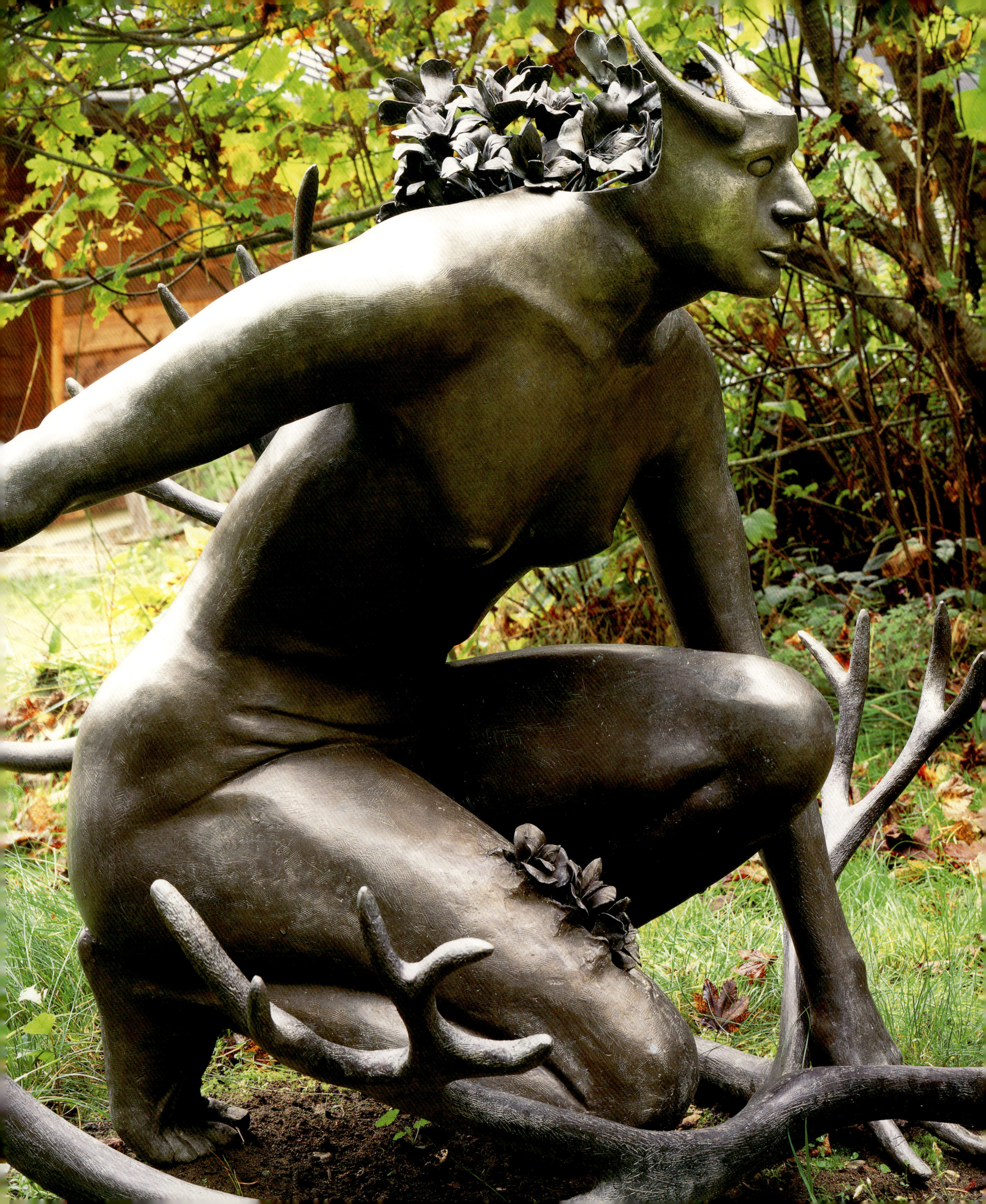

Will There Be a Place for Me?

The Goddess of Cycles is reborn as Virgin. She is growth, anticipation, and youthfulness about to spring from between the young horns of Nature itself, bringing her fruitfulness, a body filled with flowers, out into the world. Has our consciousness made a place of welcome for her? She brings with her creative possibility and the answers to how to live in a meaningful relationship to Nature. She can teach us if we will ask the right questions and listen. Will there be a place for her?

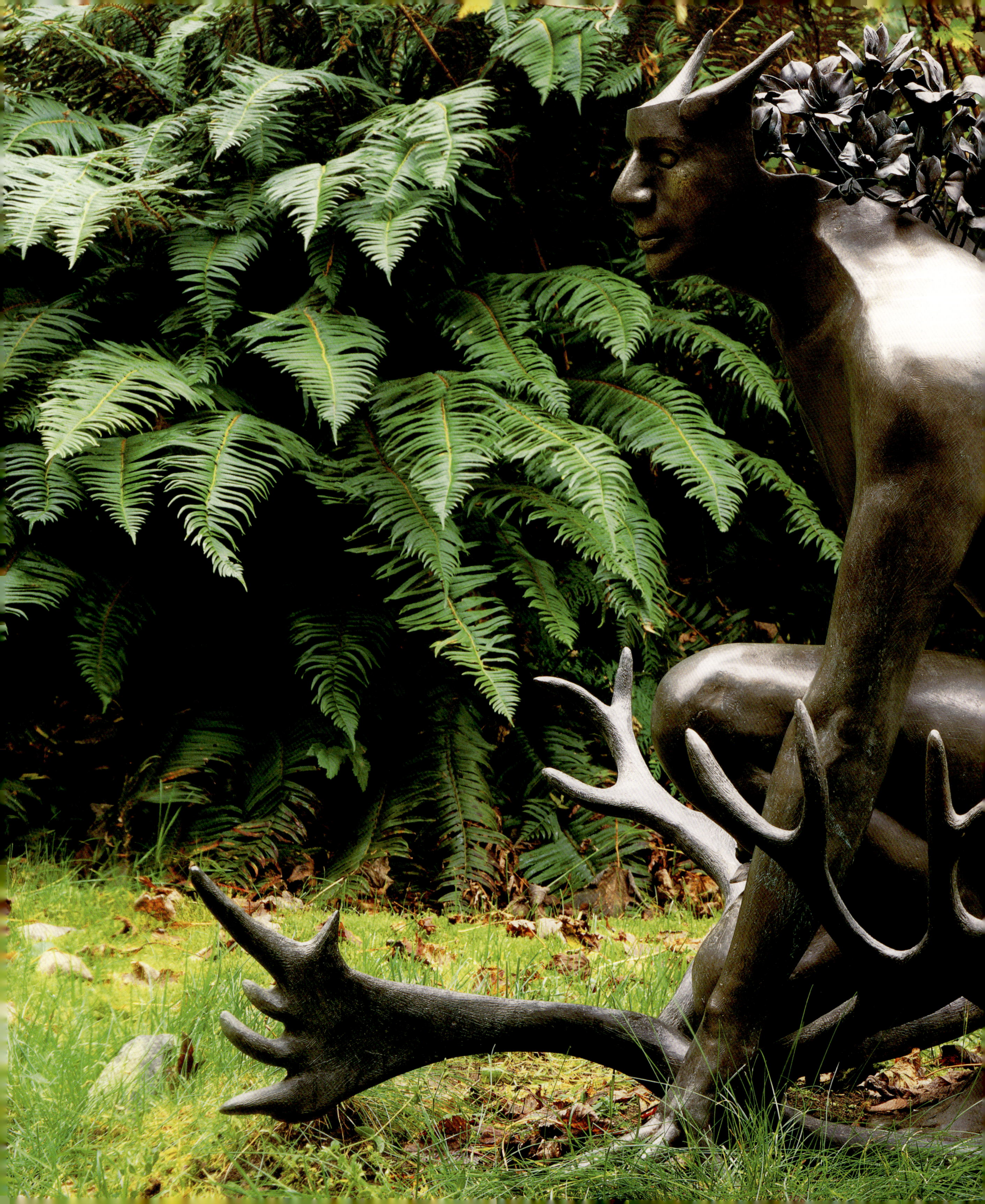

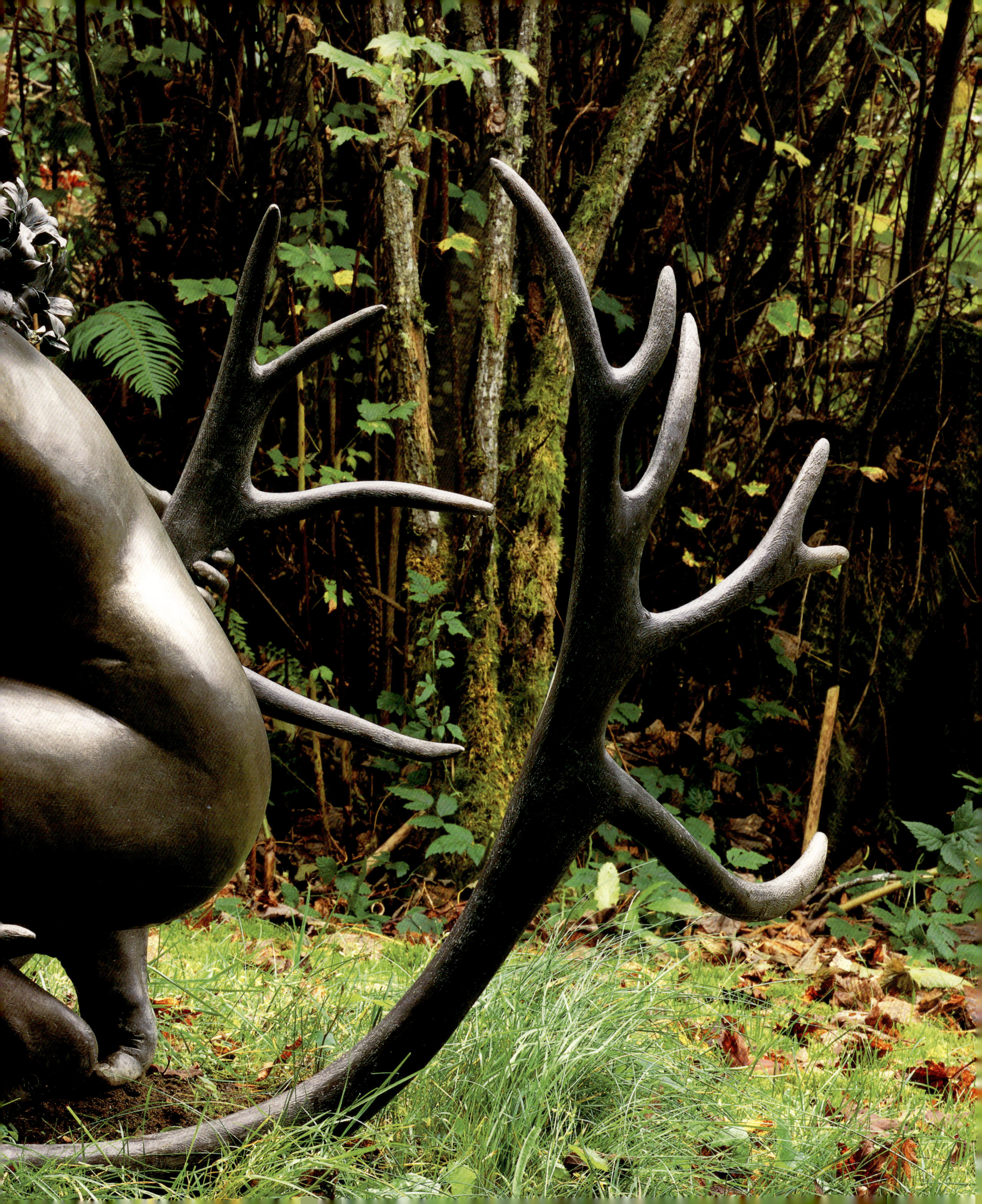

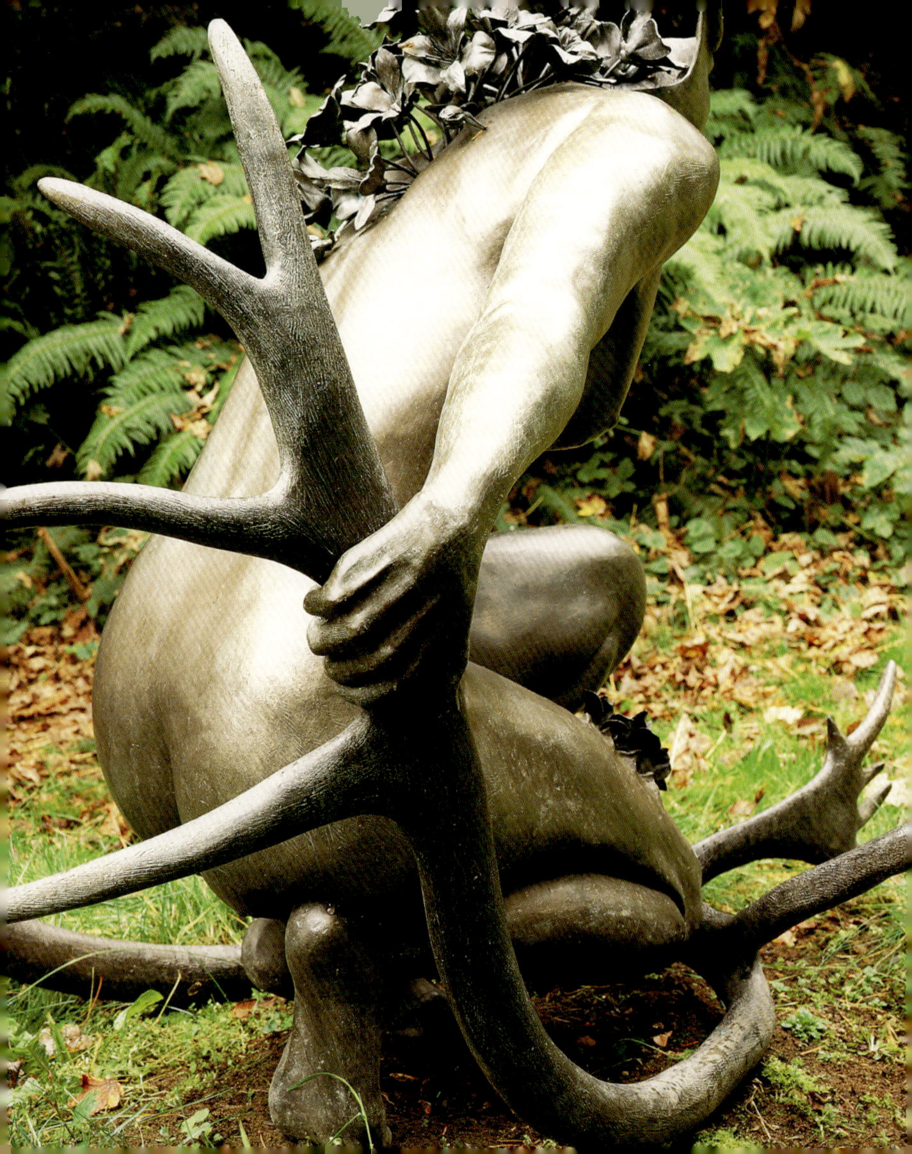

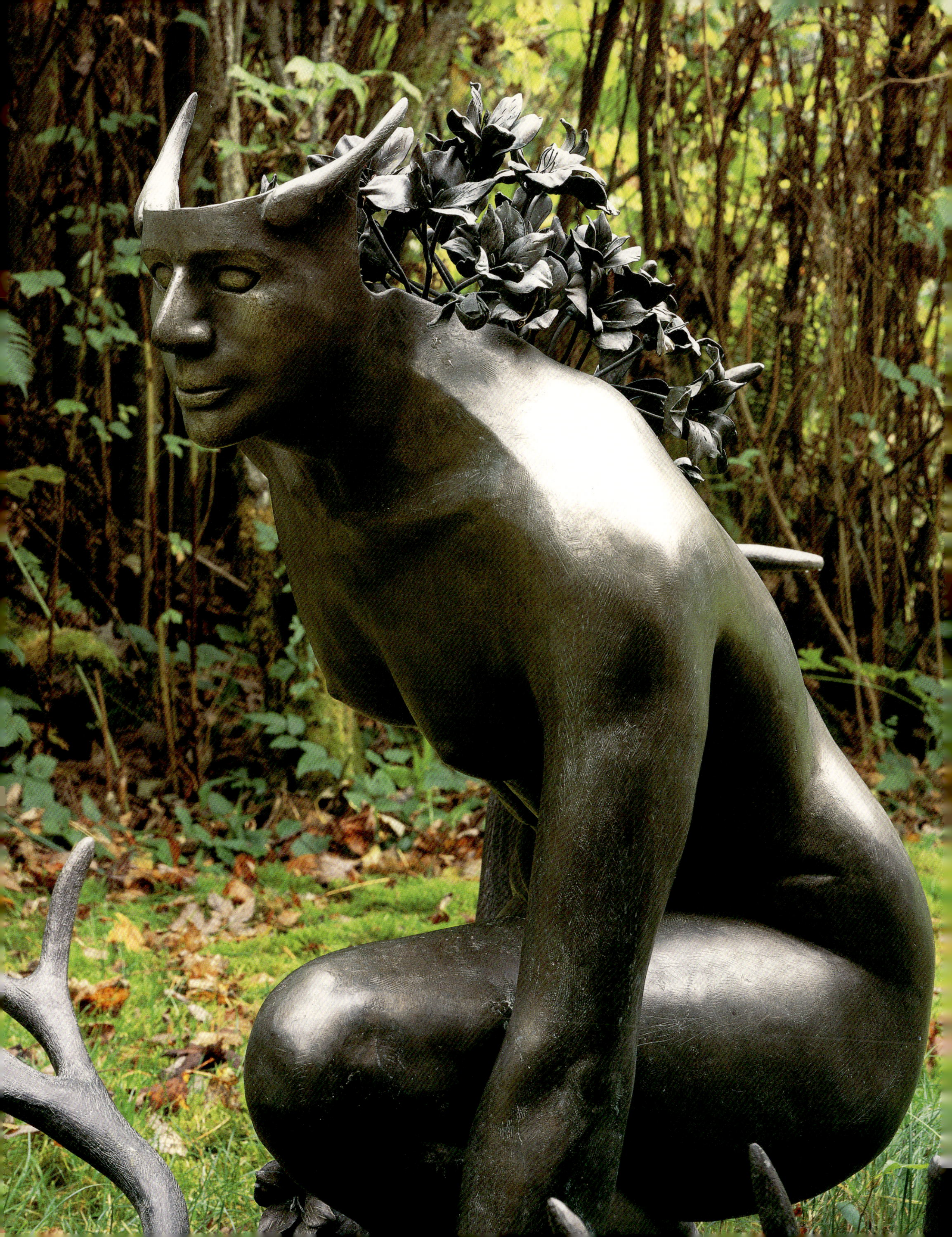

Her Cry

The mature fecund Goddess of Cycles lifts the antlers symbolic of Nature, holding them out for us to see. She cries out that Nature is in jeopardy and it is the creative human spirit which calls to the rest of us to attend to the consequences of our actions. She asks us to consider our relation to our planet—asks the question of how our undisciplined reproduction can be sustained. Does our species have the right to crowd out all the other species? The piece cries out NO! Nature will restore her own balance with or without us. She urges us to attune ourselves to her or lose.

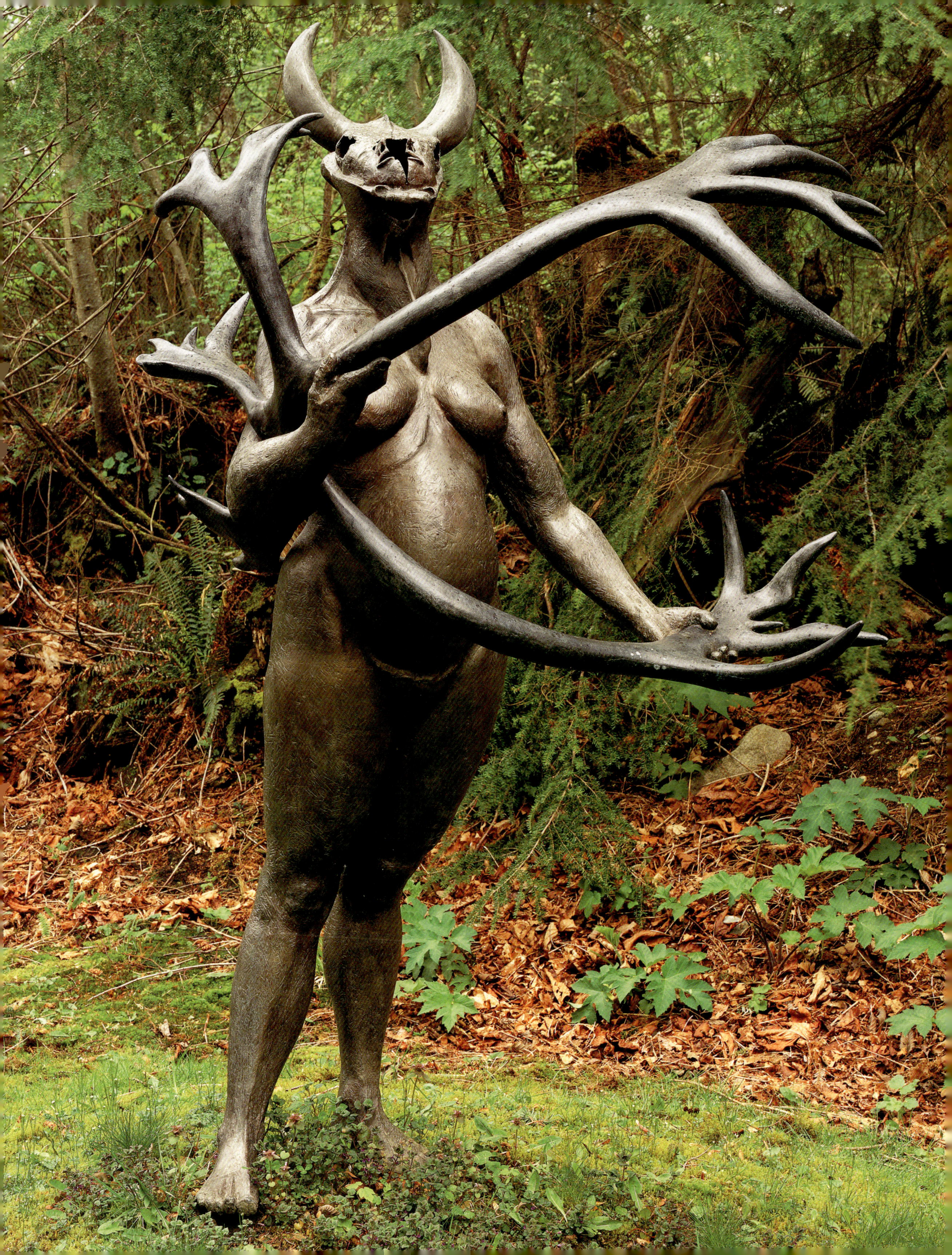

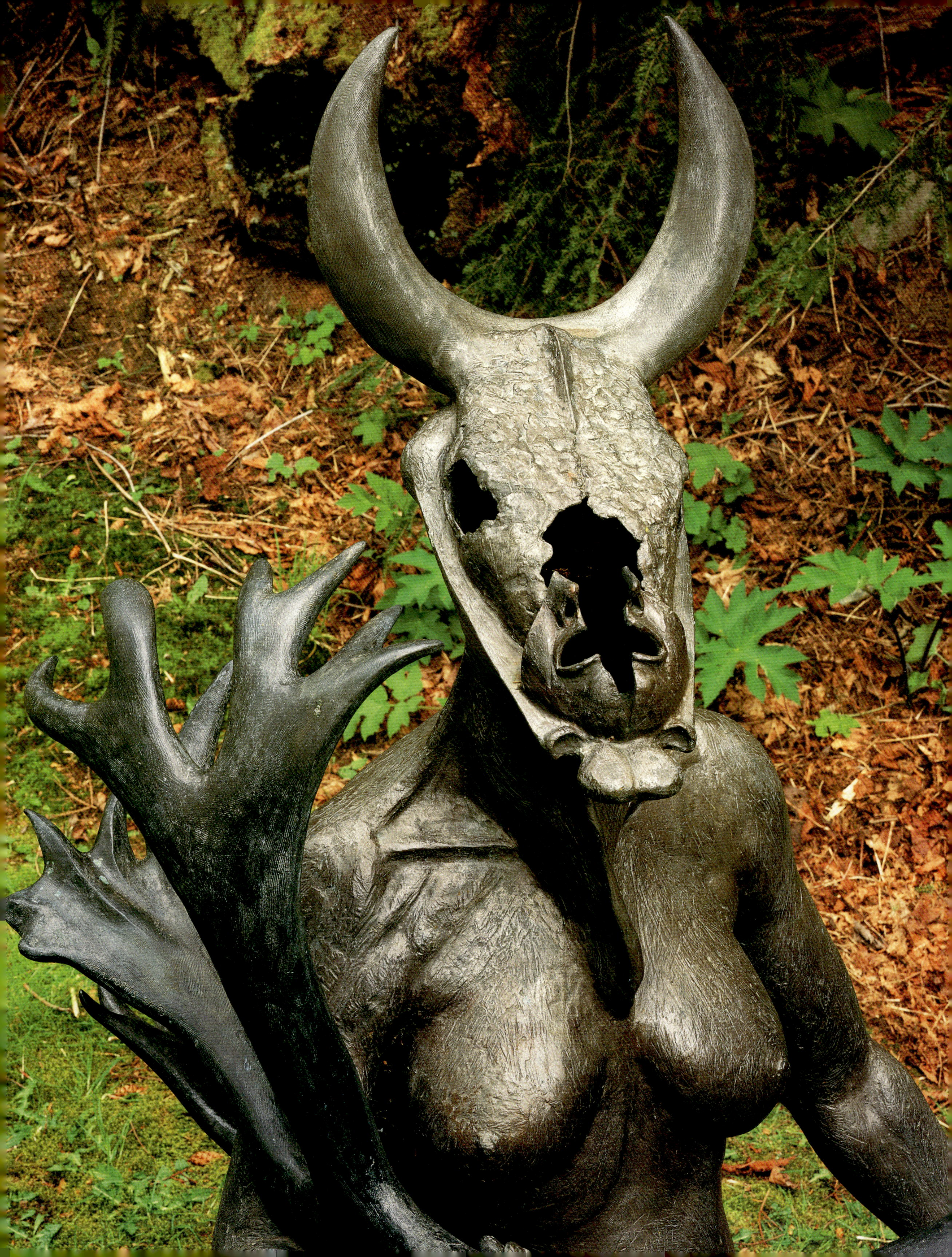

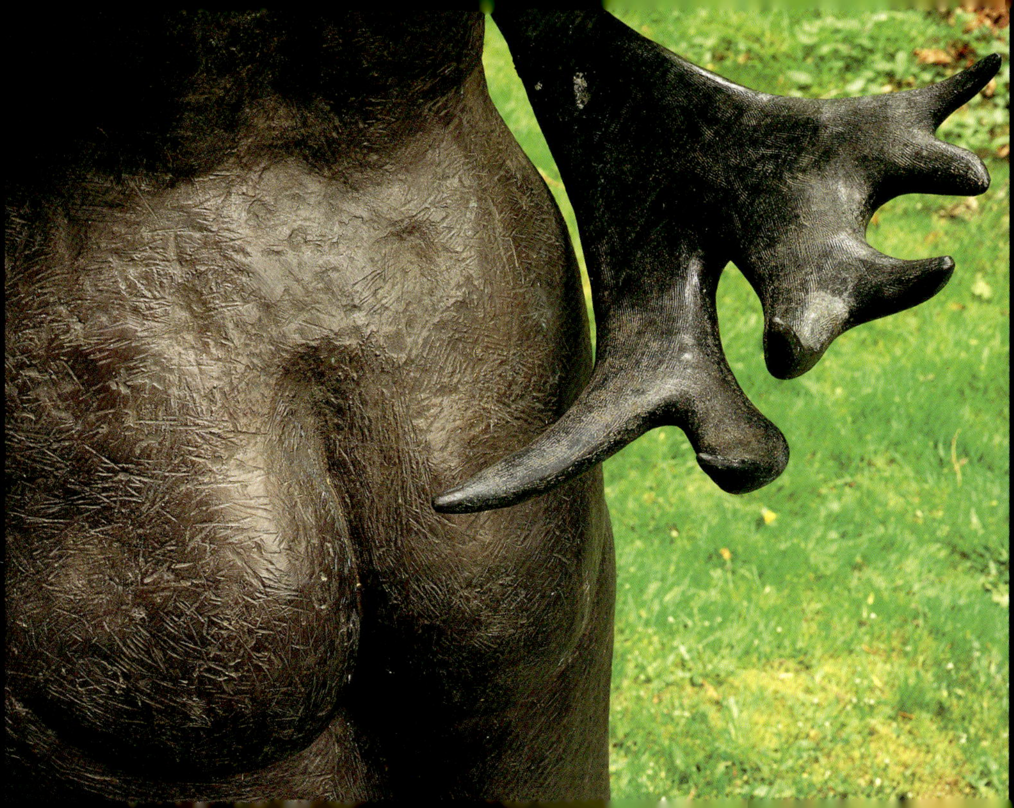

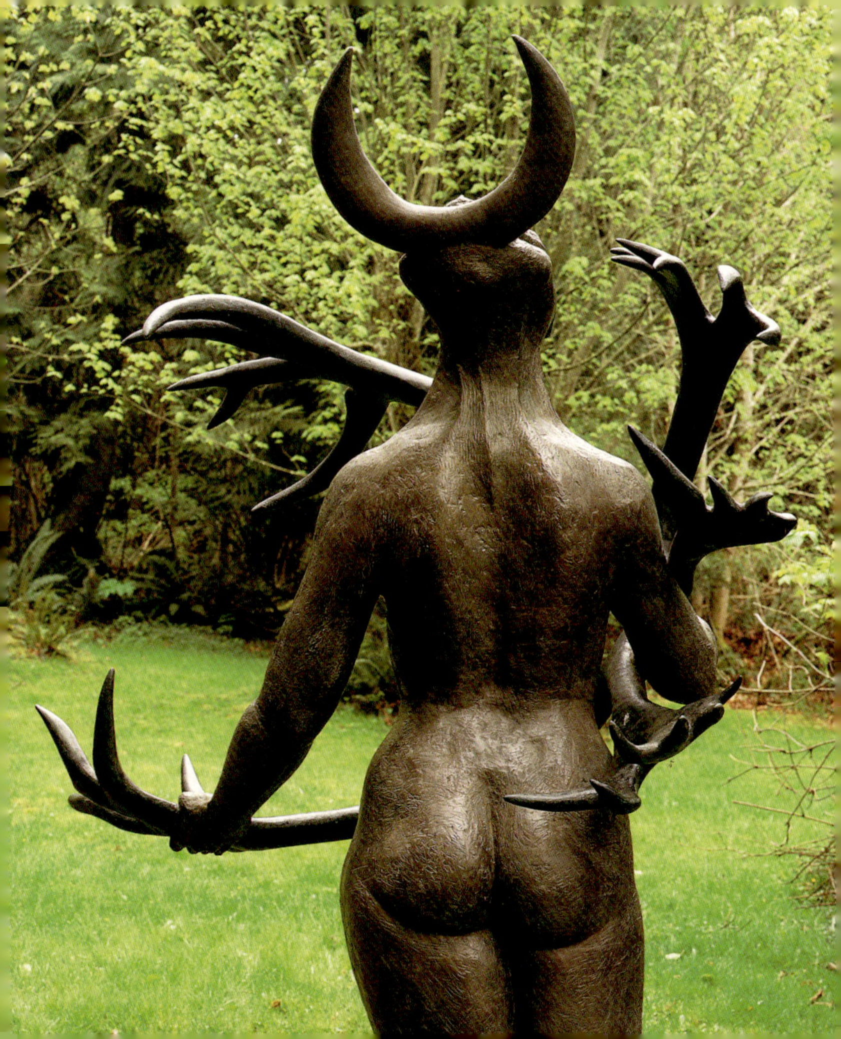

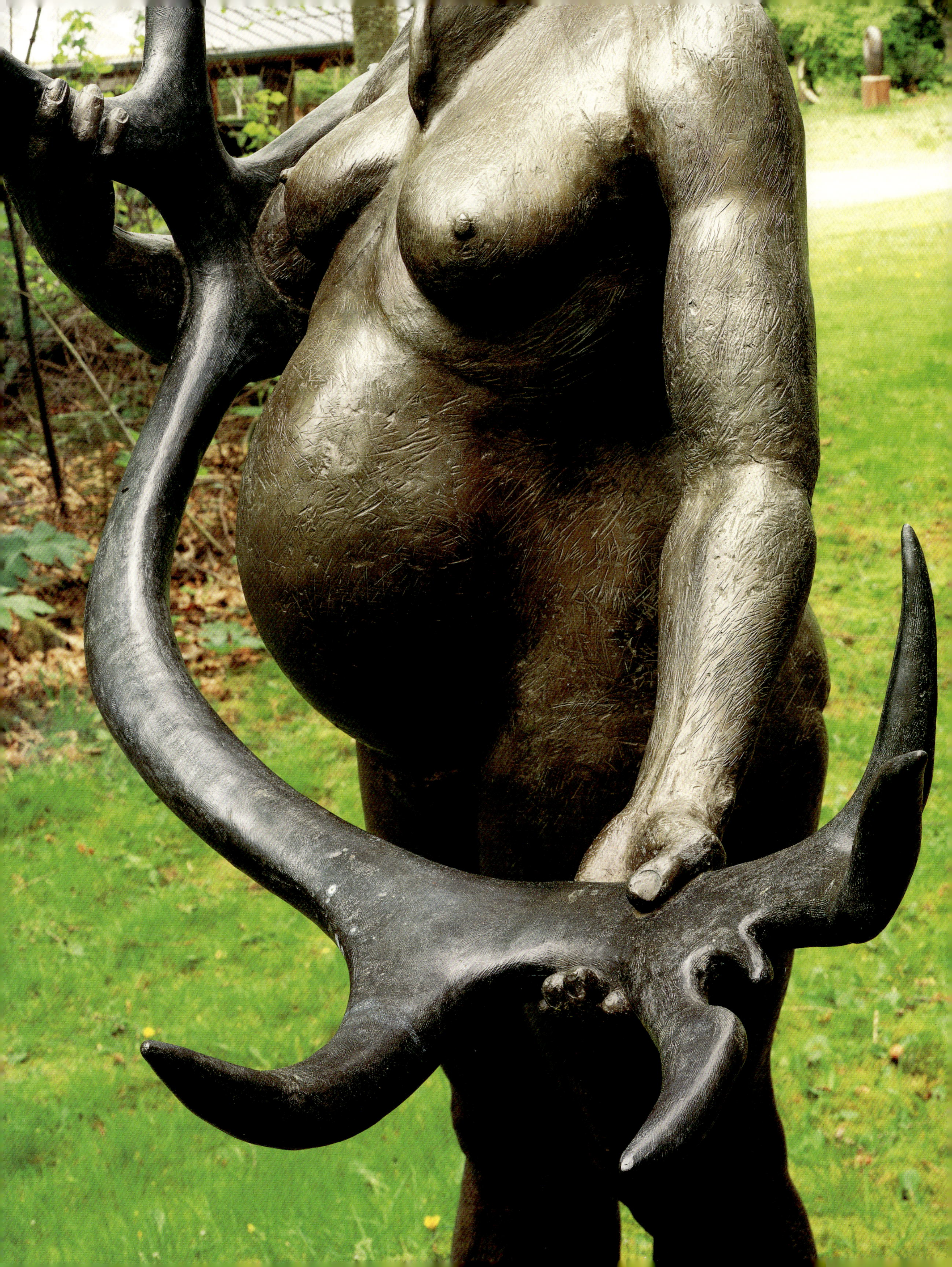

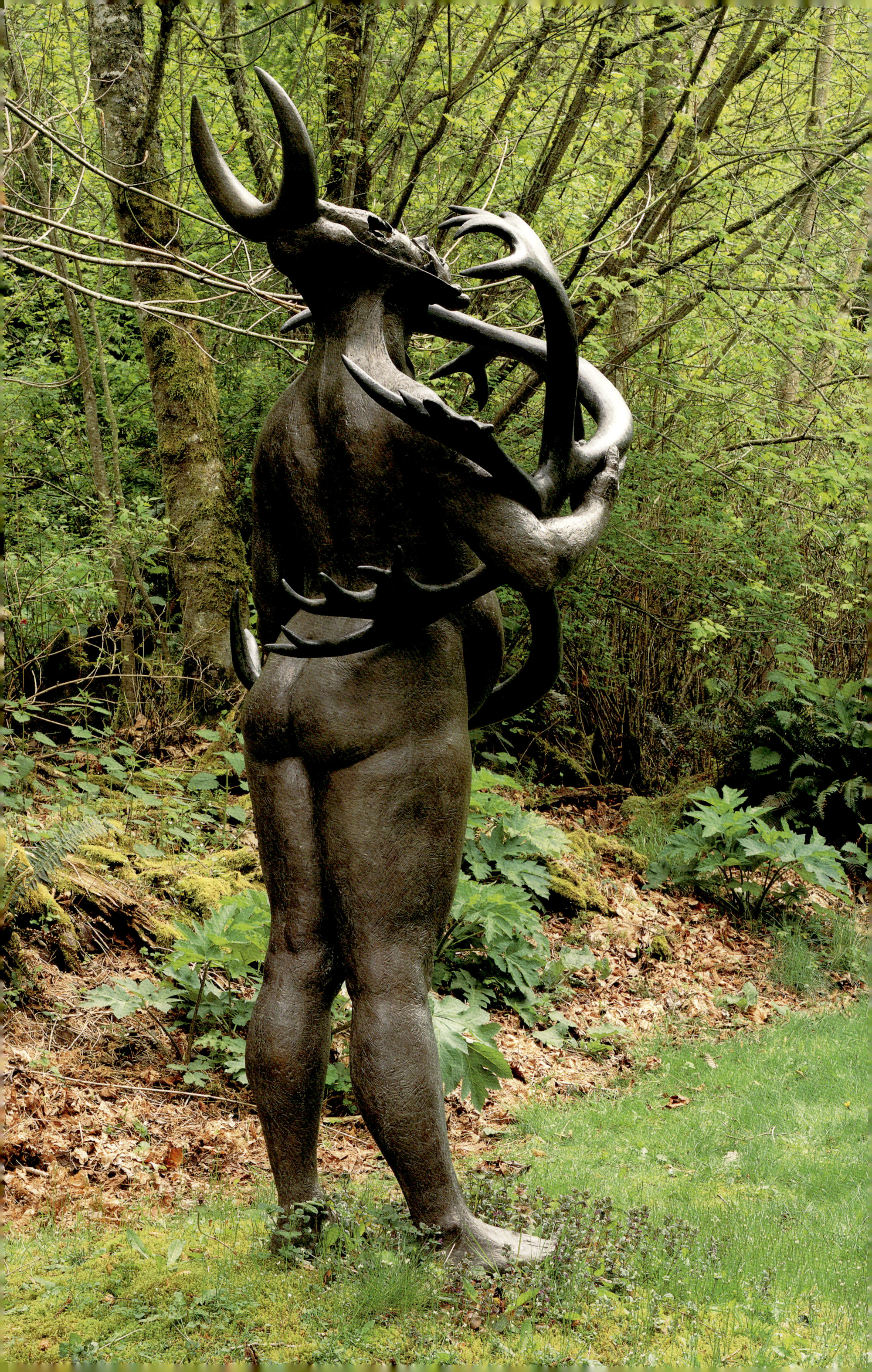

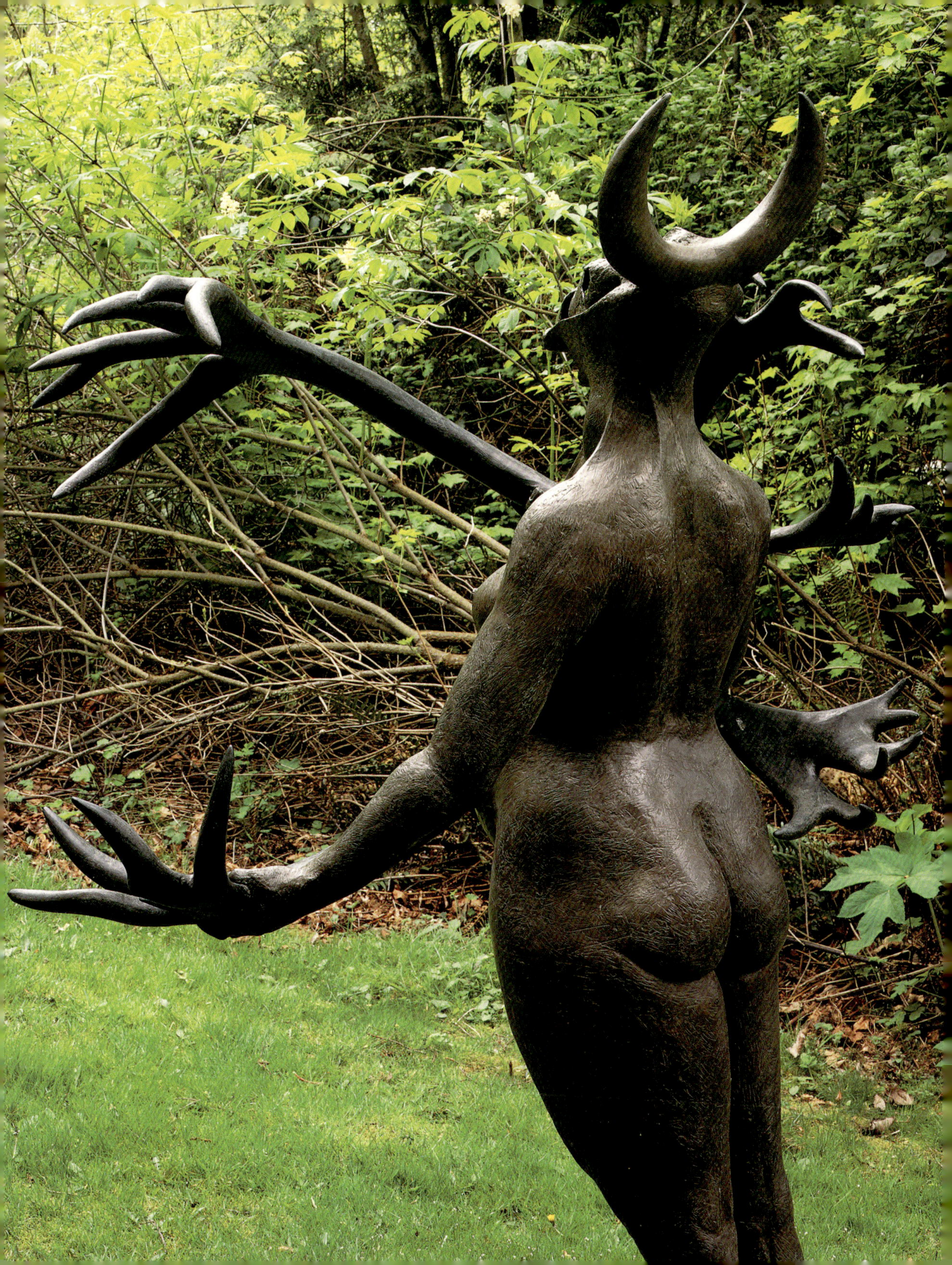

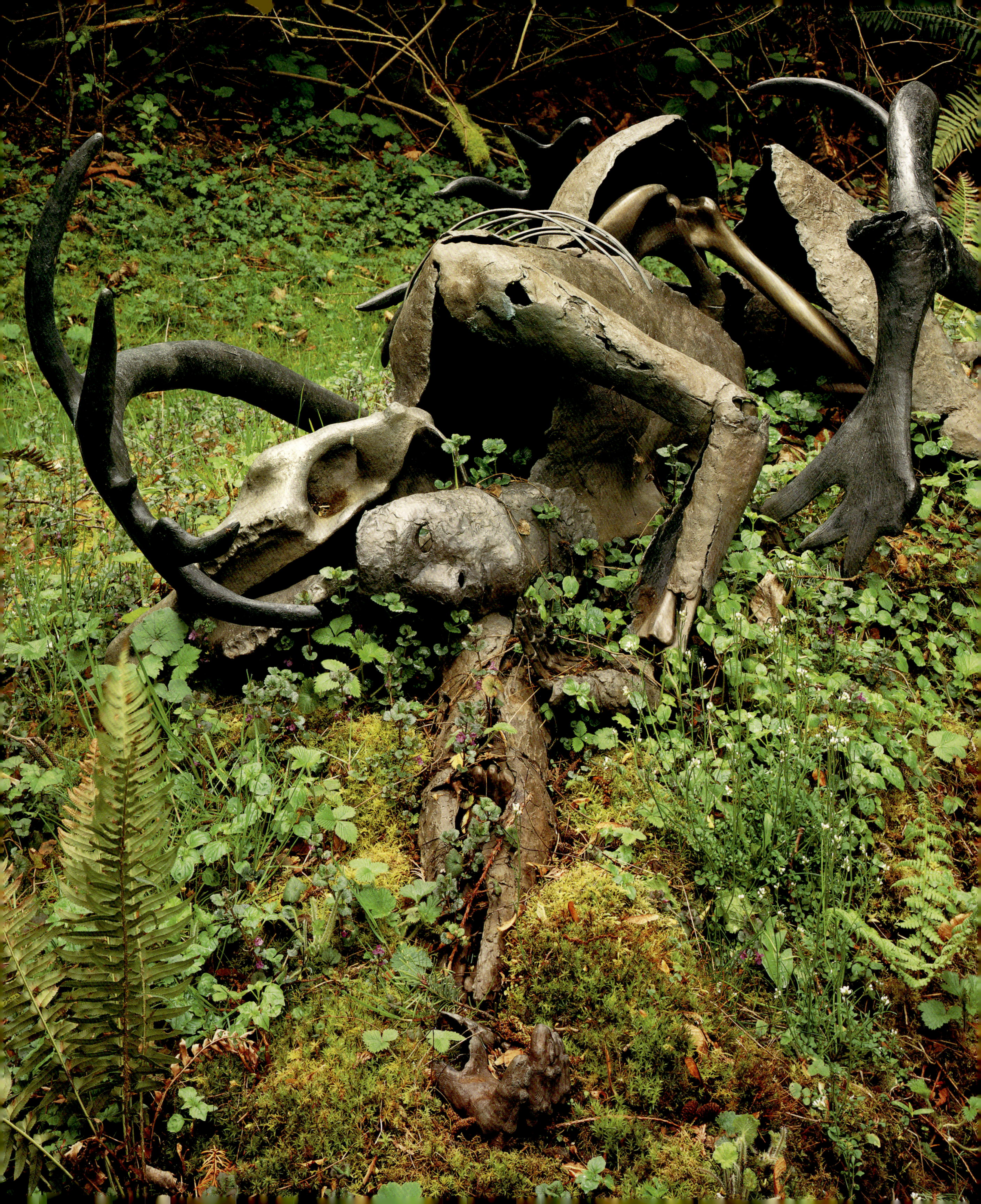

Life / Death / Life

She is the Goddess of Nature's Cycles. She knows that death feeds life, that all food is a willing death giving life to all that needs nourishment. She gives herself back to Nature as food for the others to come and is sheltered by the antlers of Nature while she rests. Her glowing bones are the indestructible life force, quietly waiting to be reborn into the Maiden Goddess who waits below her. And so it goes around and around, Life, then Death, then Life.

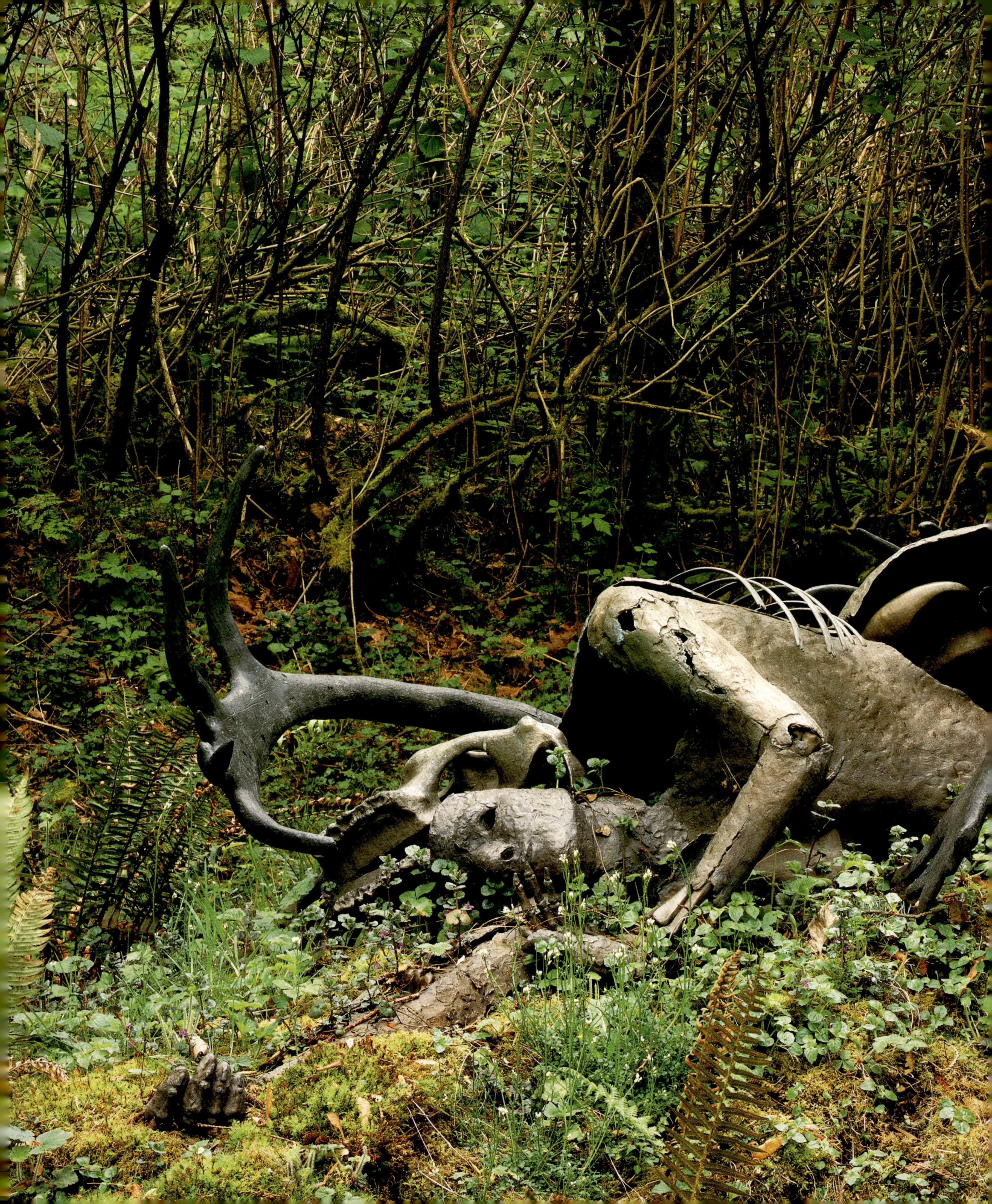

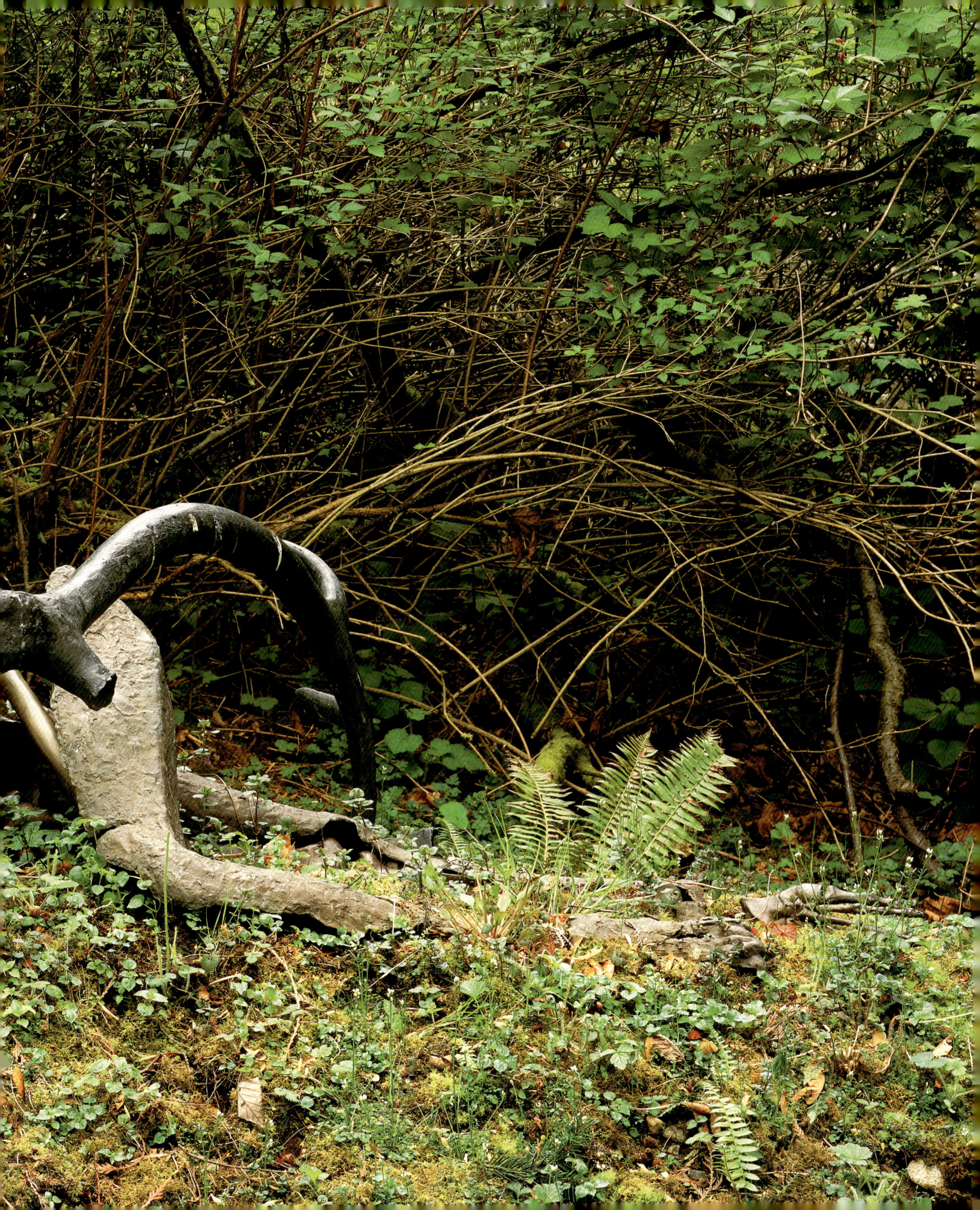

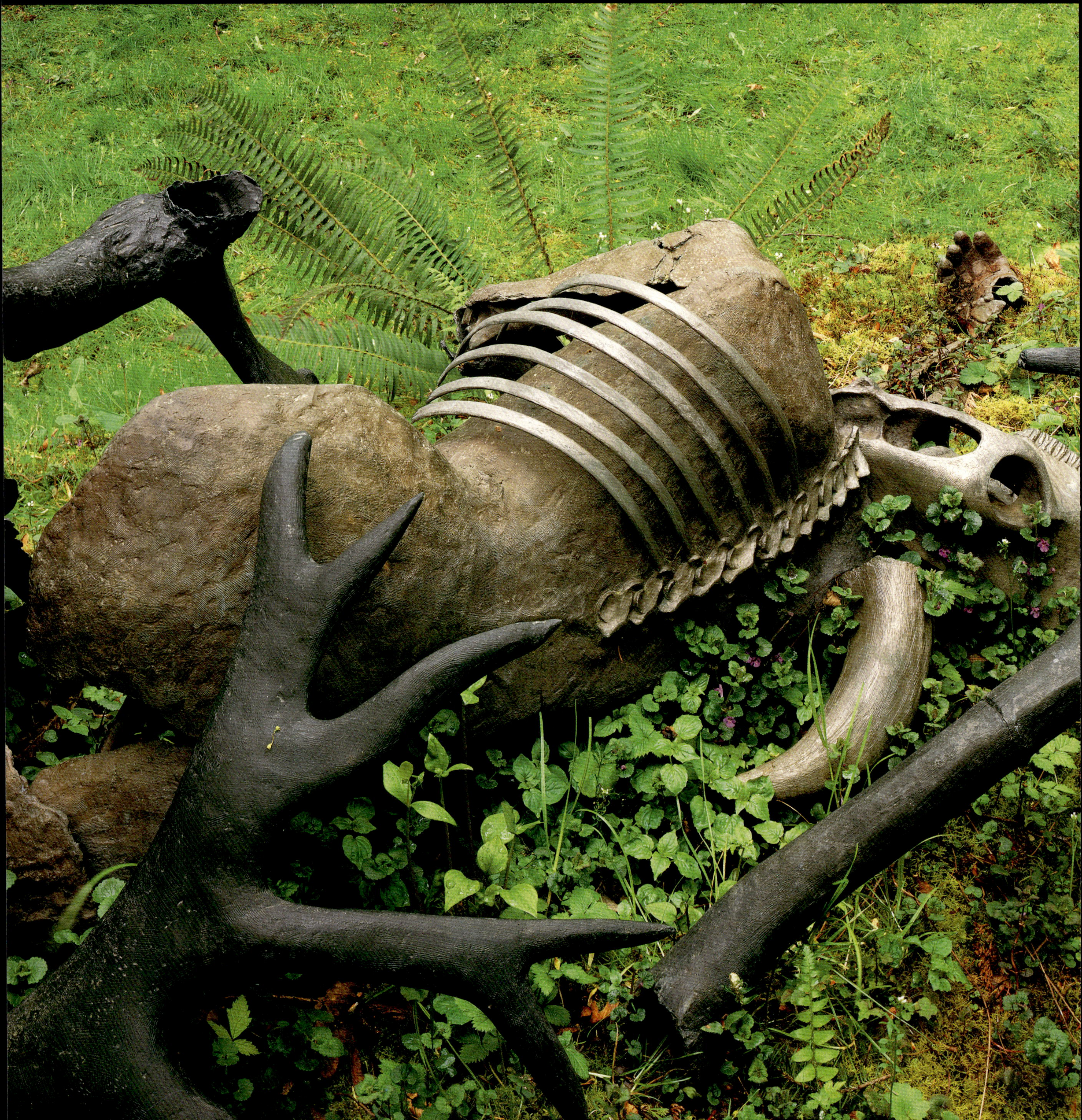

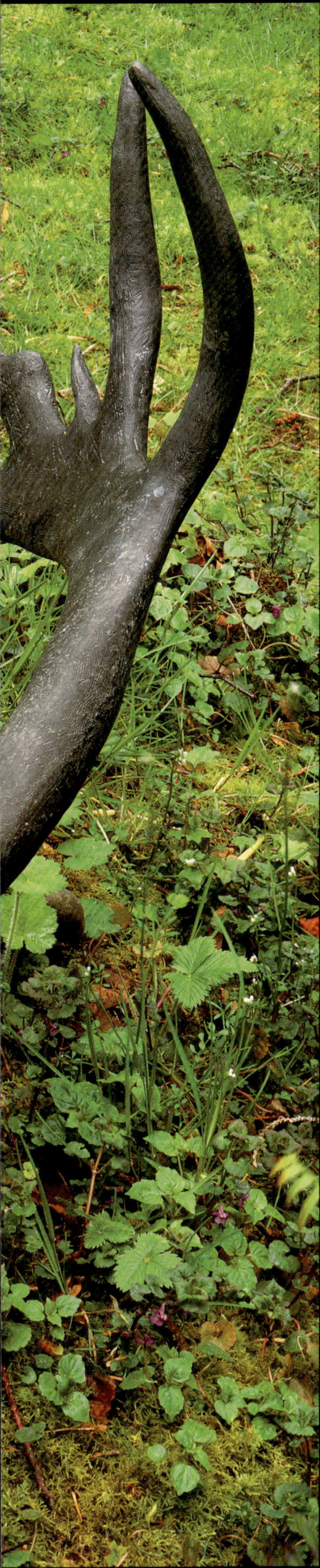

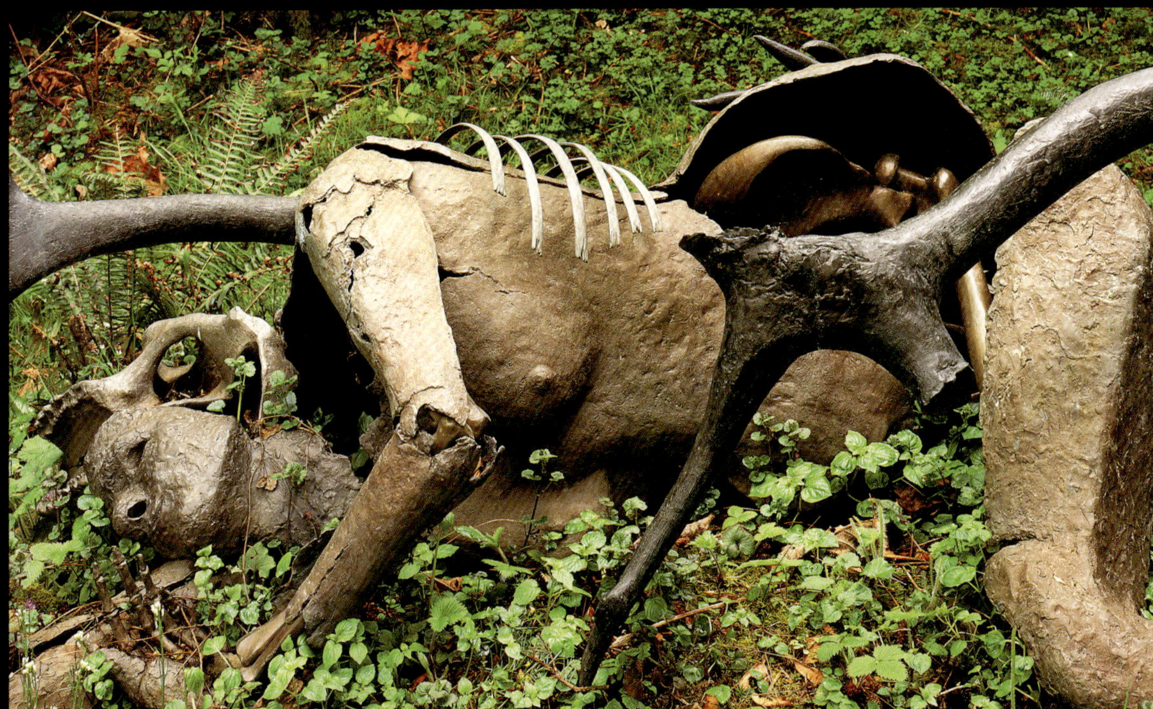

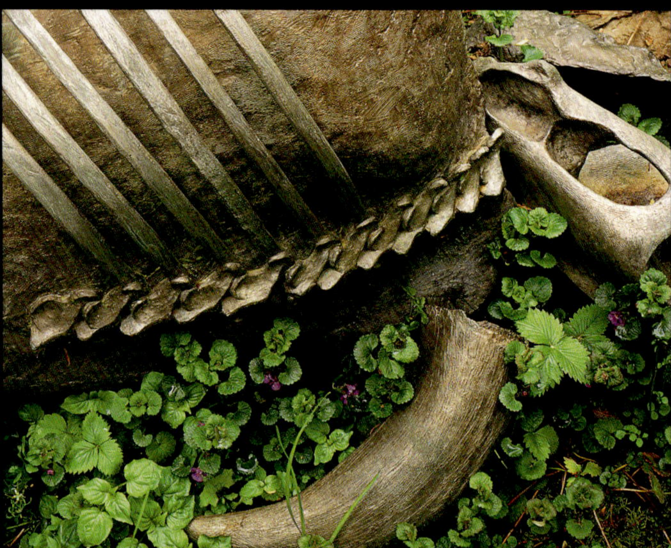

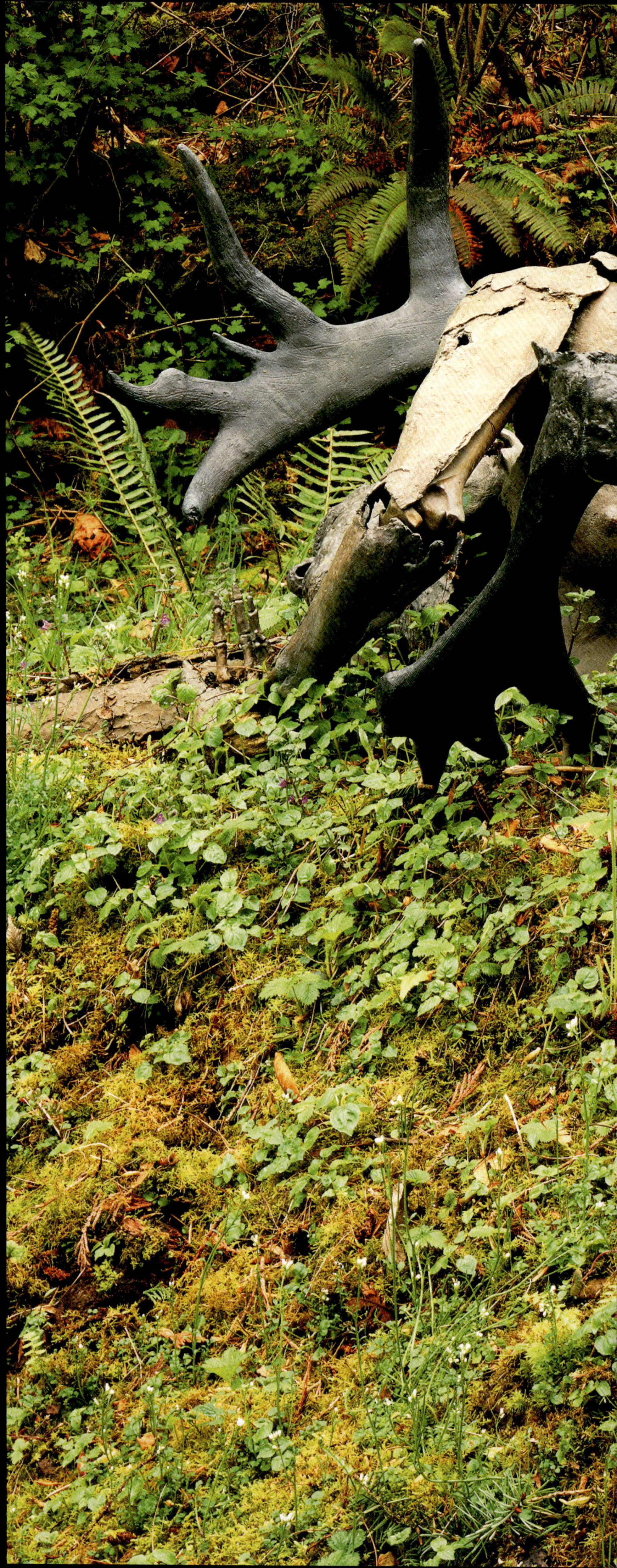

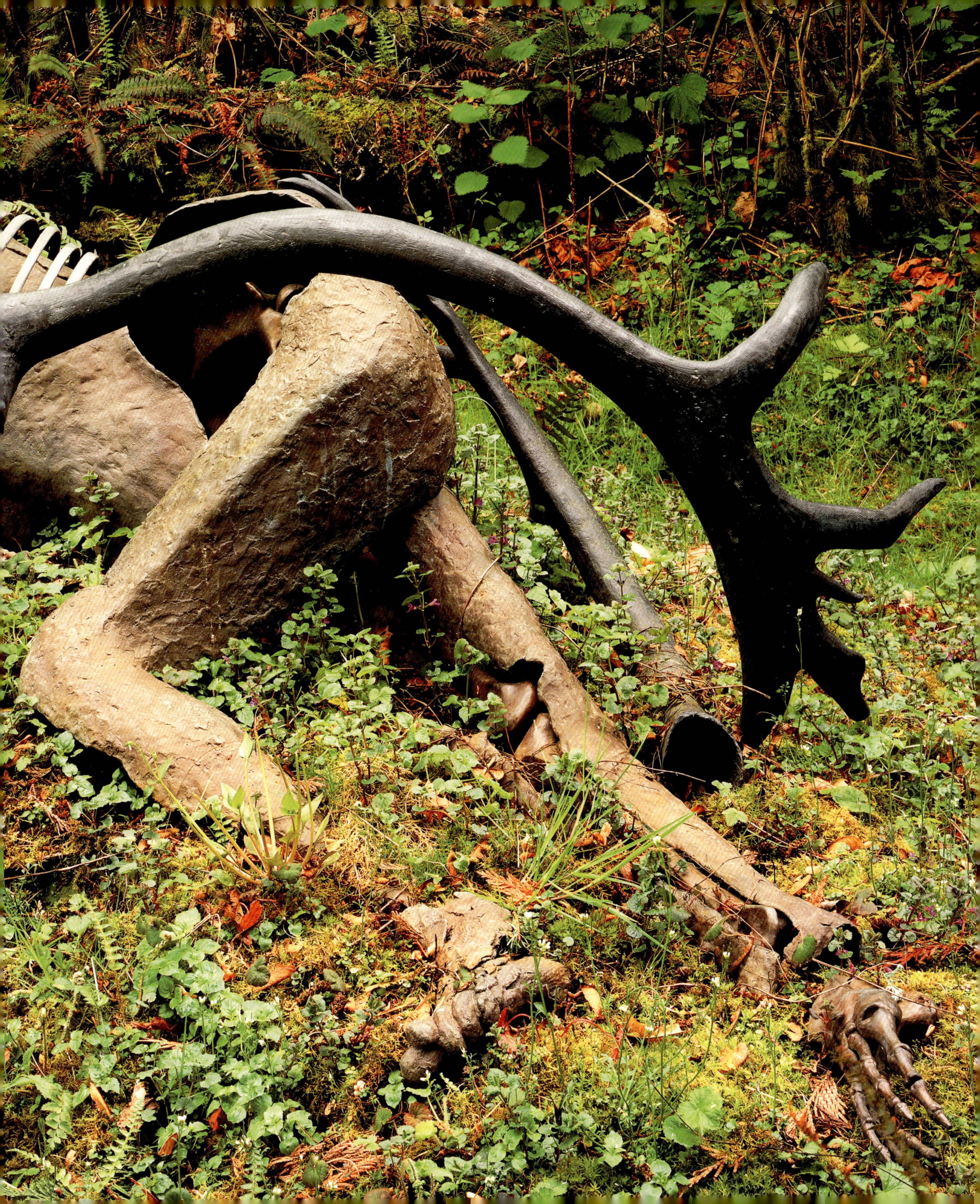

The women who voluntarily journey into the inner labyrinth will discover and can release joyous instinctual masculinity. Willingly encountered by the female, the masculine no longer needs to hide in shame, but shines with his true power when joined with her. Together they are the spontaneous Dance of Life from which all creativity springs. The internally integrated masculine and feminine spirits in us all dance the world into being.

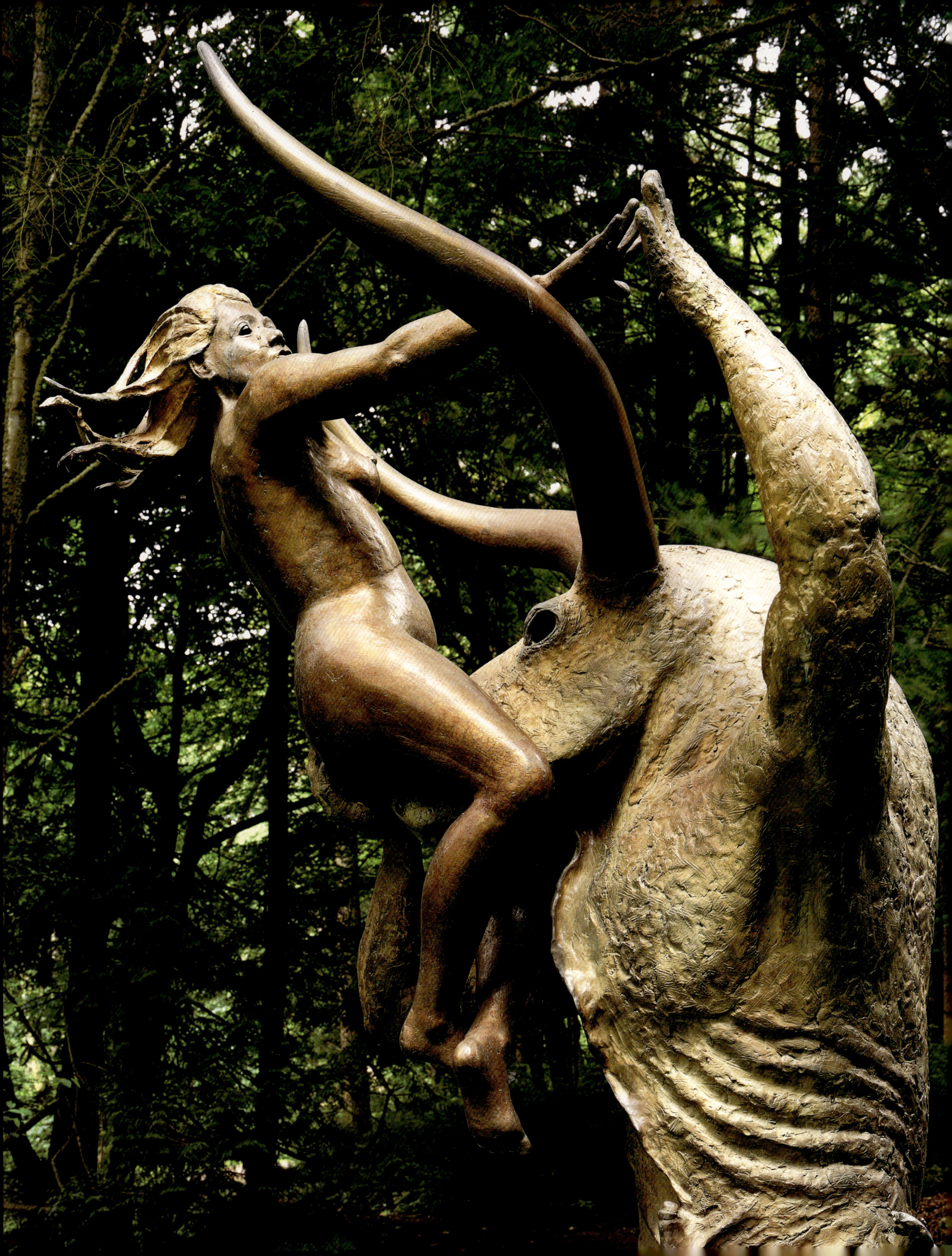

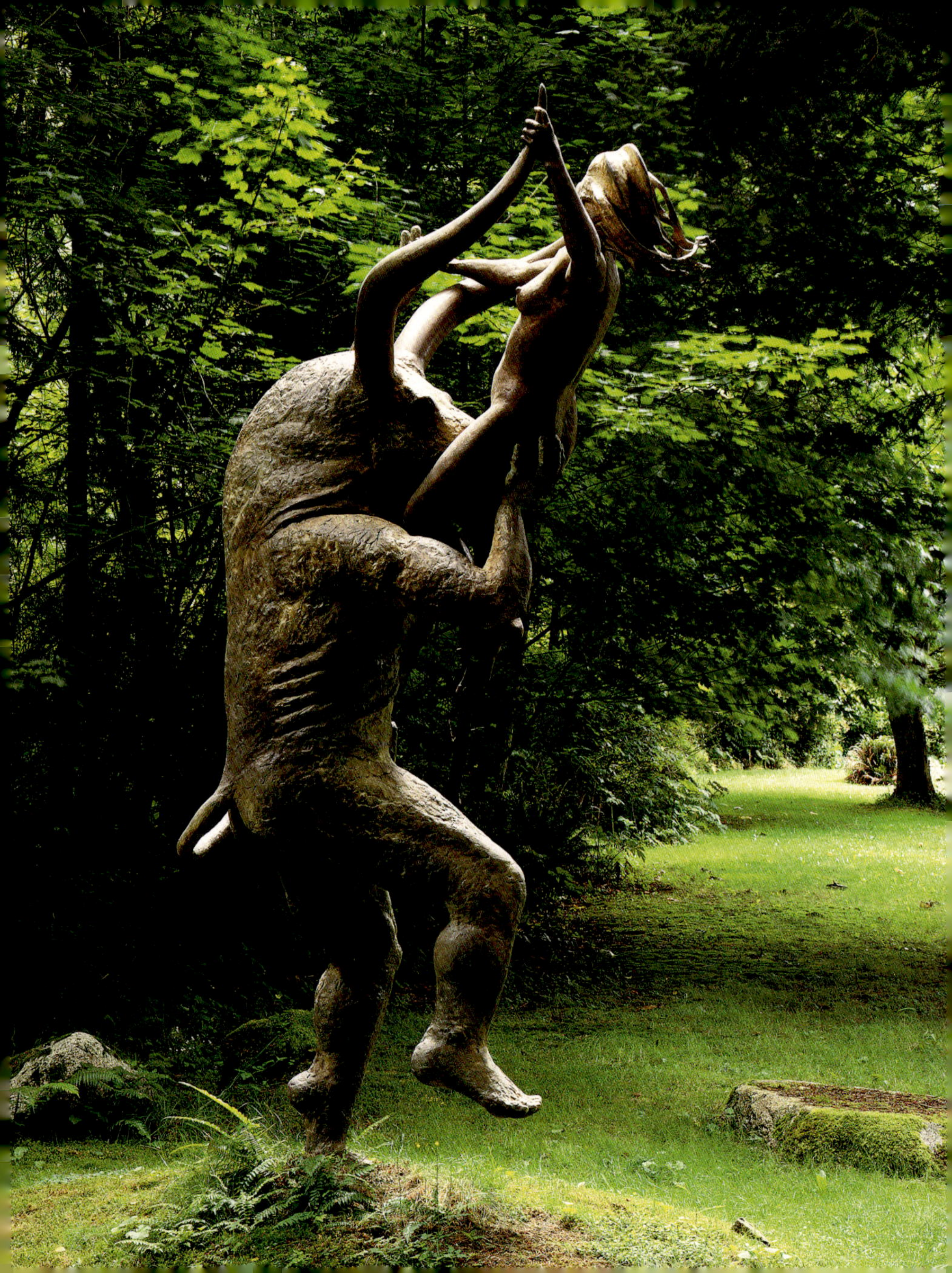

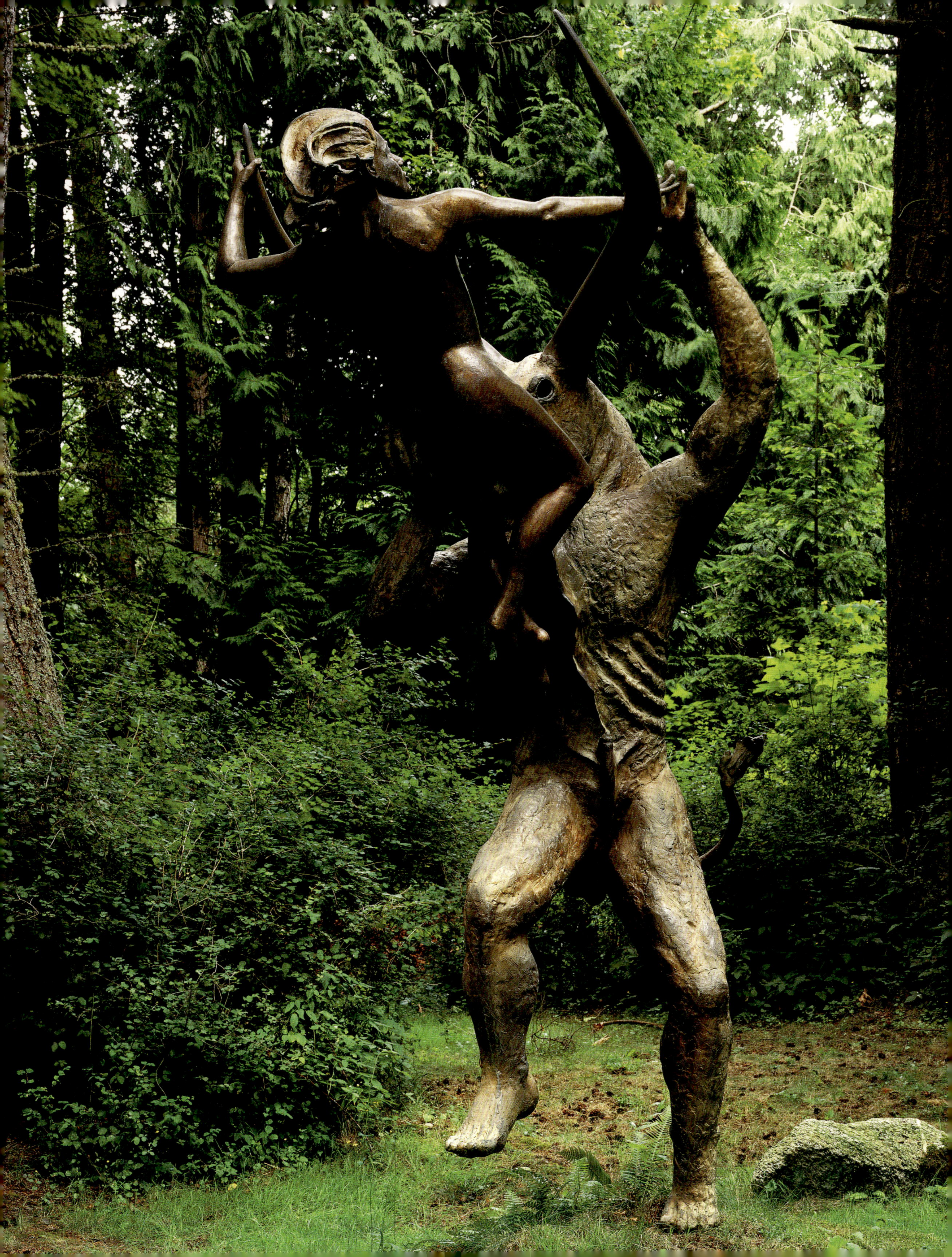

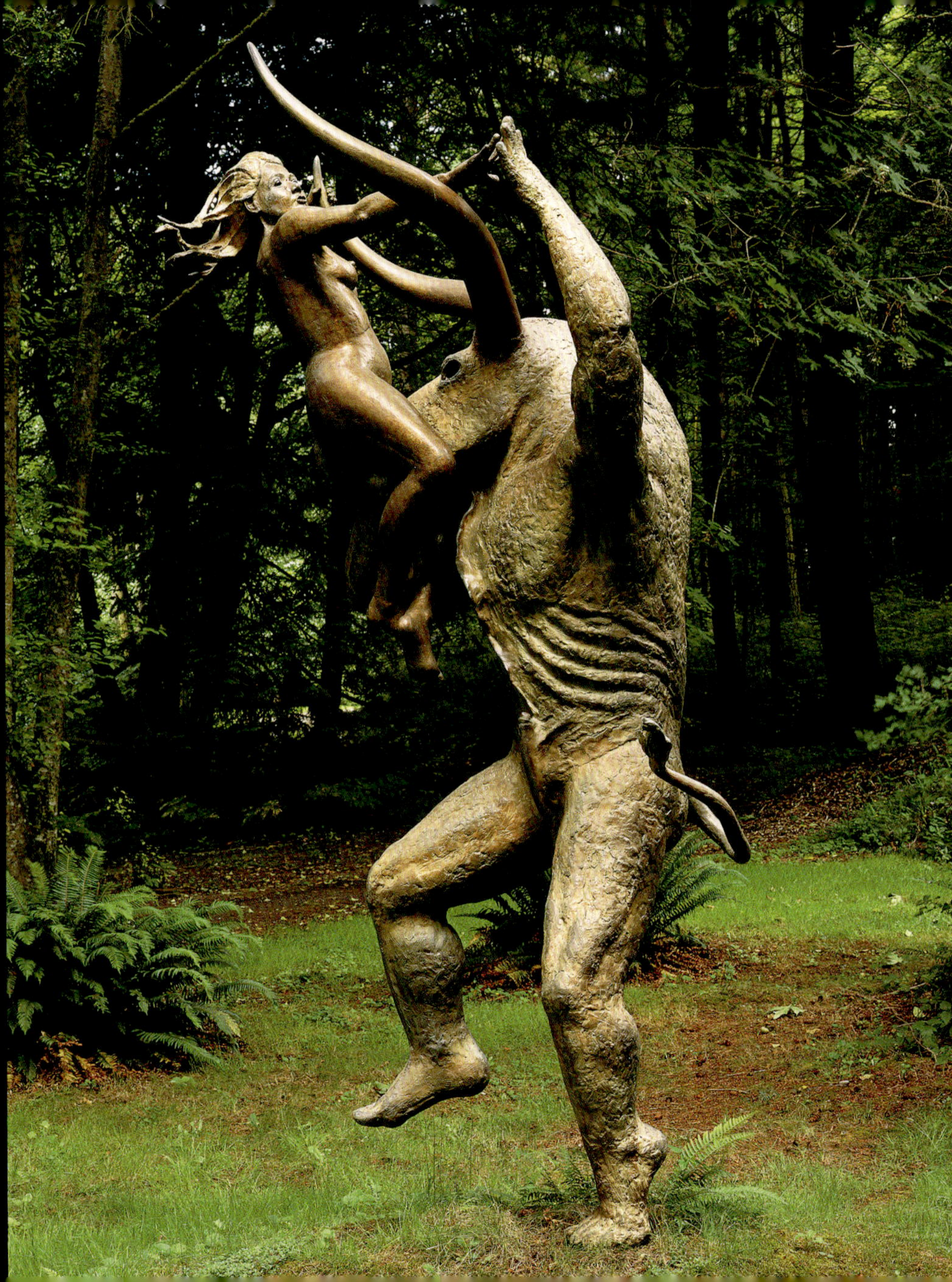

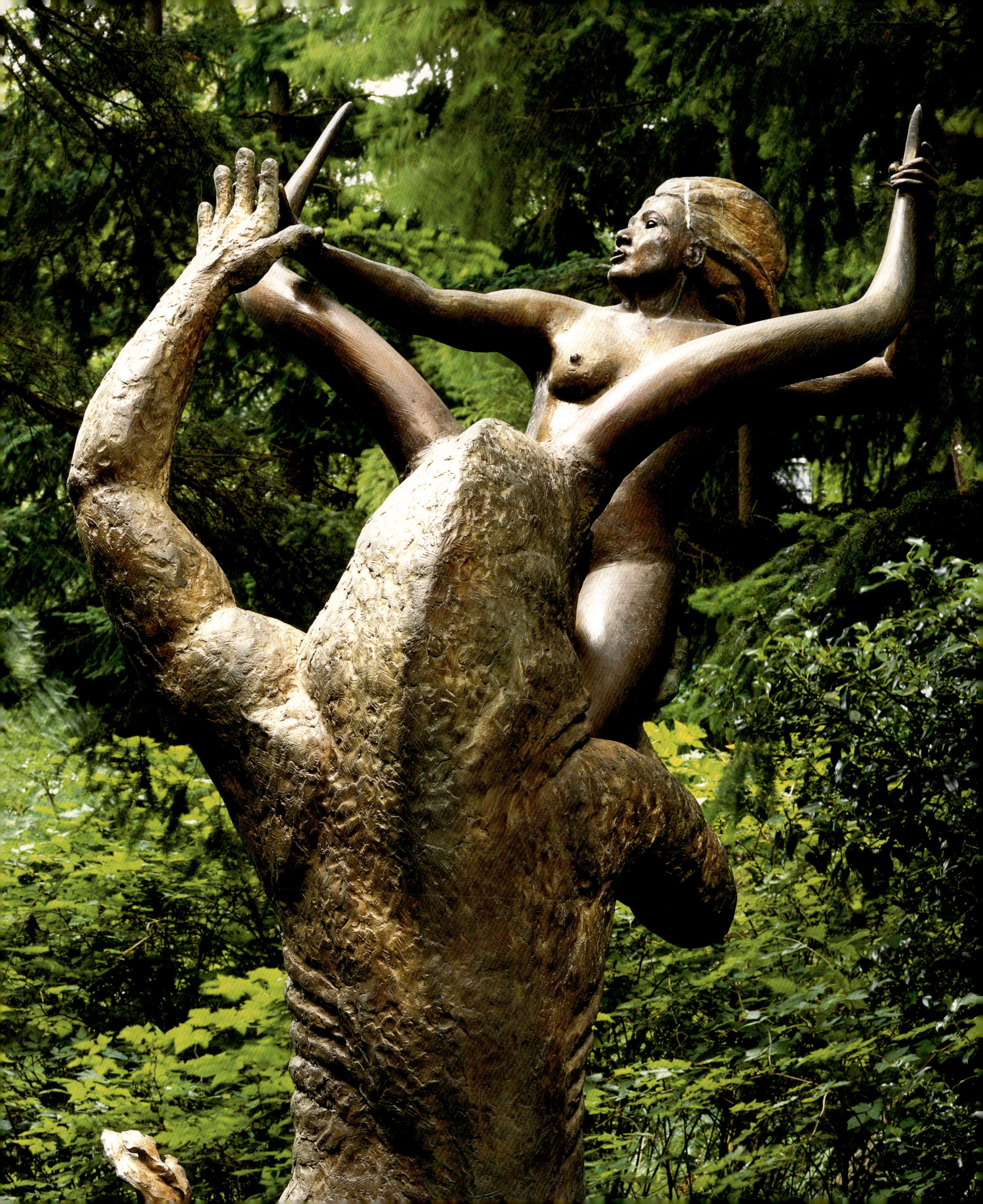

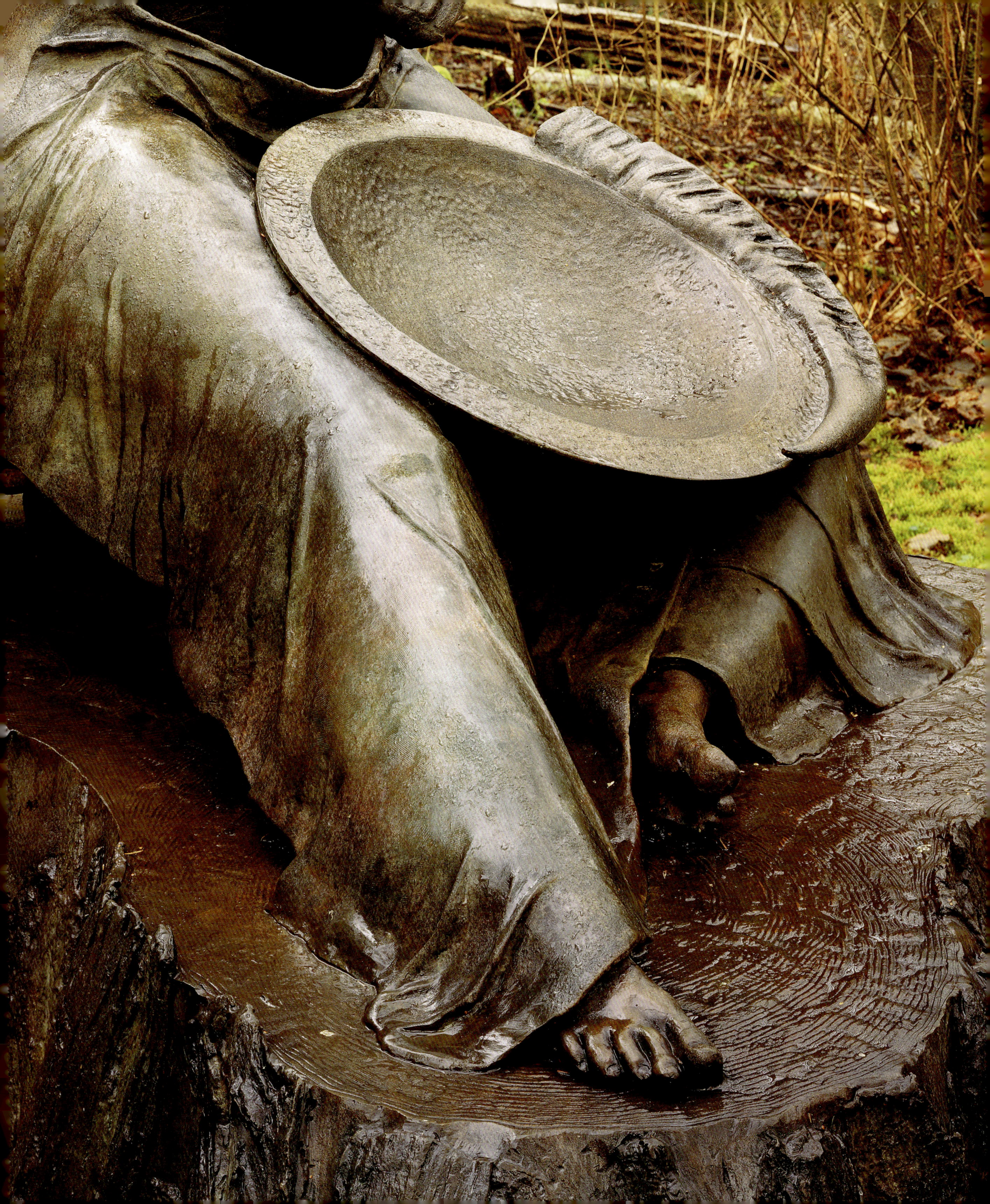

Ask Gaia

The Earth Mother as Oracle-in-20th-Century-Guise is seated on the three-horned cauldron, home of the snake of feminine wisdom; she awaits us. The winds of our disbelief blow through her, but the horns of Nature hold her firm. Her dish of plenty upon her ample lap holds little now. The place where she sits has been cut, yet she will always remain. Have we the courage to ask her to prophesy our human future? Dare we do as she asks? Dare we not?

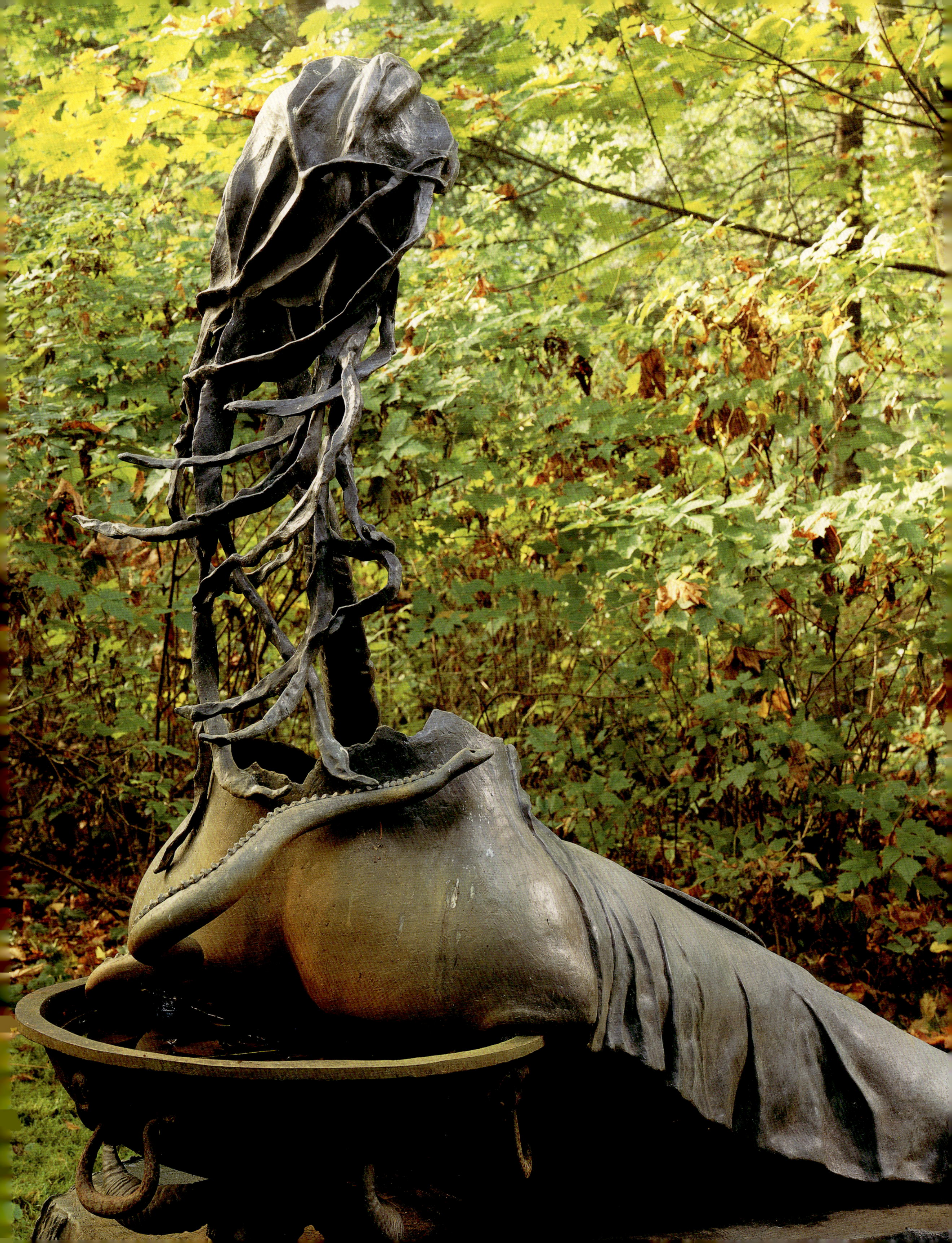

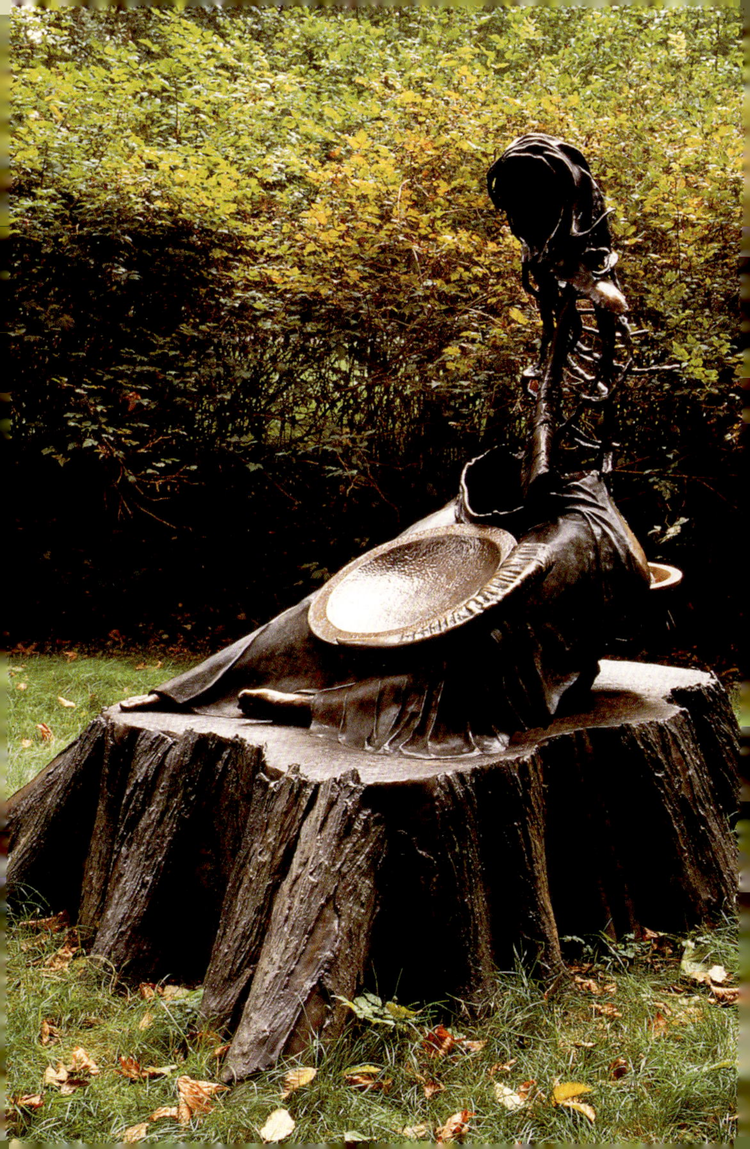

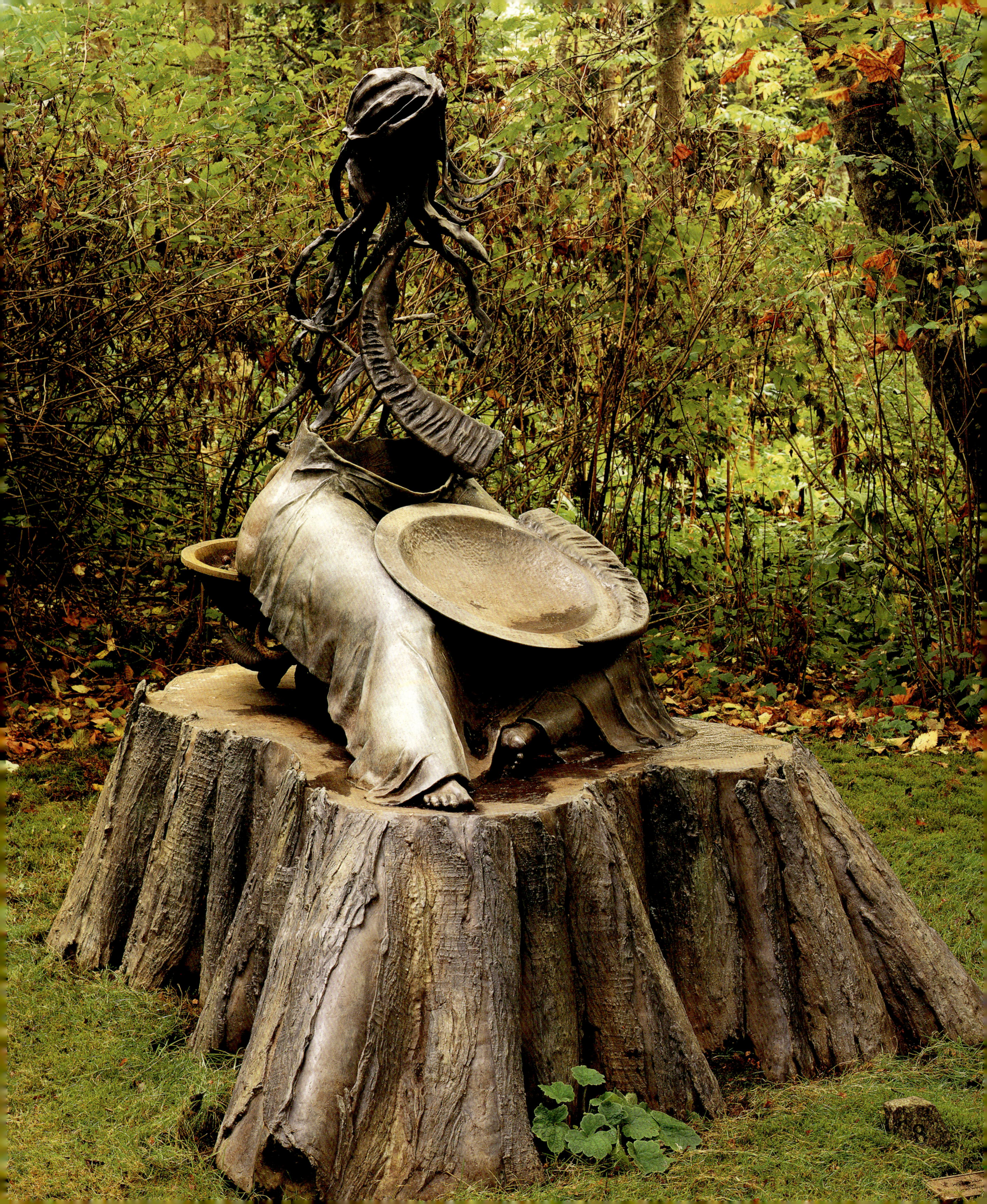

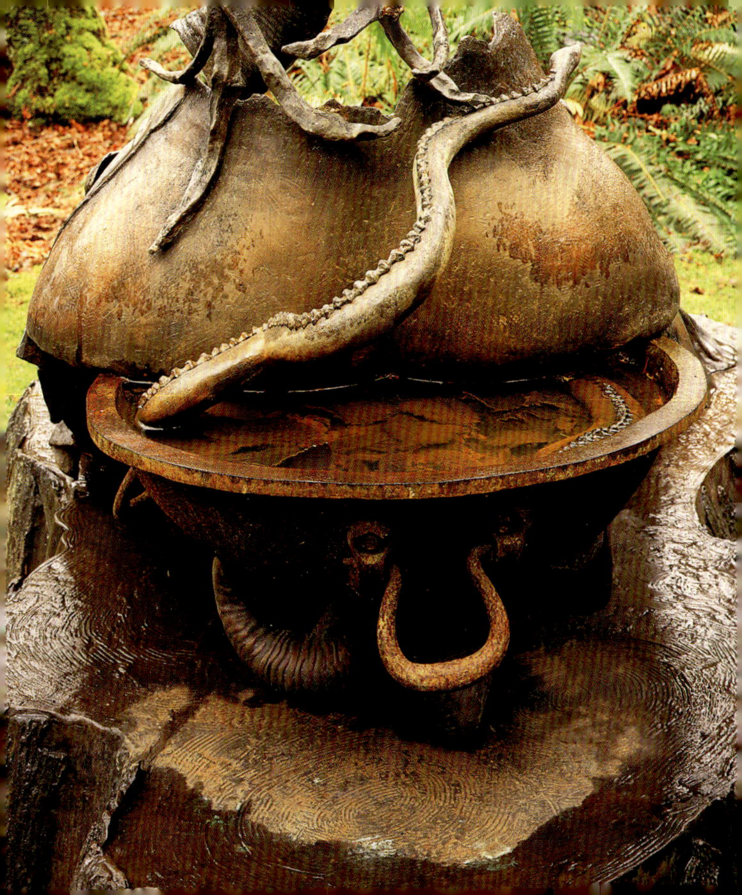

Gifting the Giver

Our psychic wholeness is the joining of the masculine and the feminine. Being whole, we know it to be a gift, and joining our humanness with all other natural forces, we offer our lives back to the Universe. We gift ourselves to the Universal Giver.

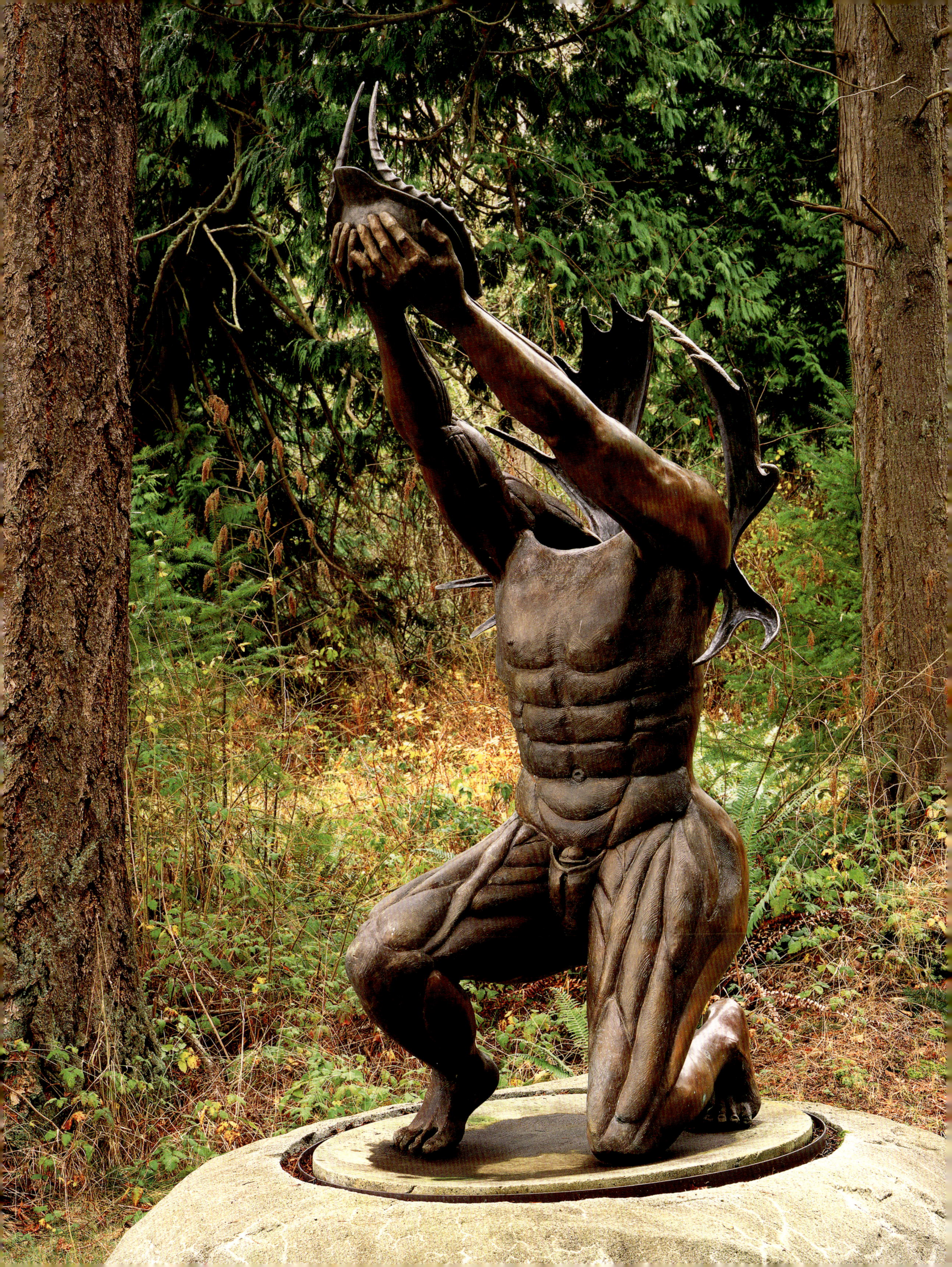

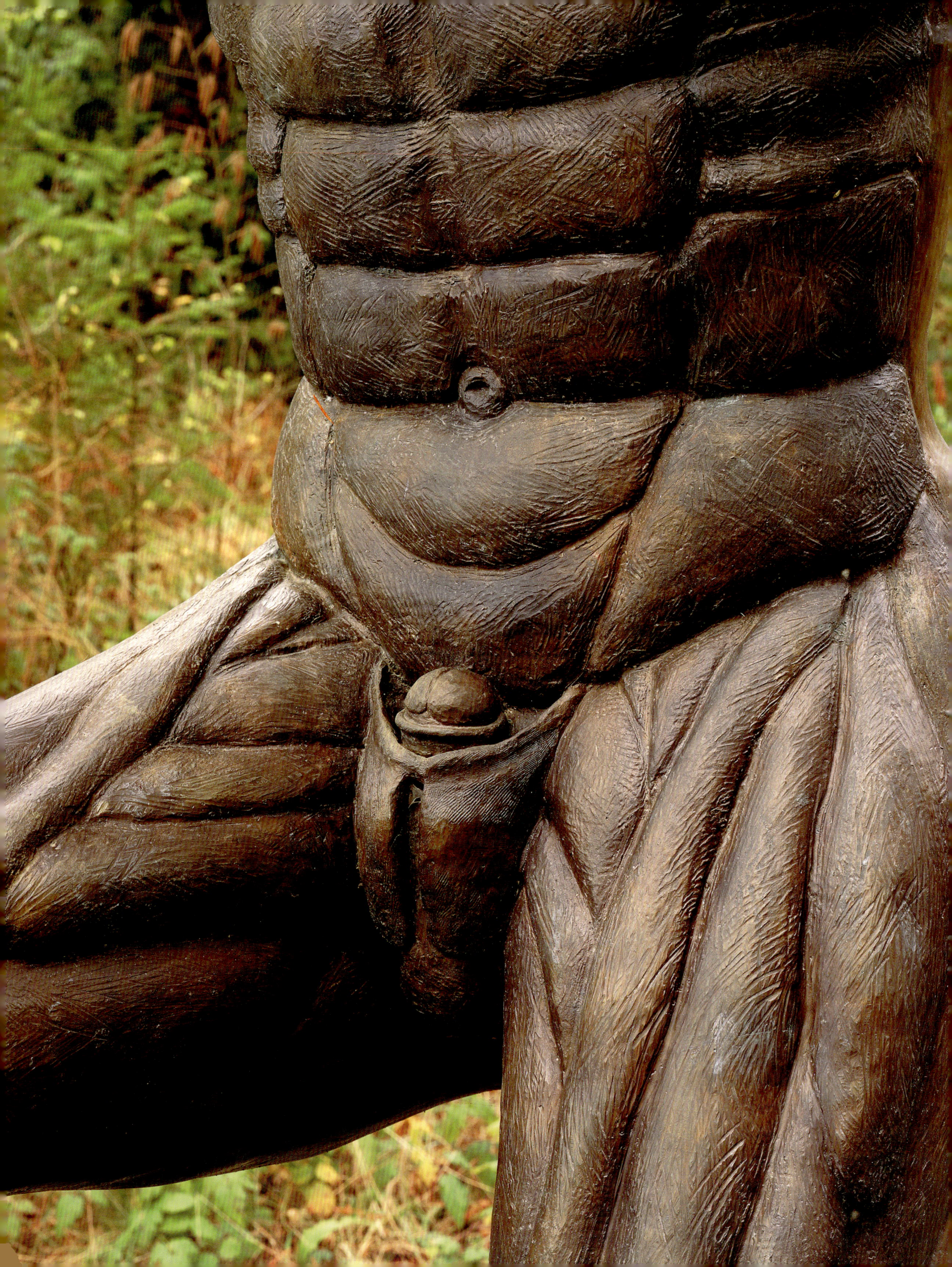

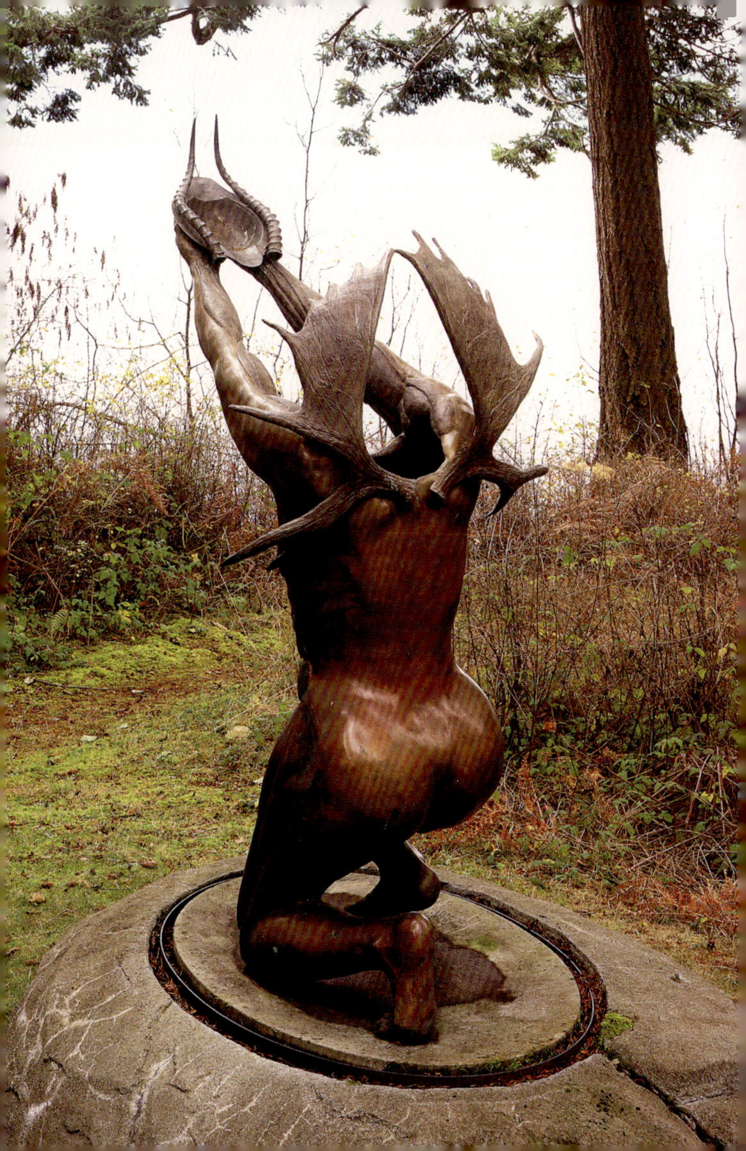

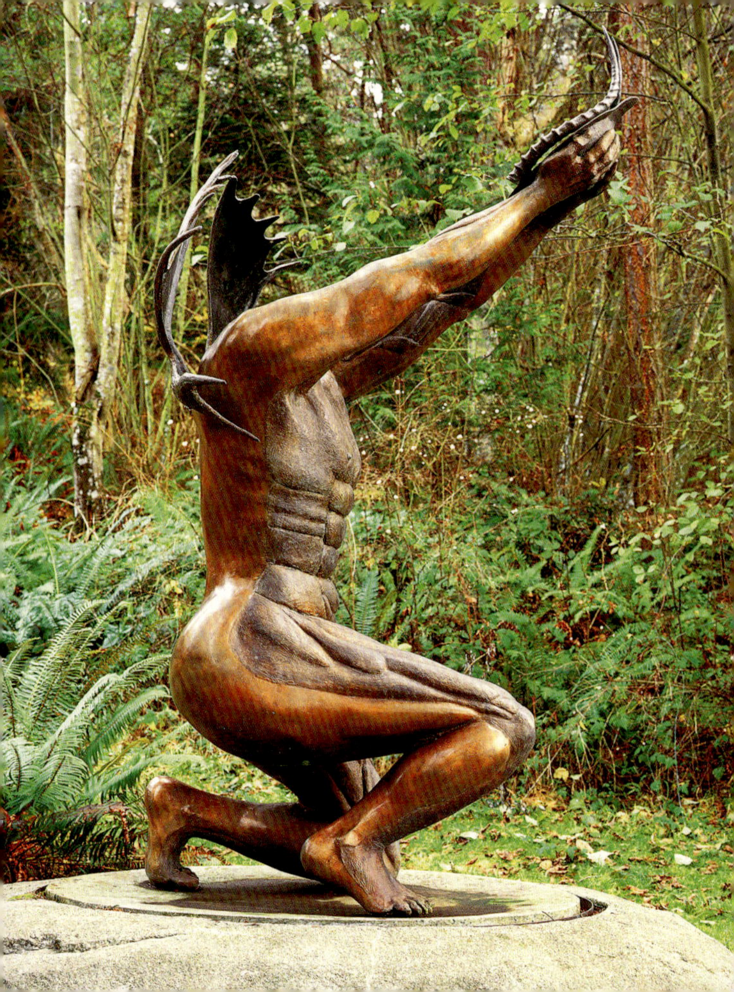

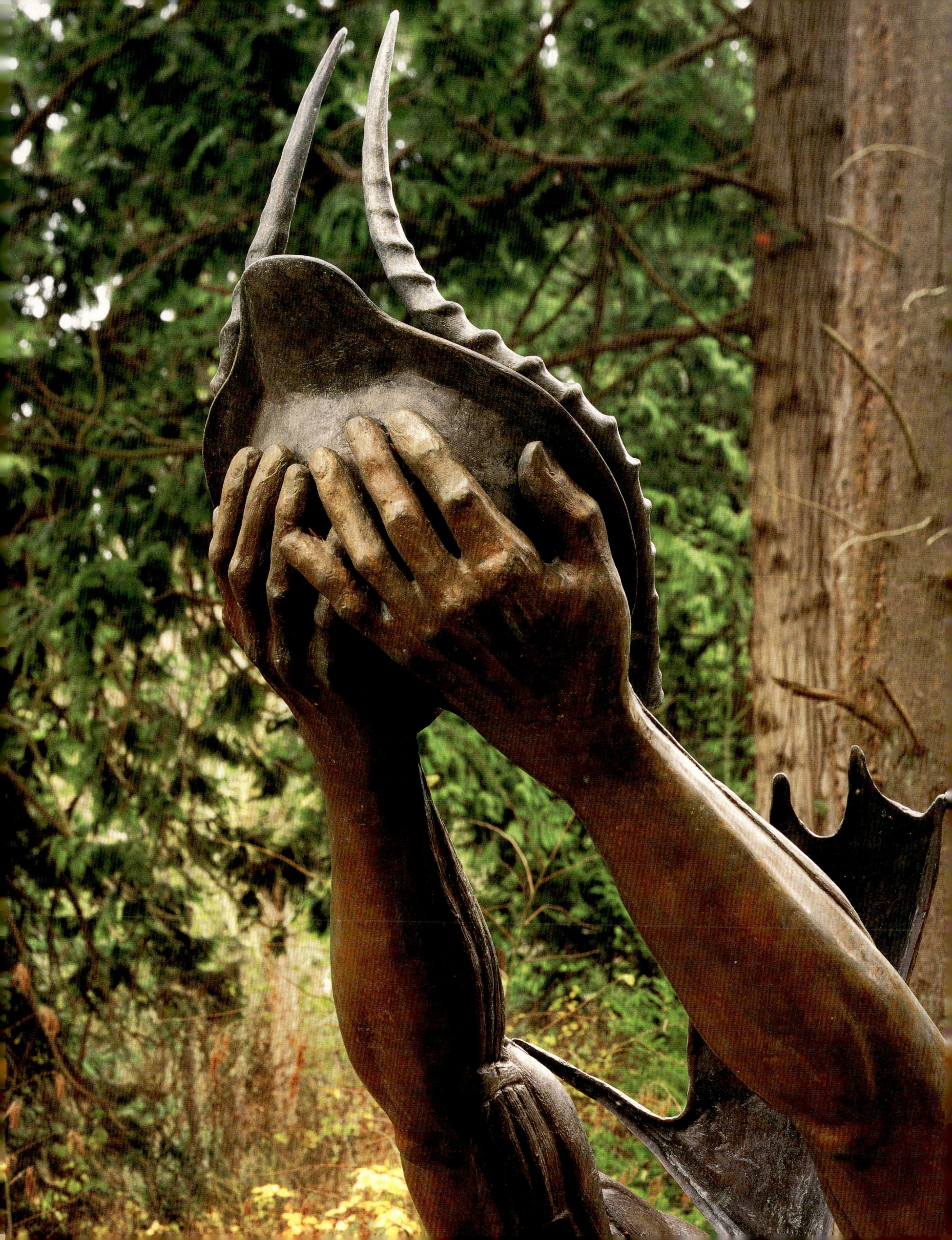

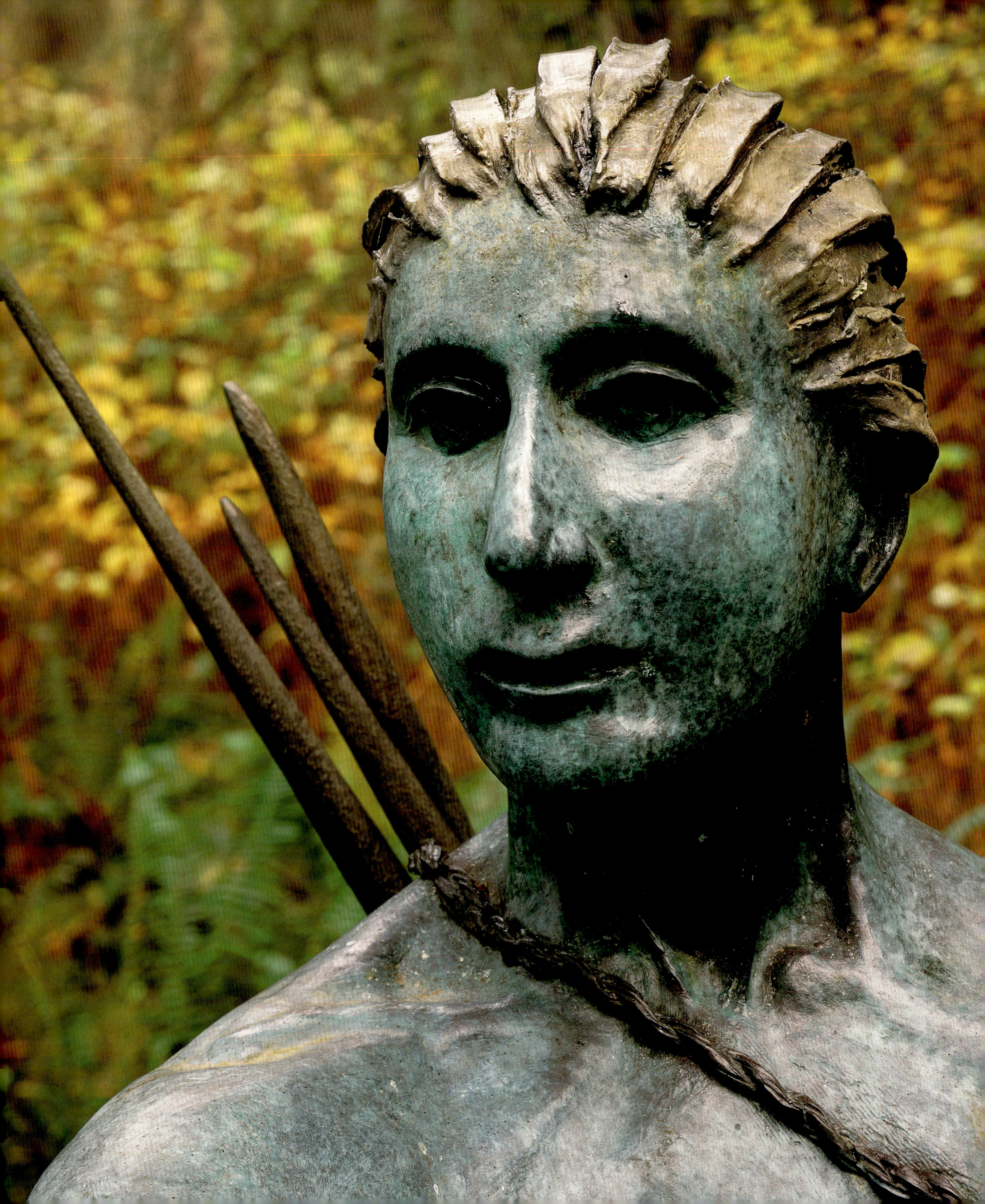

Becoming Merlin

The youthful Merlin is born from the Feminine. On his handmade cart he pulls his blanket of leaves, her talisman. The horns were once his crib, the others, his tools for the future. He is a model of psychic wholeness in harmony with Nature. He is what we seek to become.

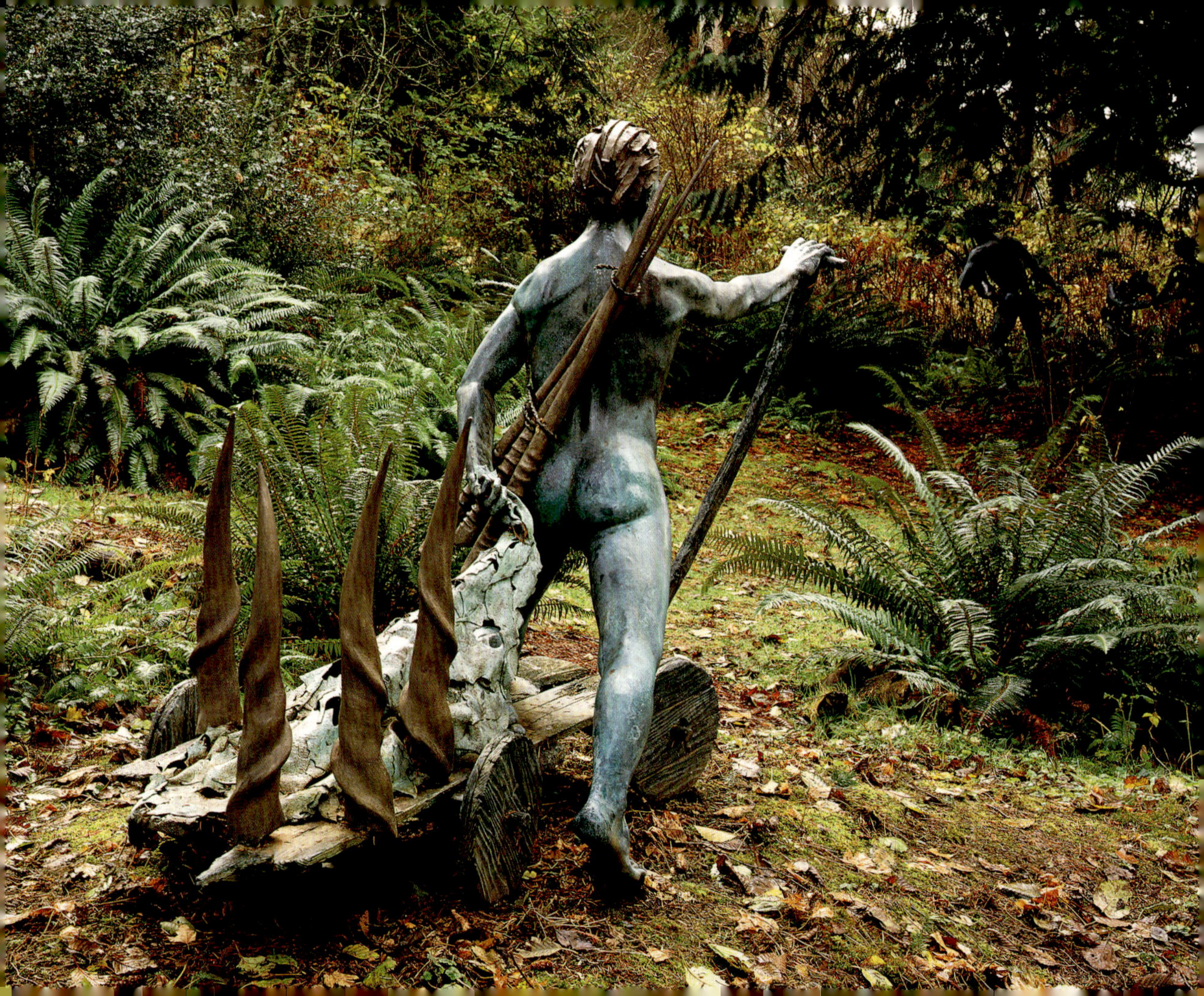

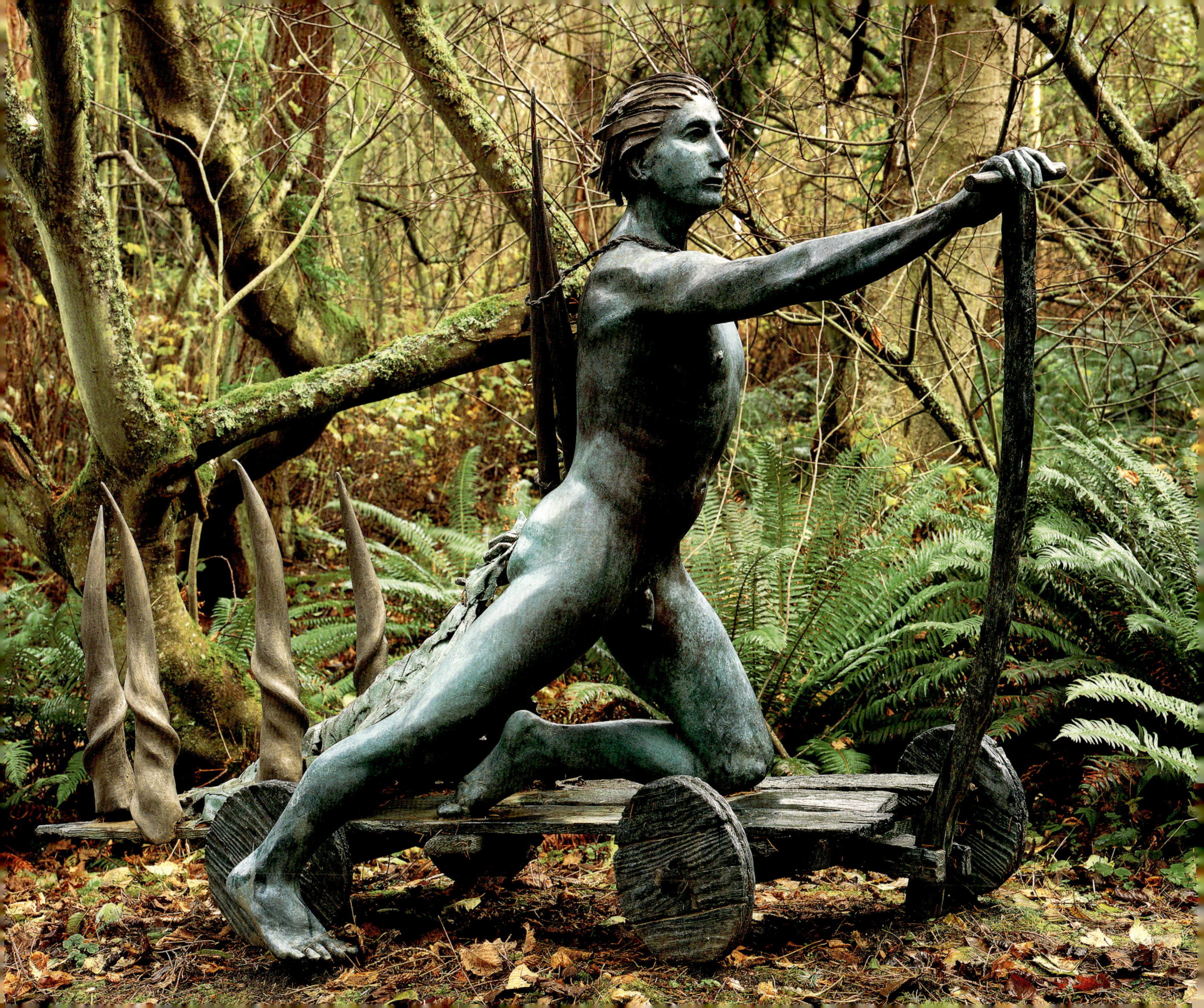

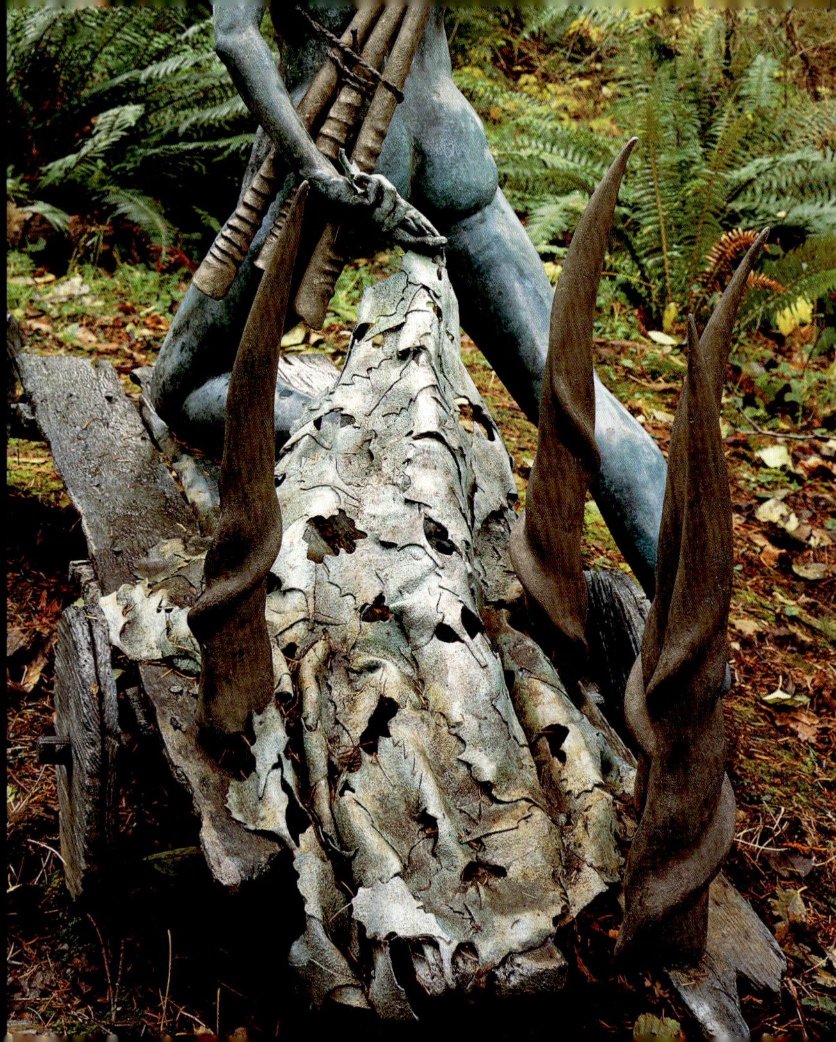

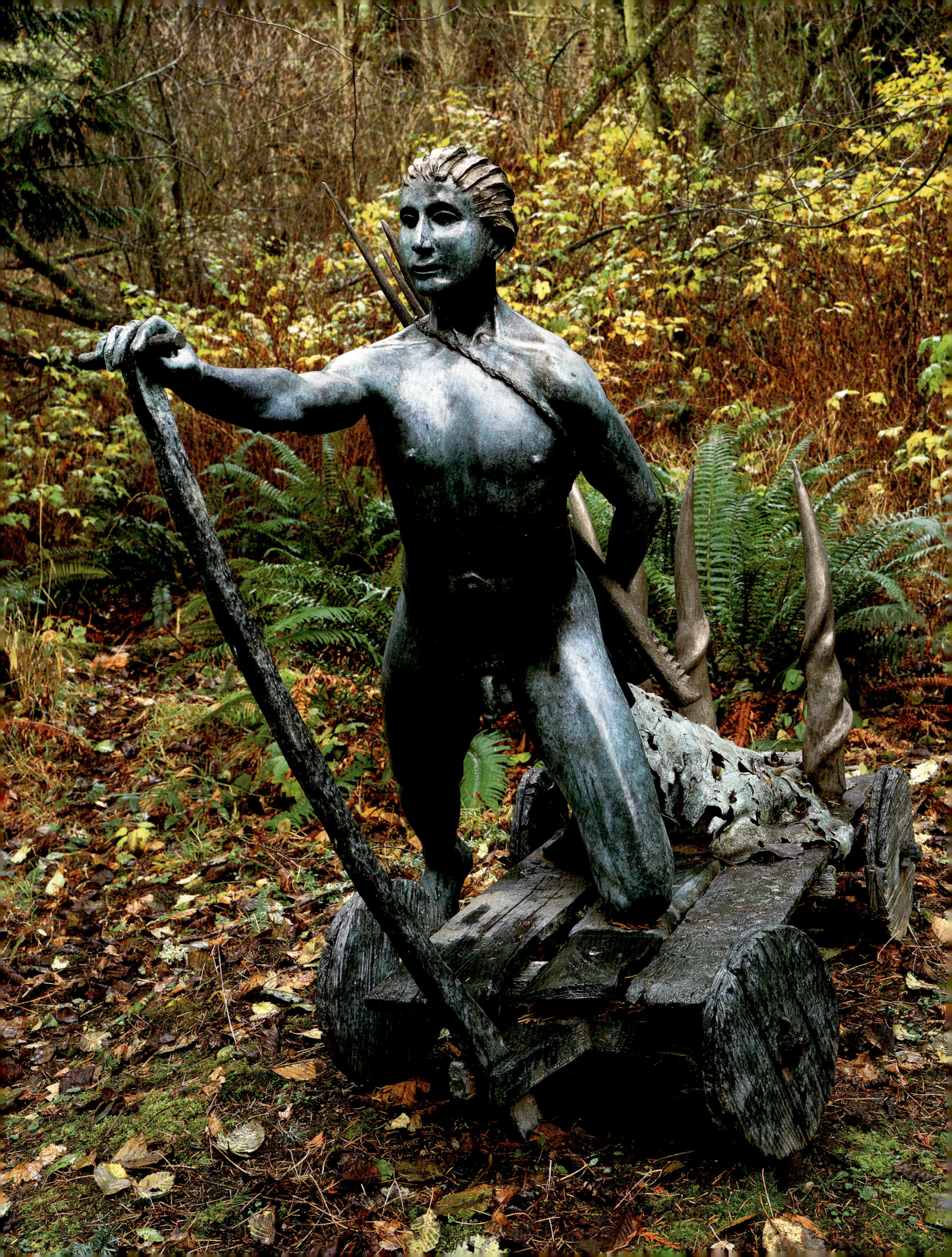

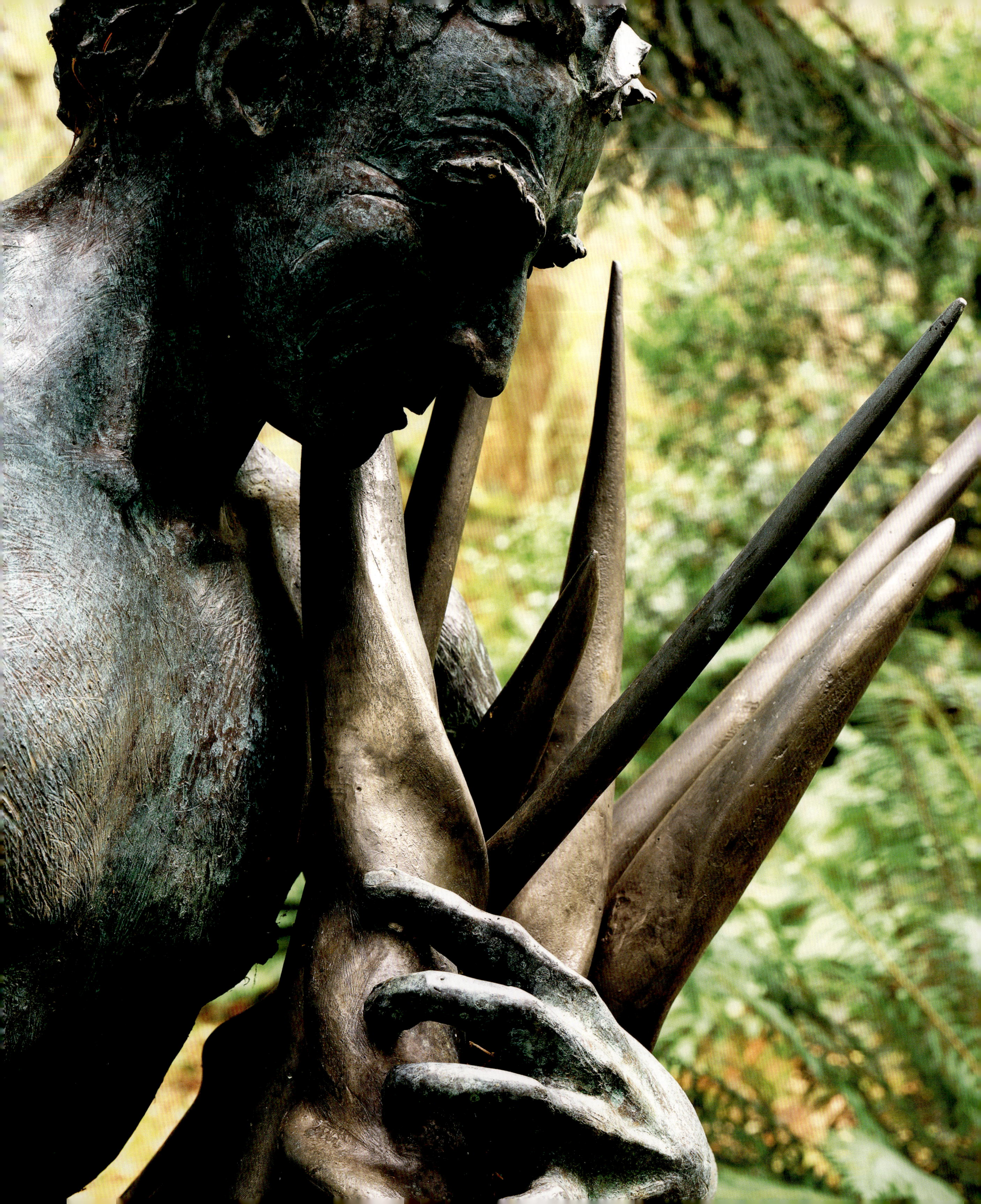

He clutches the horns which symbolize the spiraling cycles of Nature. As a commodity he claims them as his. His abdomen is empty—insatiable. His hand wards off the Feminine whose clasped hands provide a seat for him. He desires to control Nature, scorning his rightful relationship with the feminine land. Wisdom is lost to him. She will await his return, dancing in the light

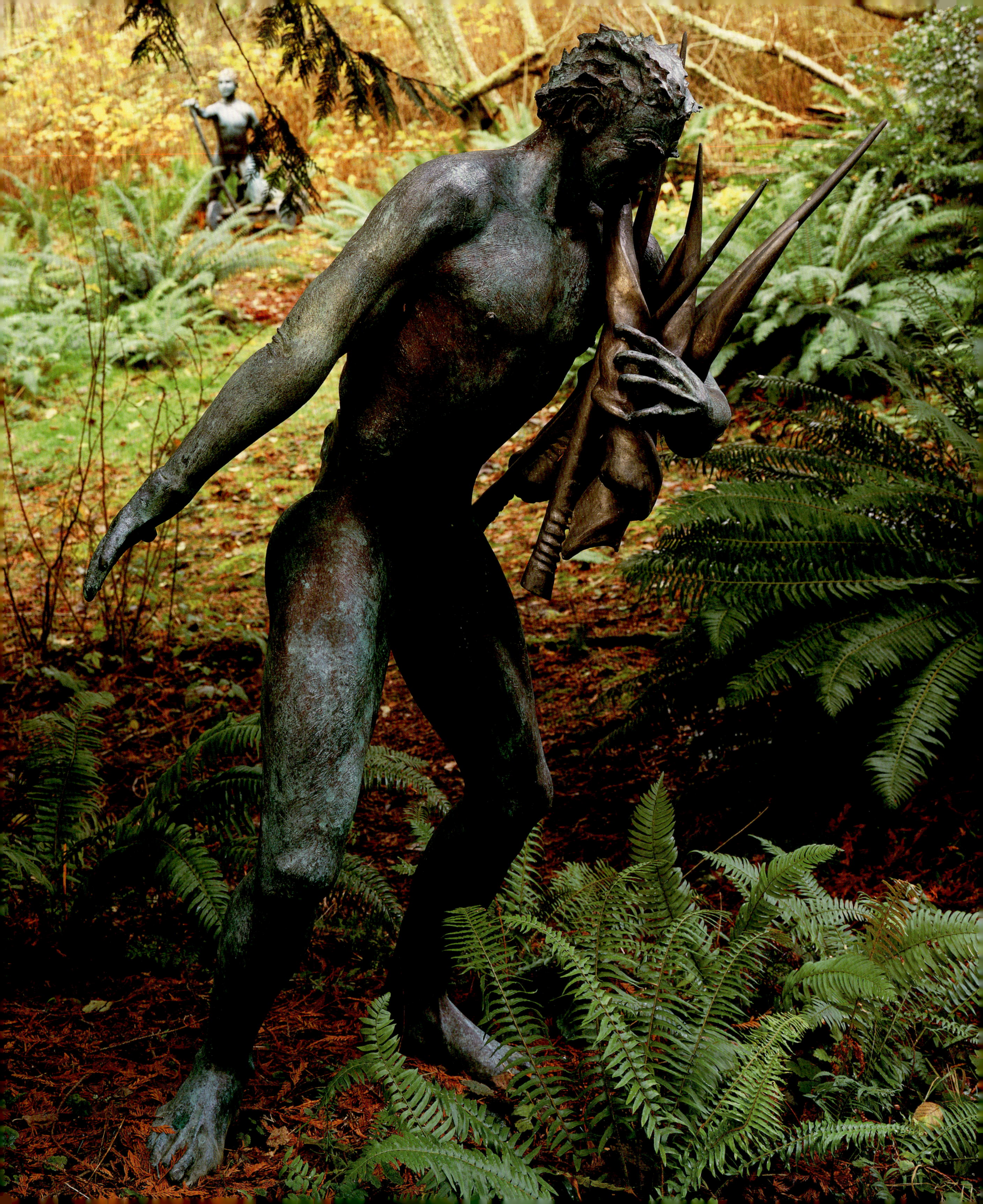

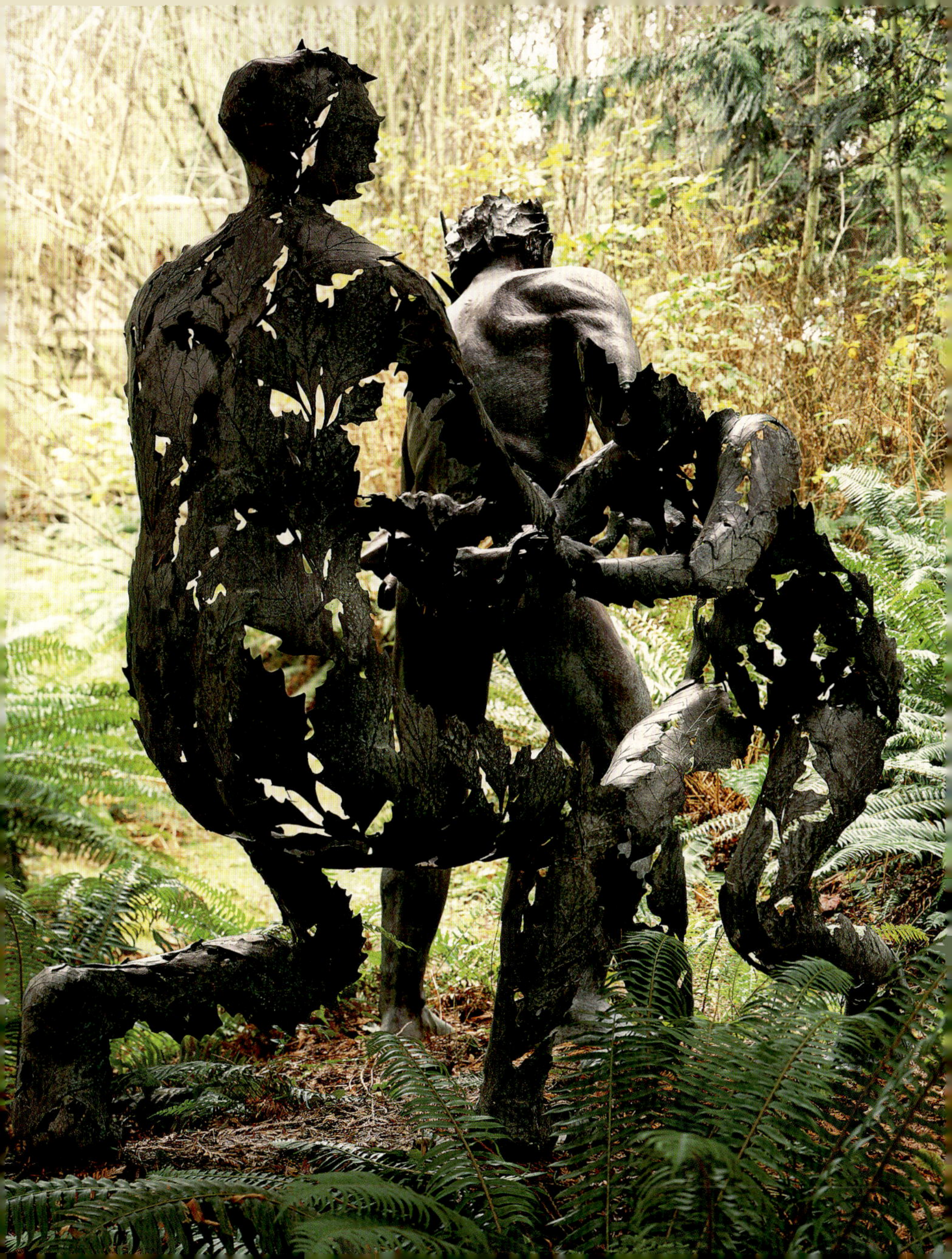

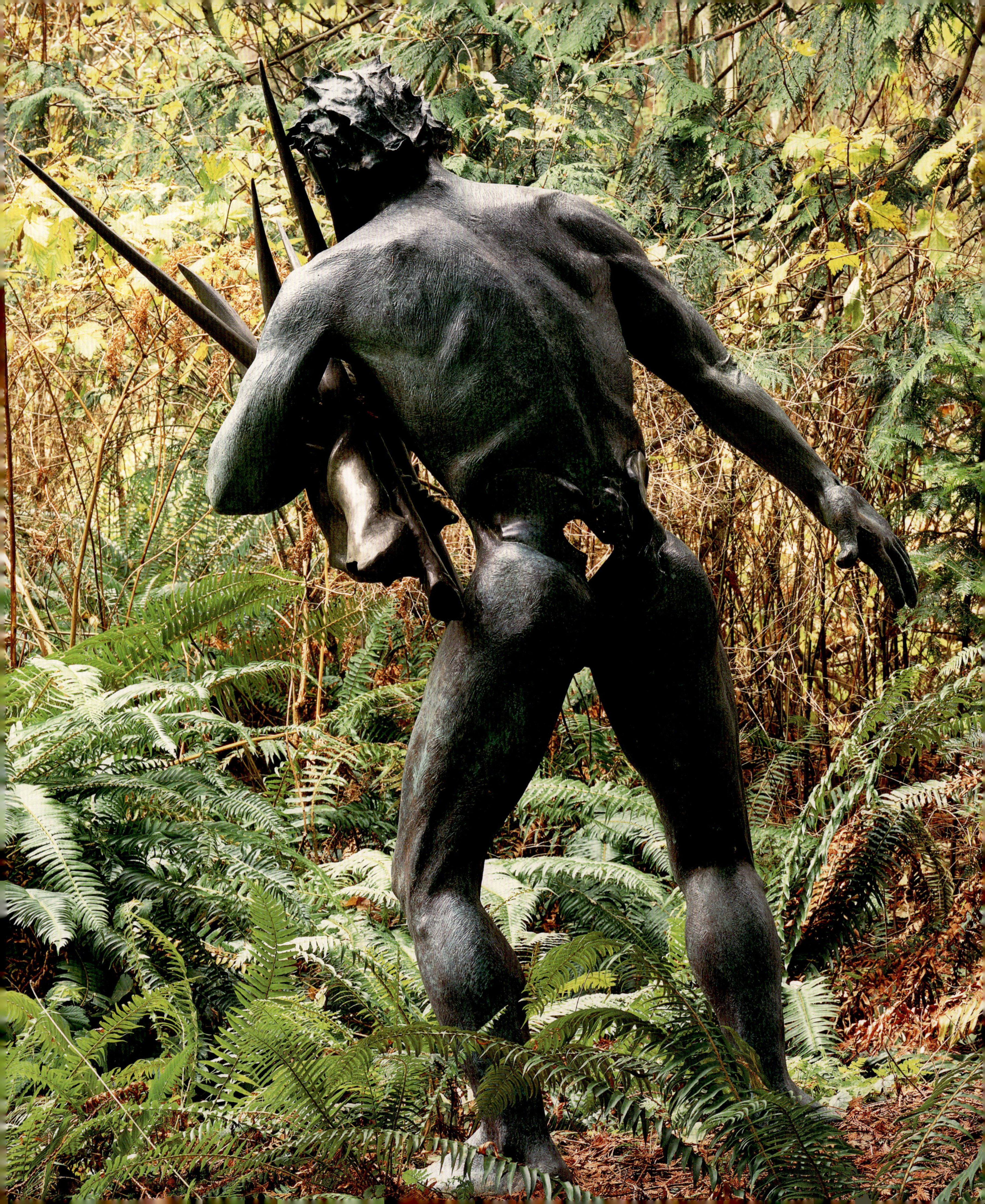

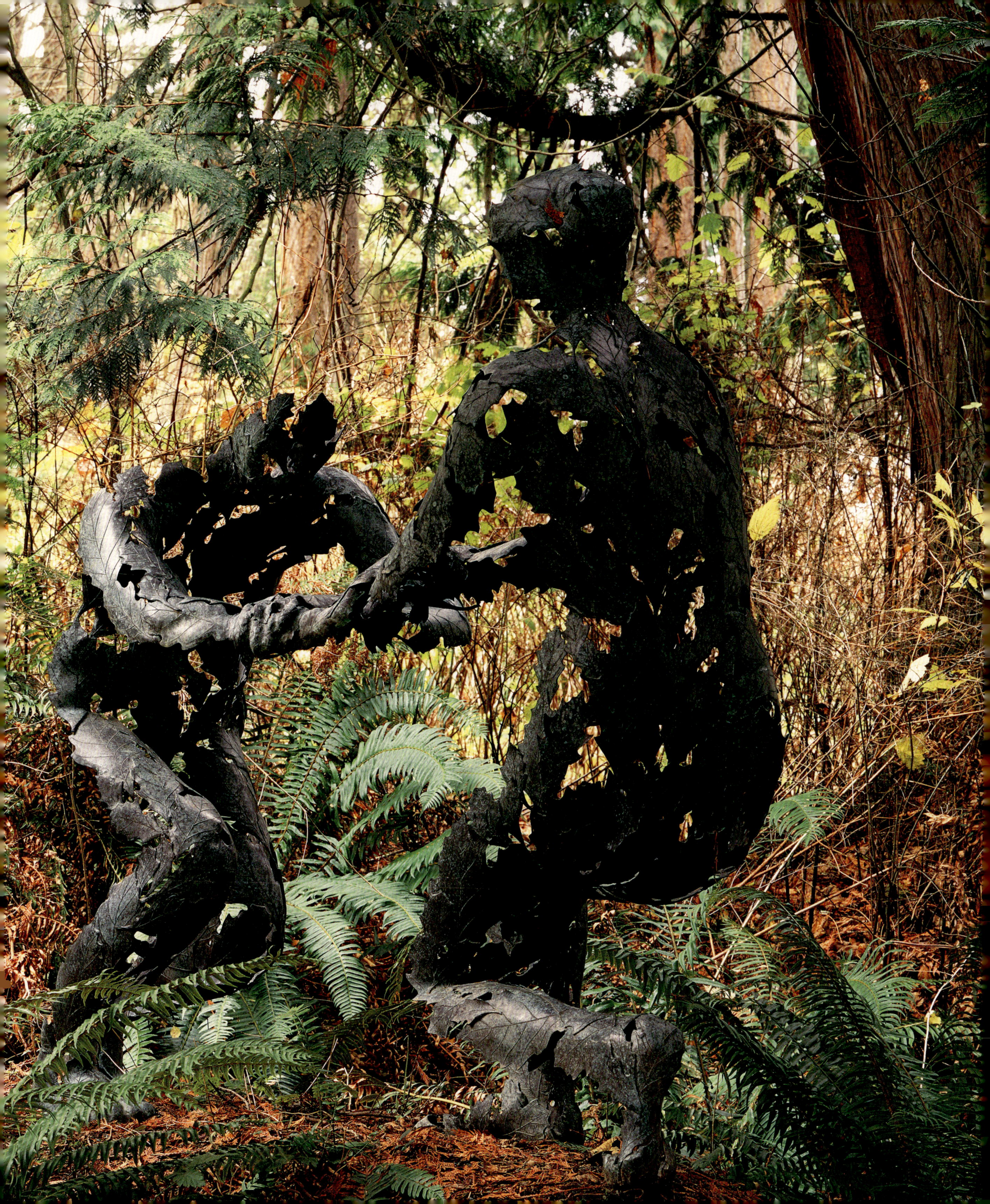

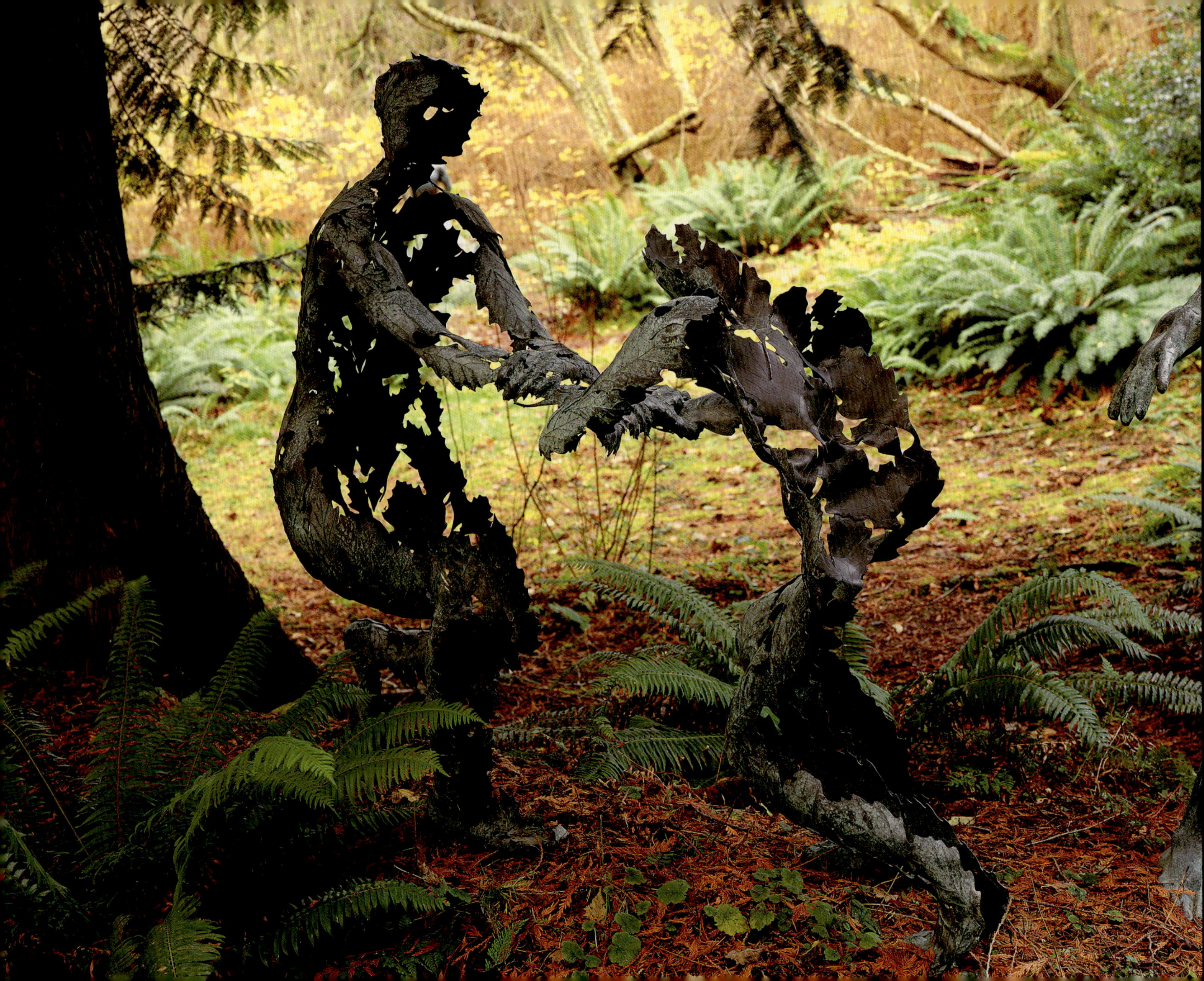

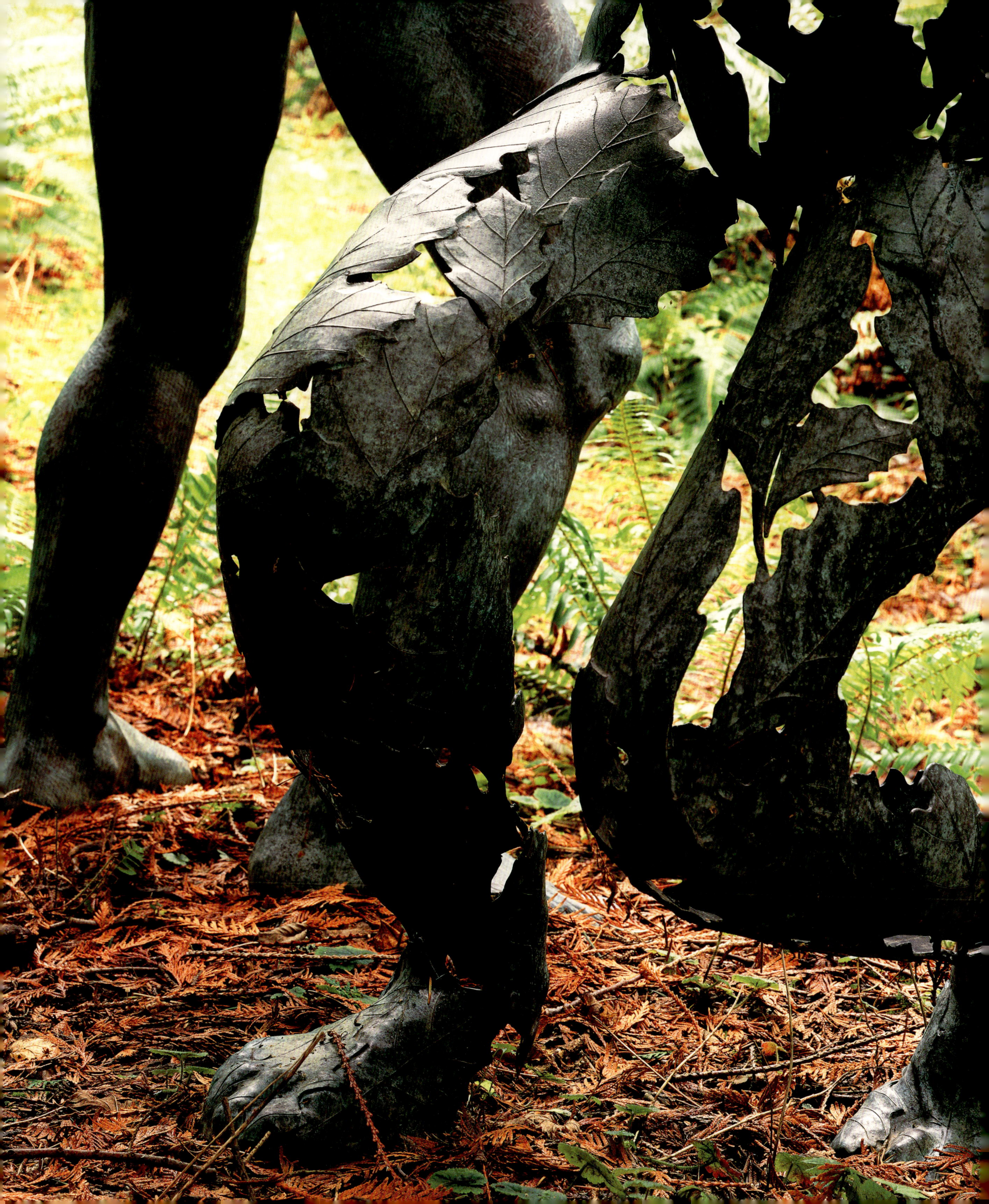

Merlin, the archetype of the Seer, is joined with the tree, the feminine potency of the Earth; a requisite for Kingship from Celtic times—the basis of our Merlin legend. Supported by a staff of horns symbolizing the spiraling cycles of Nature, he is wedded to the land. The Seer in our time is balanced between unconscious sleep and awakening. Will Merlin Wake? Will it be in time?

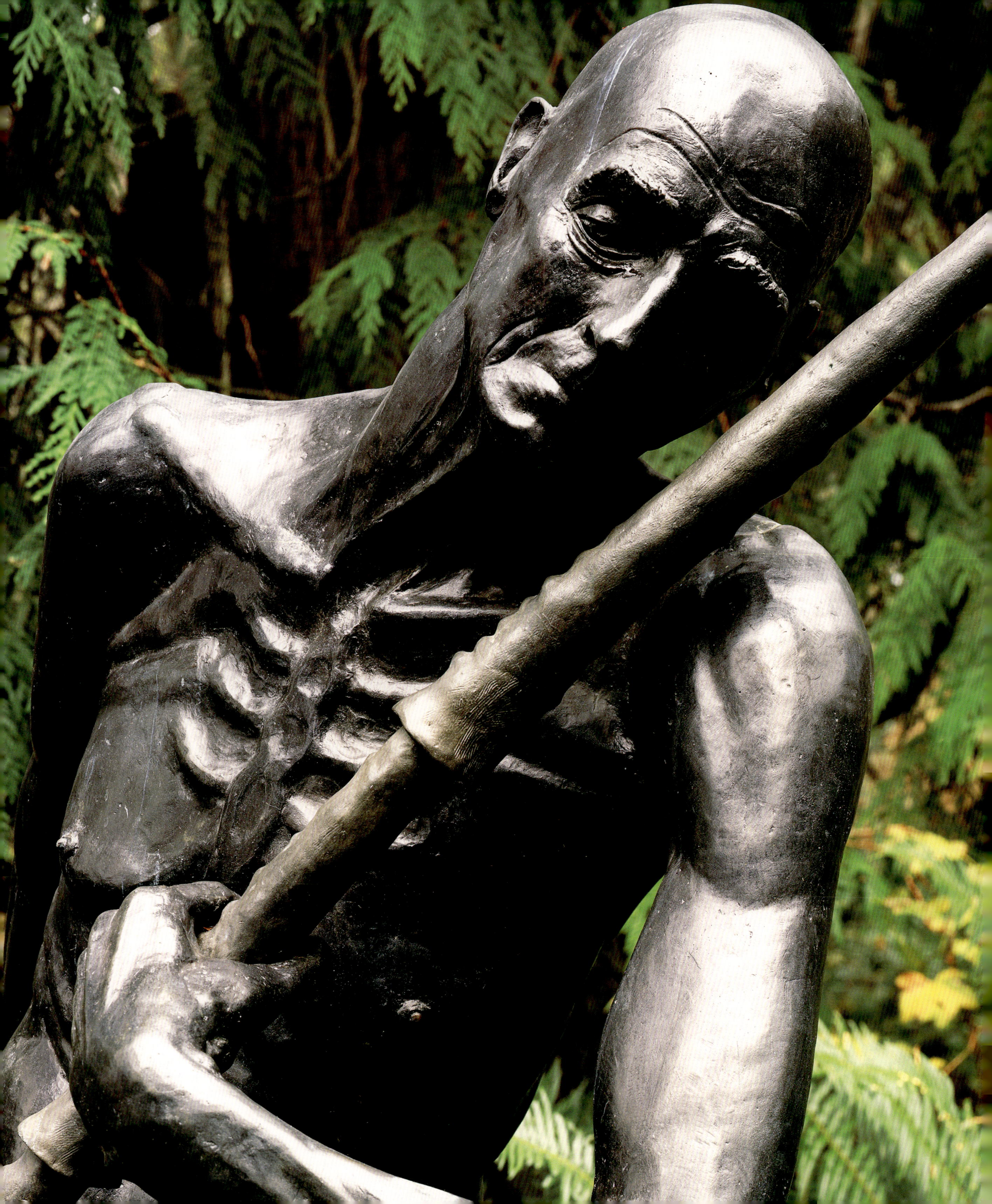

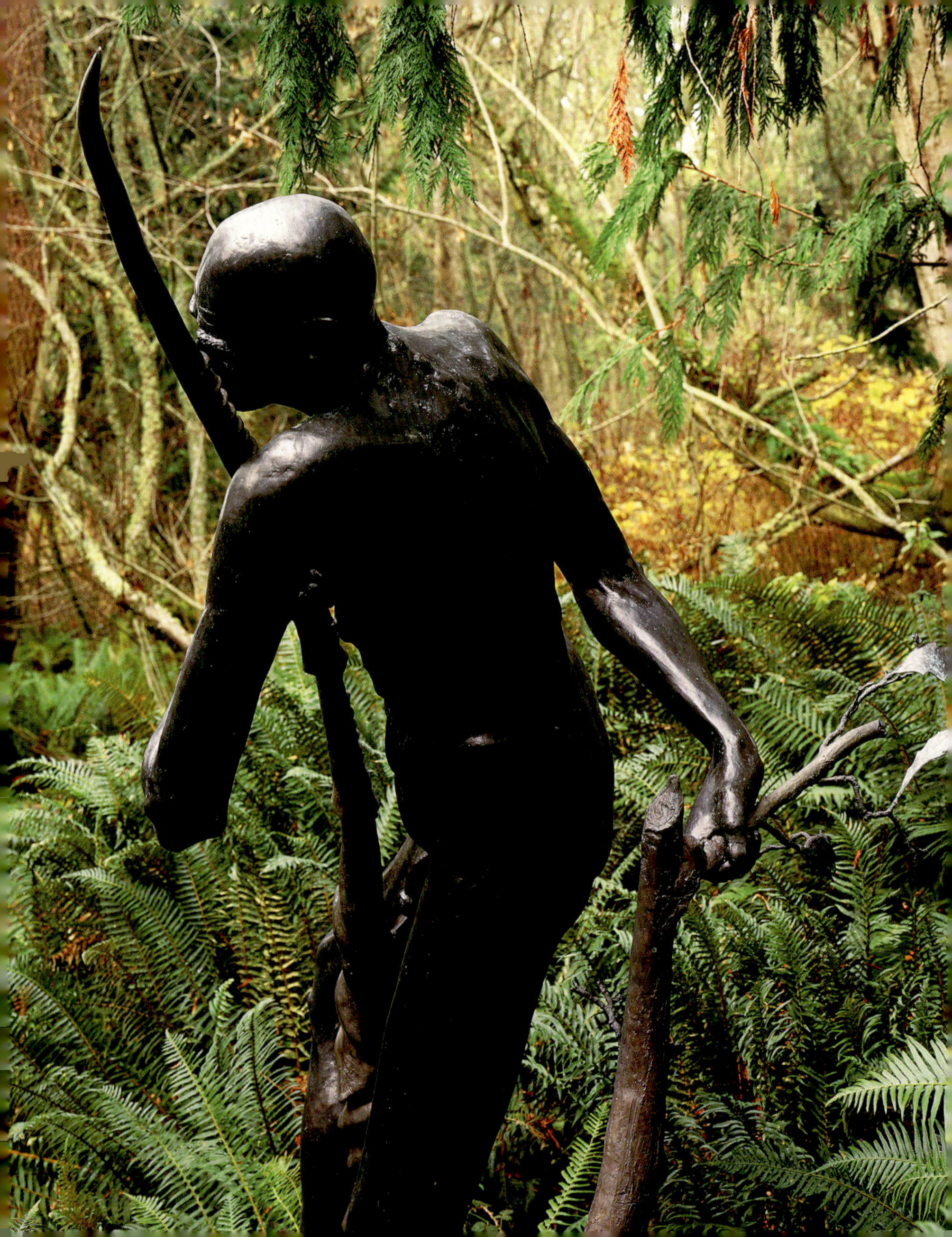

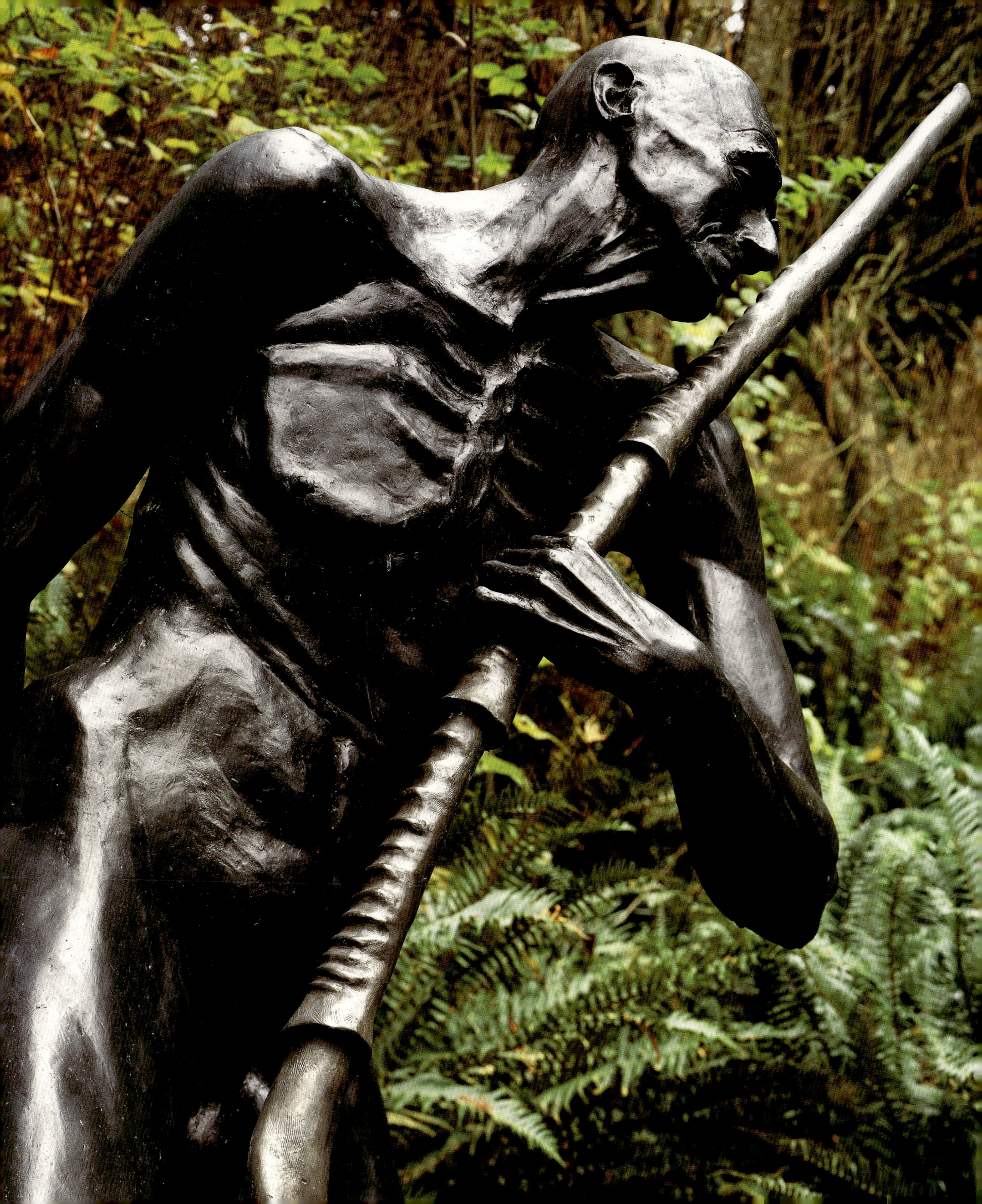

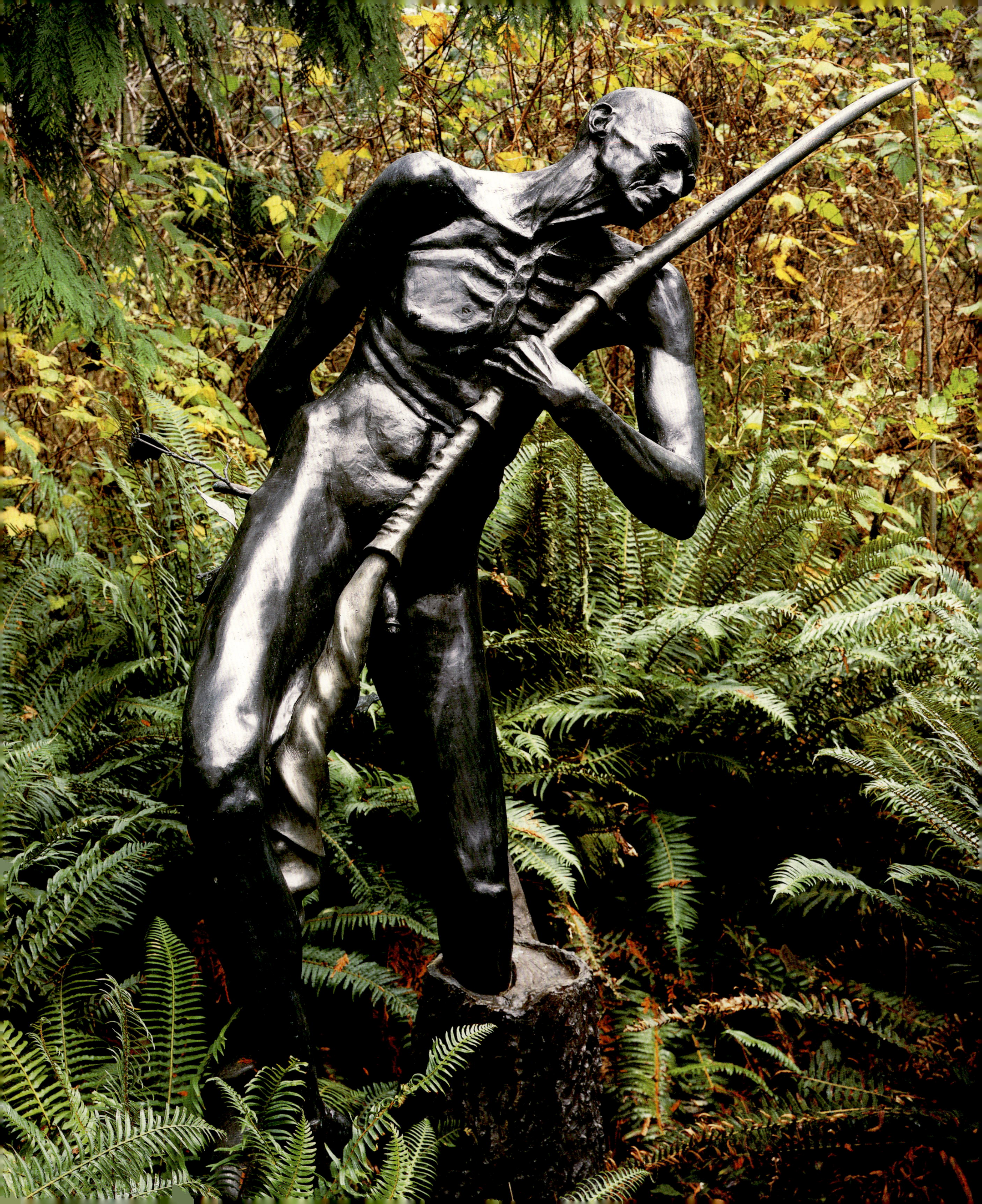

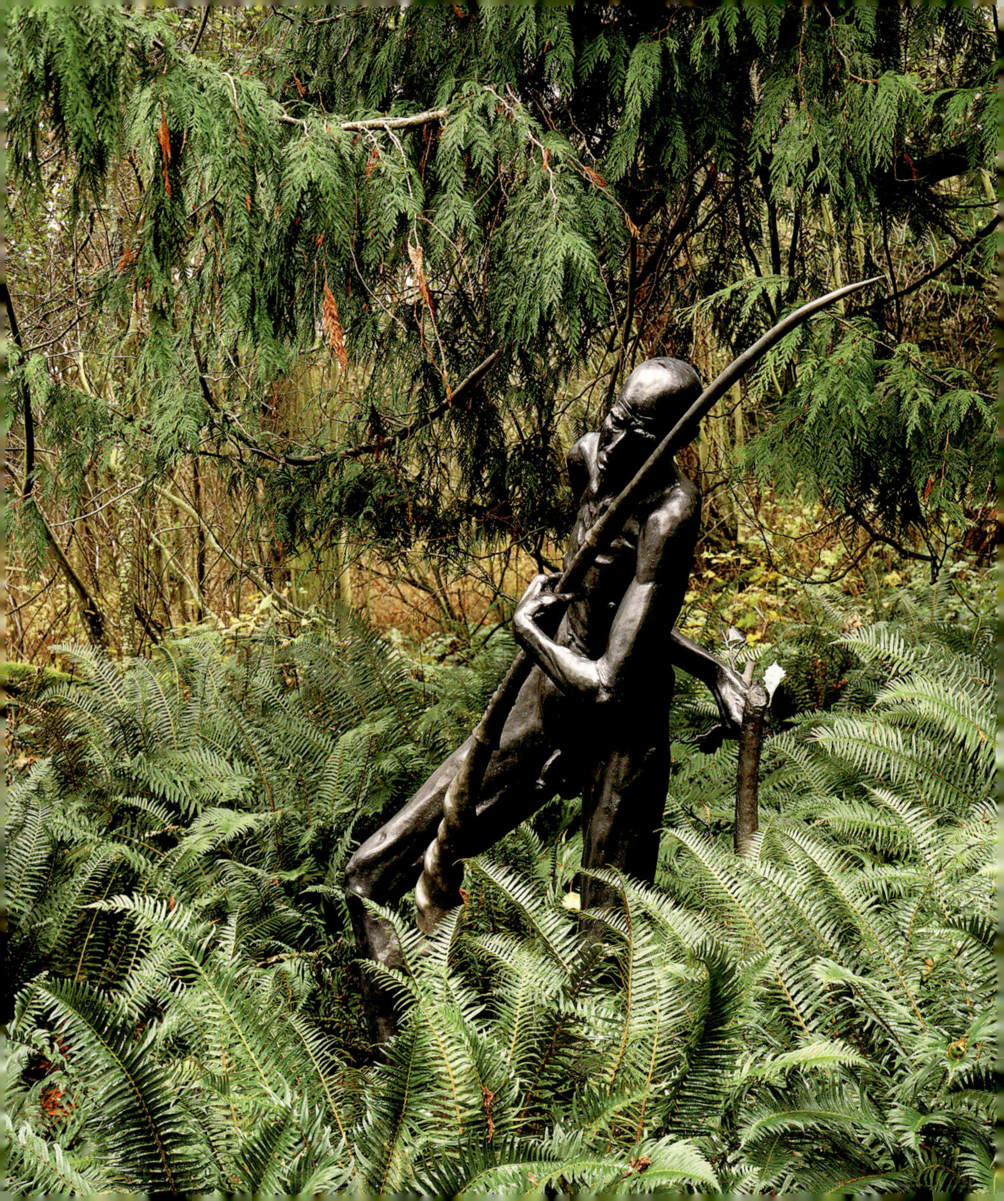

Acceptance of Sorrow

She stands grieving, reflected in the water of her tears. Her fingers have grown into Nature Herself, the green ferns of the woods now protect her. The fish fin pool contains her. Upon this reflection she stands strong in full acceptance of her sorrow, one of the many threads of all life.

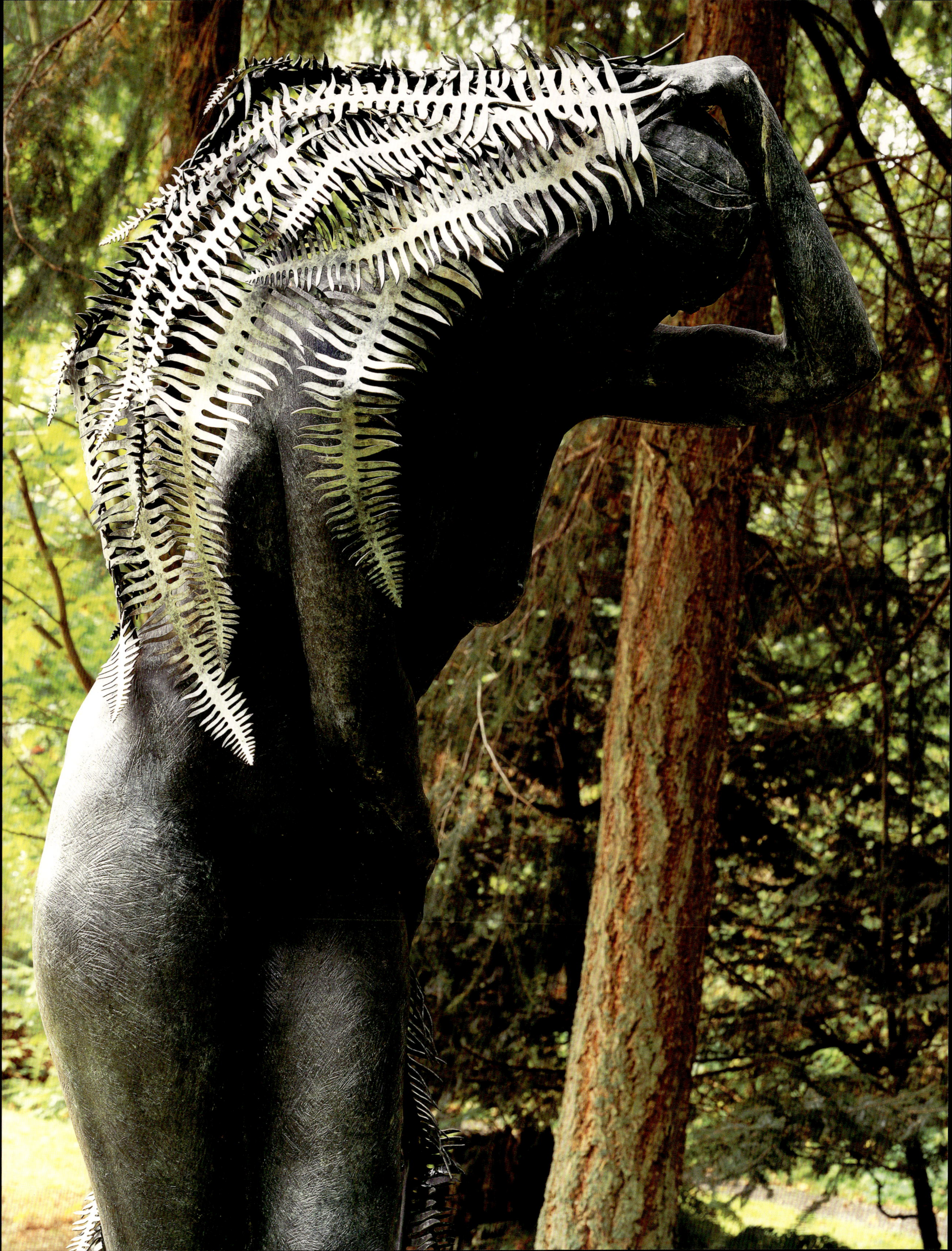

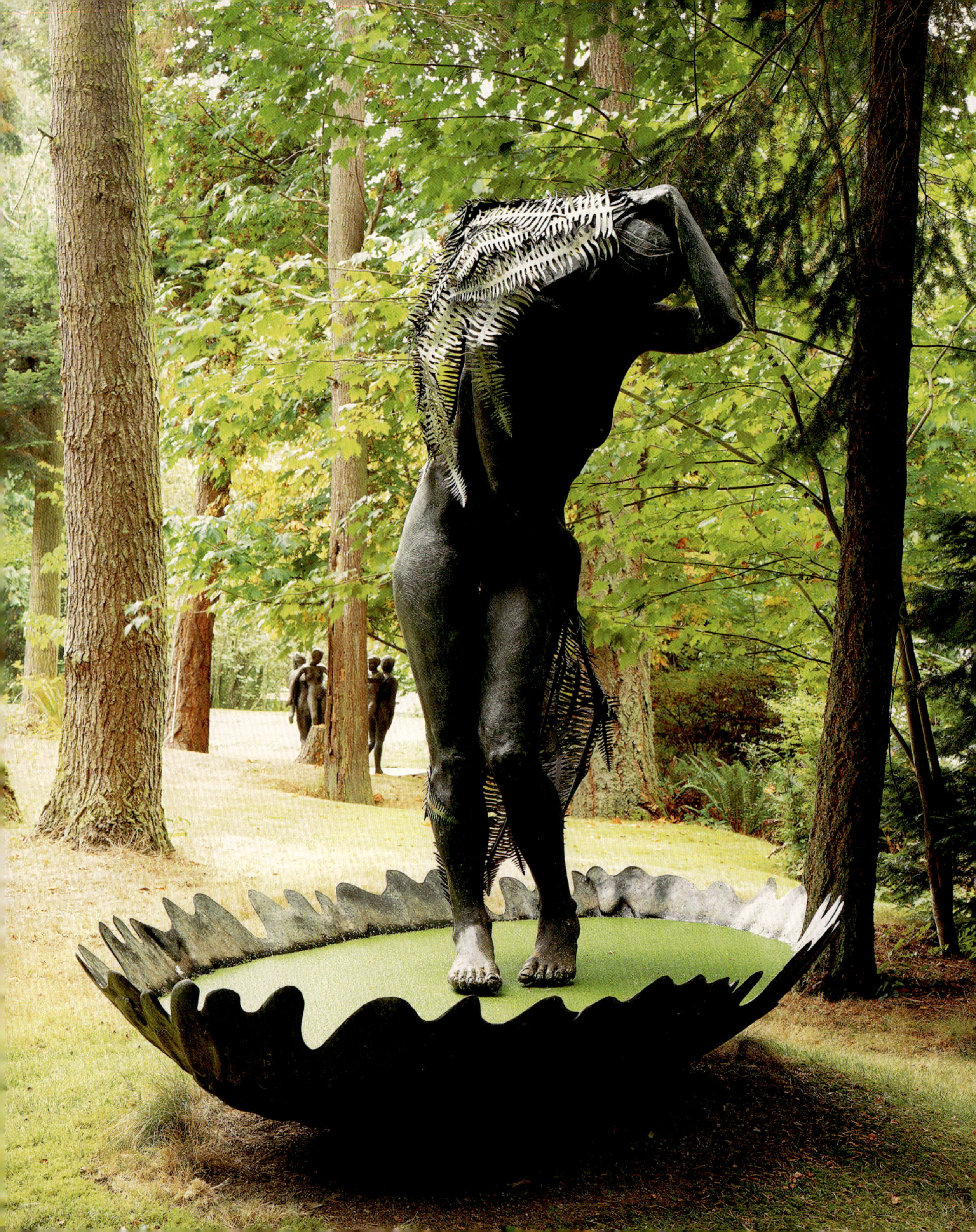

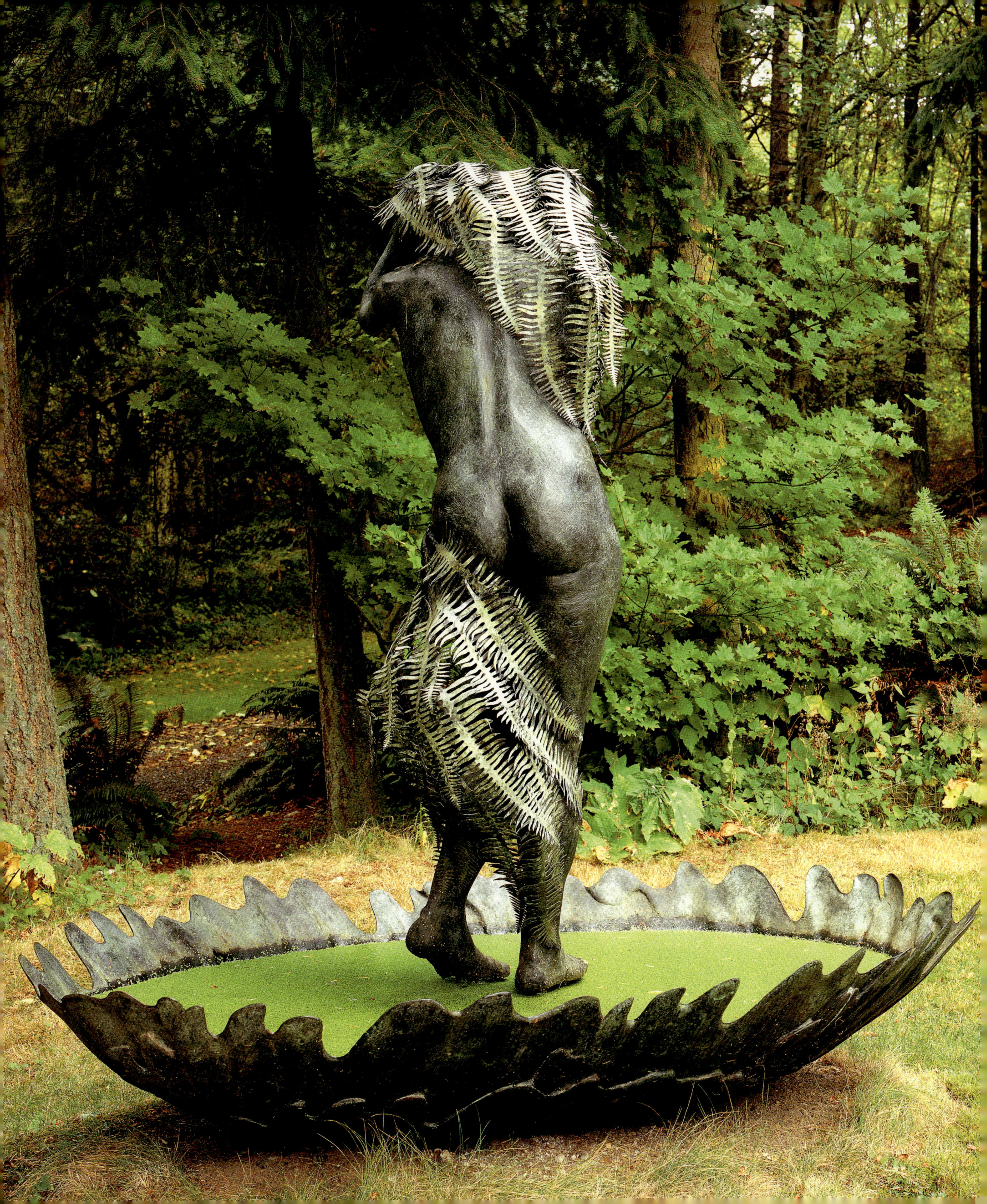

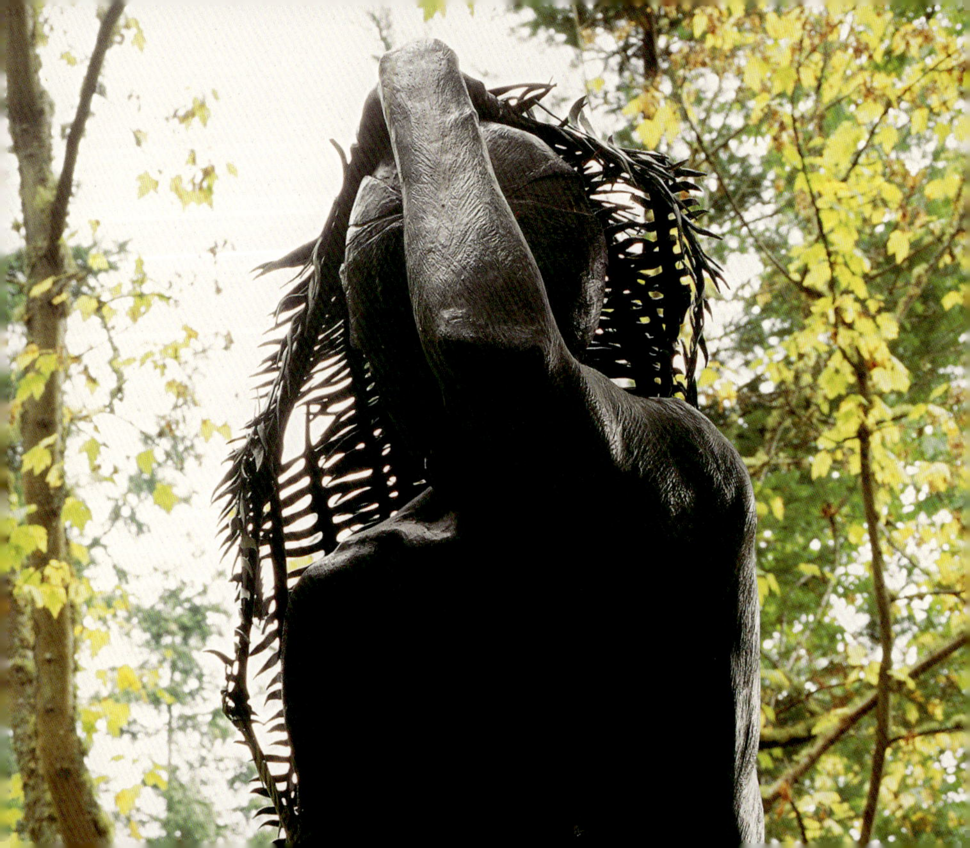

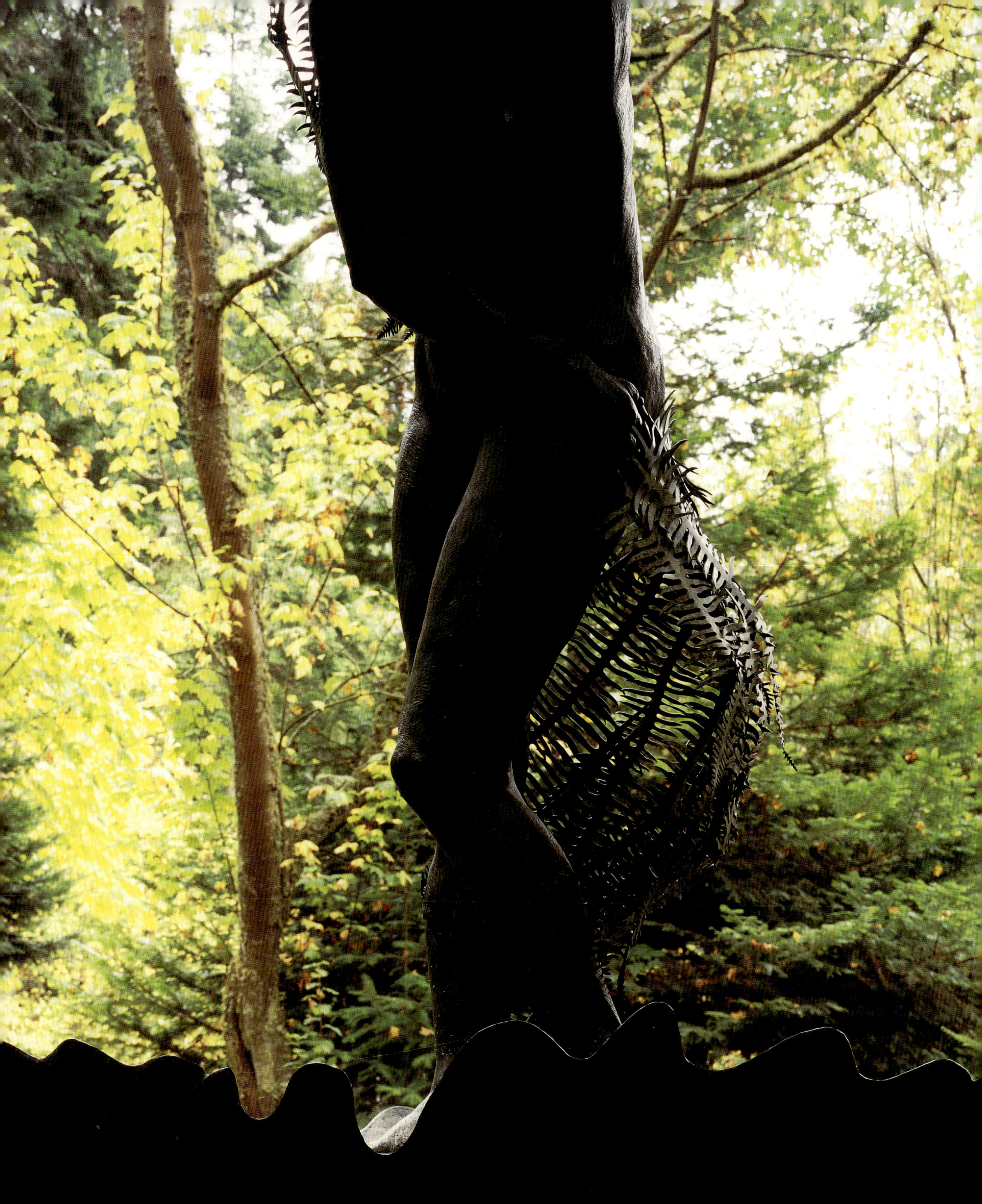

Backbone of the Universe

The backbone of the four-footed ones on which humans depend, encircled by our ancestors.The woman gives birth to agriculture, the hunter must shift. Will woman still depend on him? What will their relationship be? Humans, plants, animals, the backbone of the Universe.

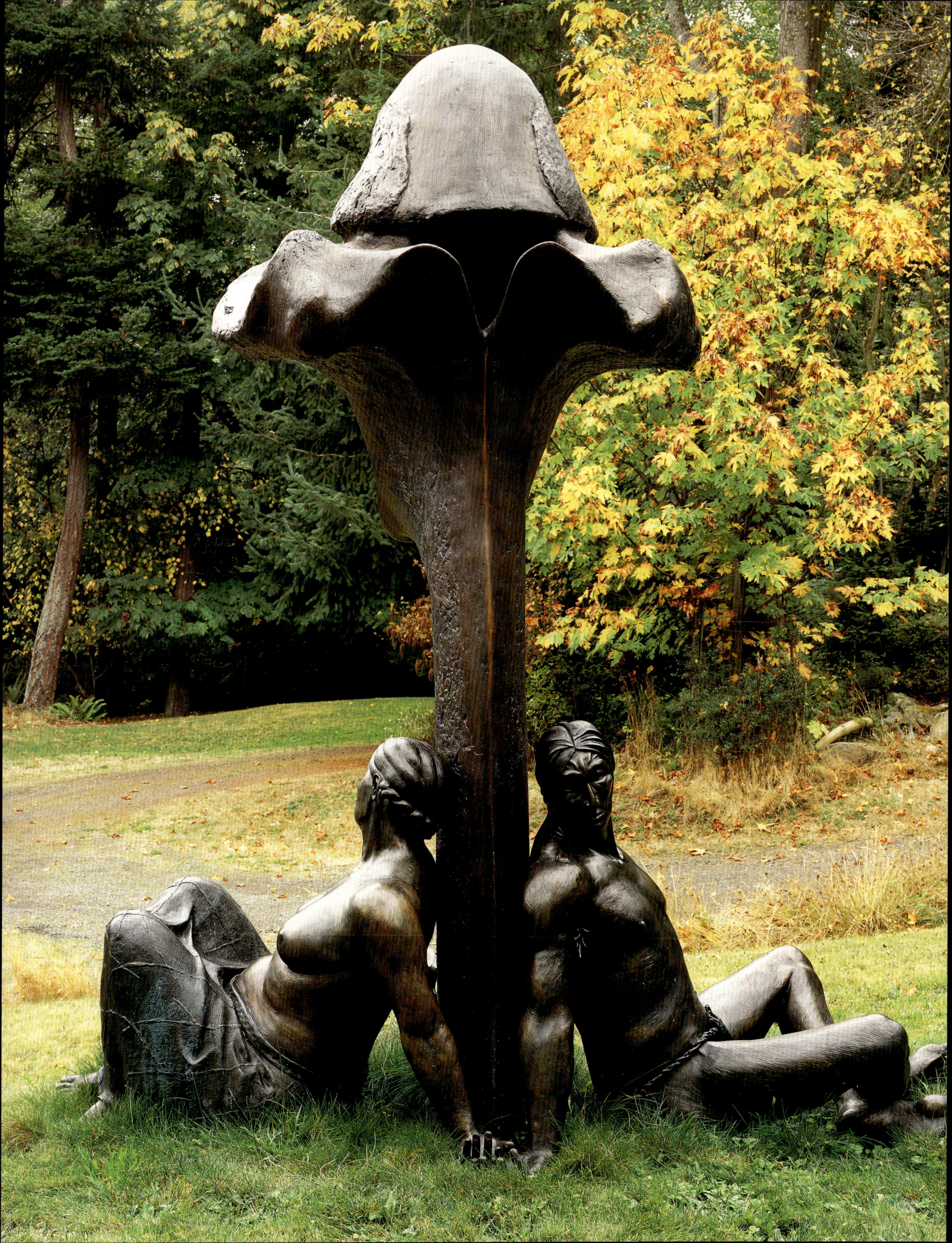

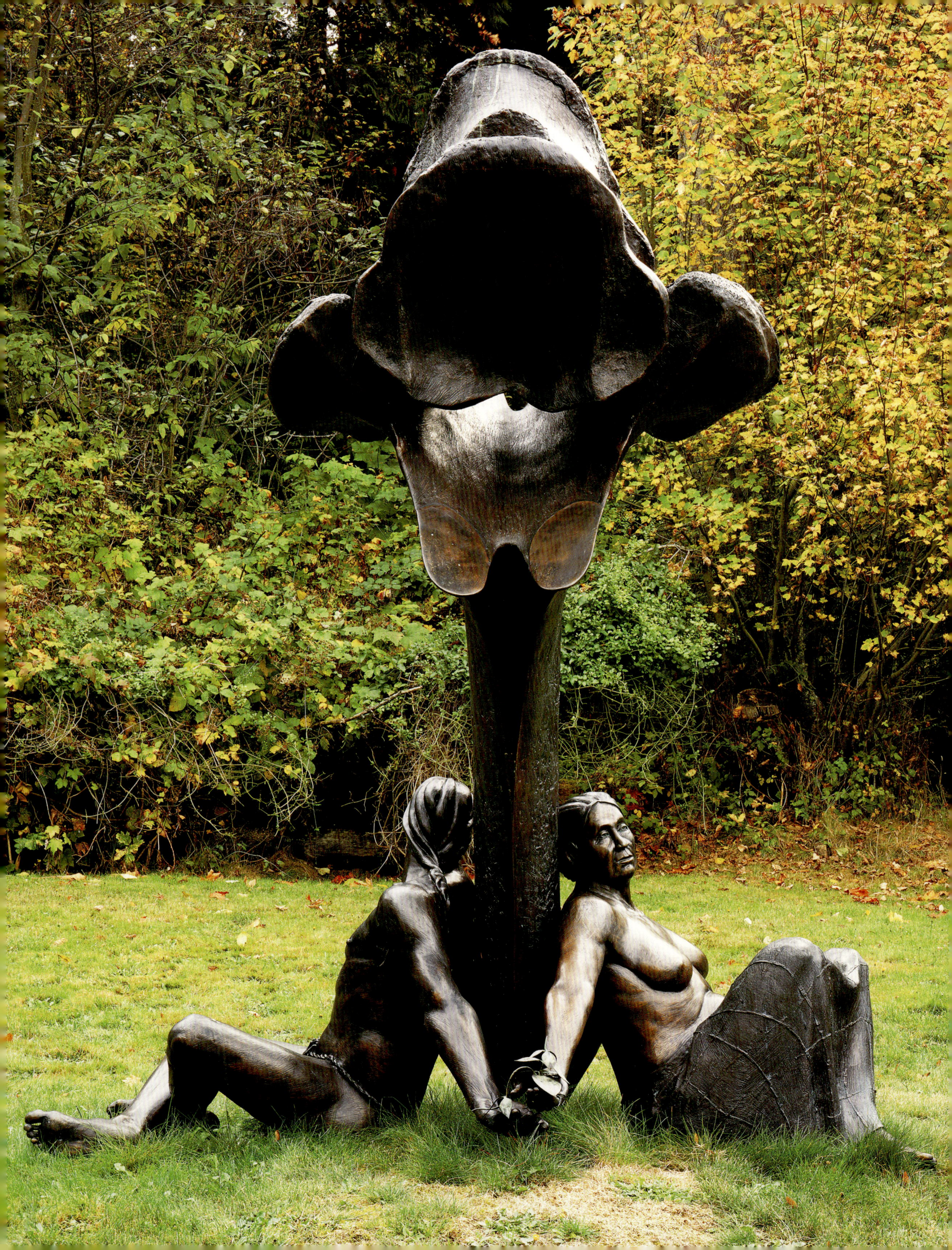

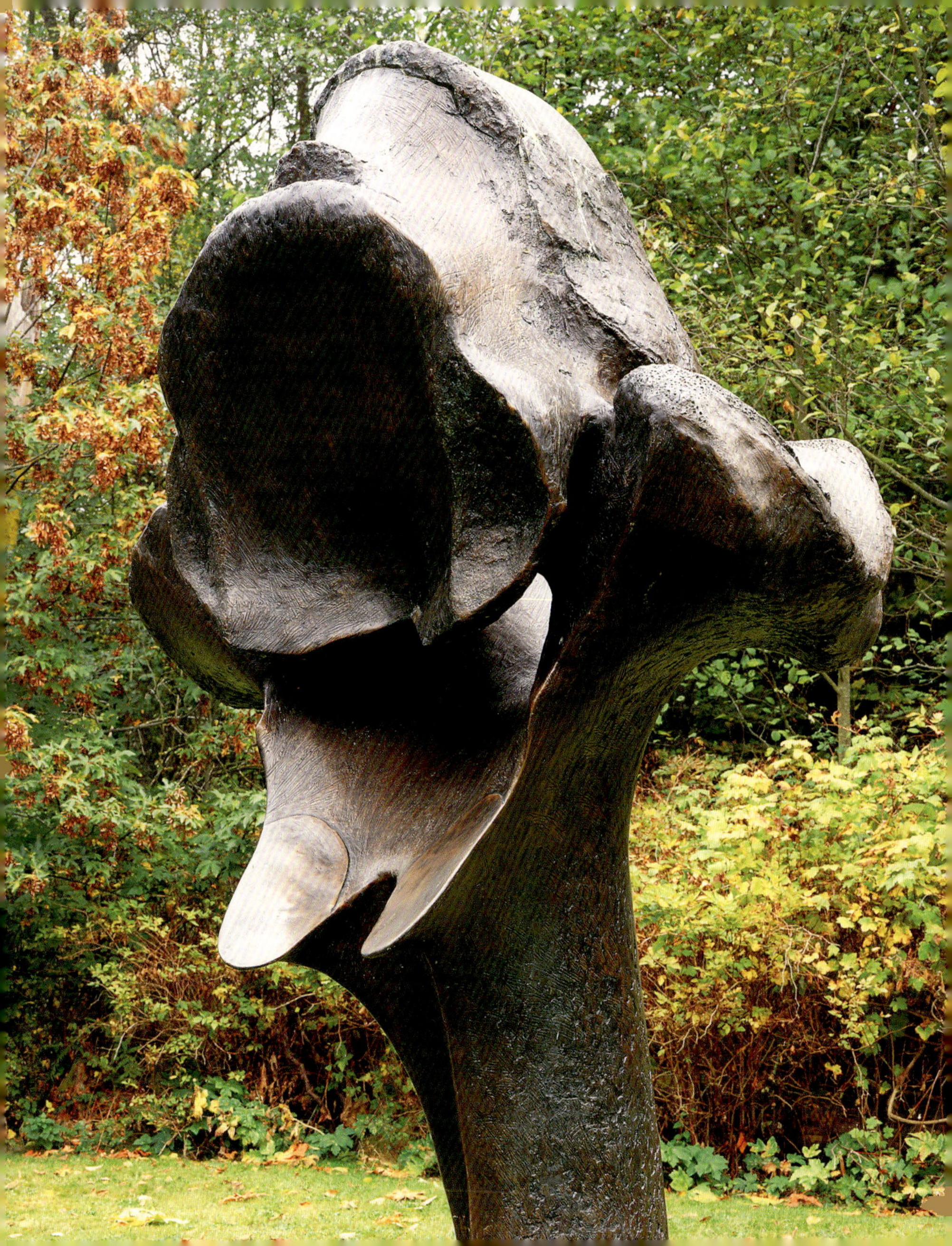

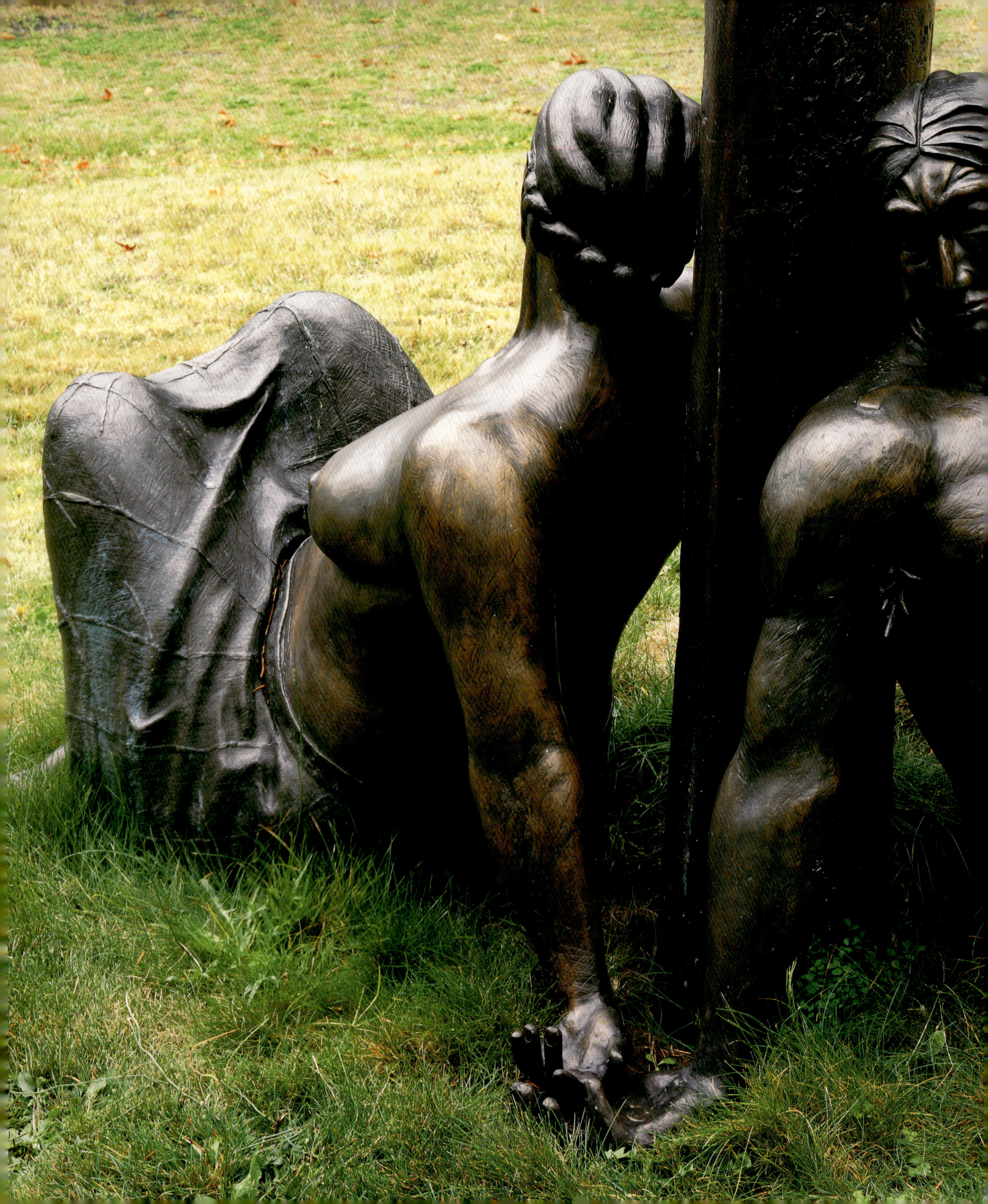

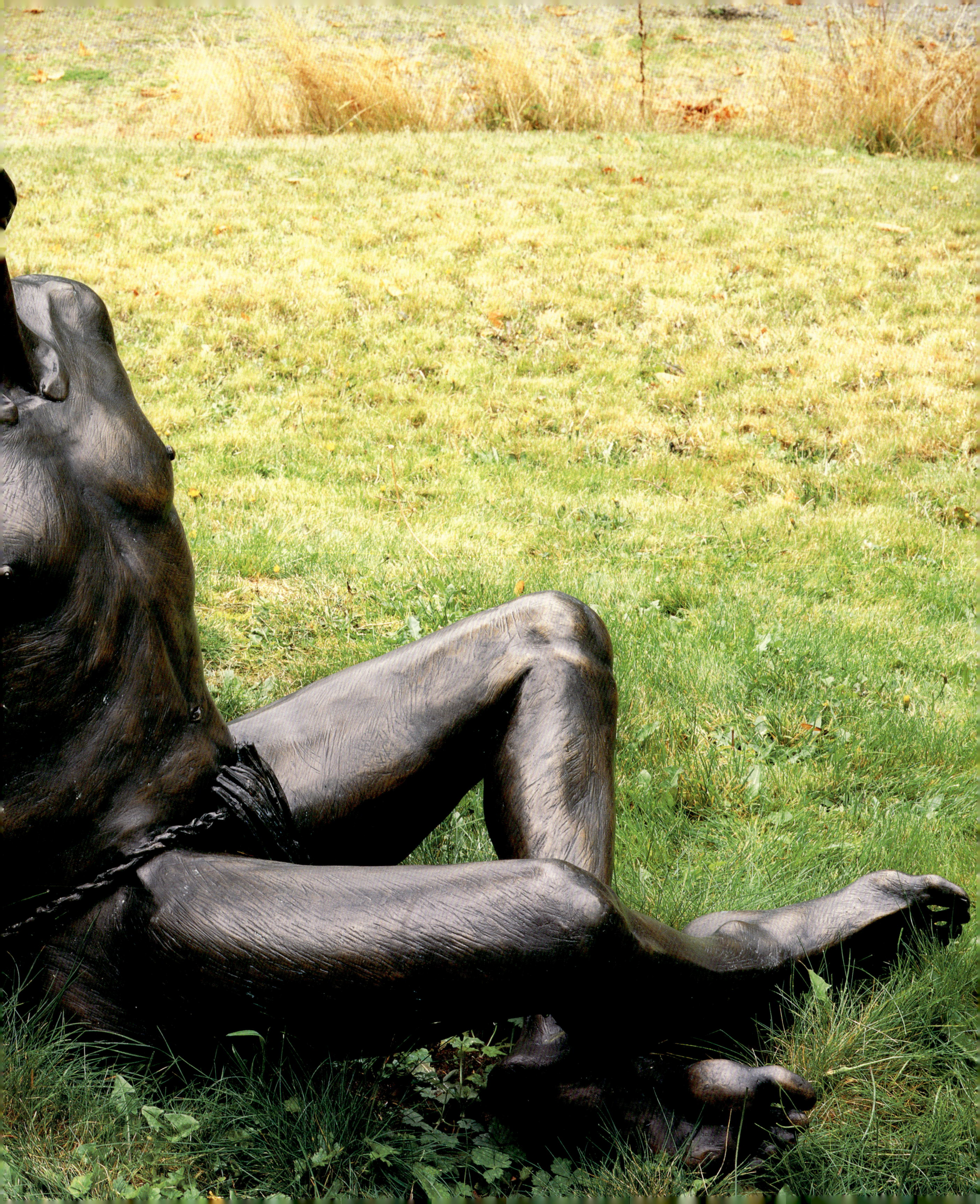

Trinity

Skeletons of plant, animal, and human, related by structure, related by need, mutually dependent upon one another for life itself. Have we the capacity to honor this need, to allow the plants and animals their own required realm which humans do not impinge upon? Or will we only consider human needs, invade their respective spaces, leaving only the skeletal remains of this vital trinity of dependence as a record of our folly?

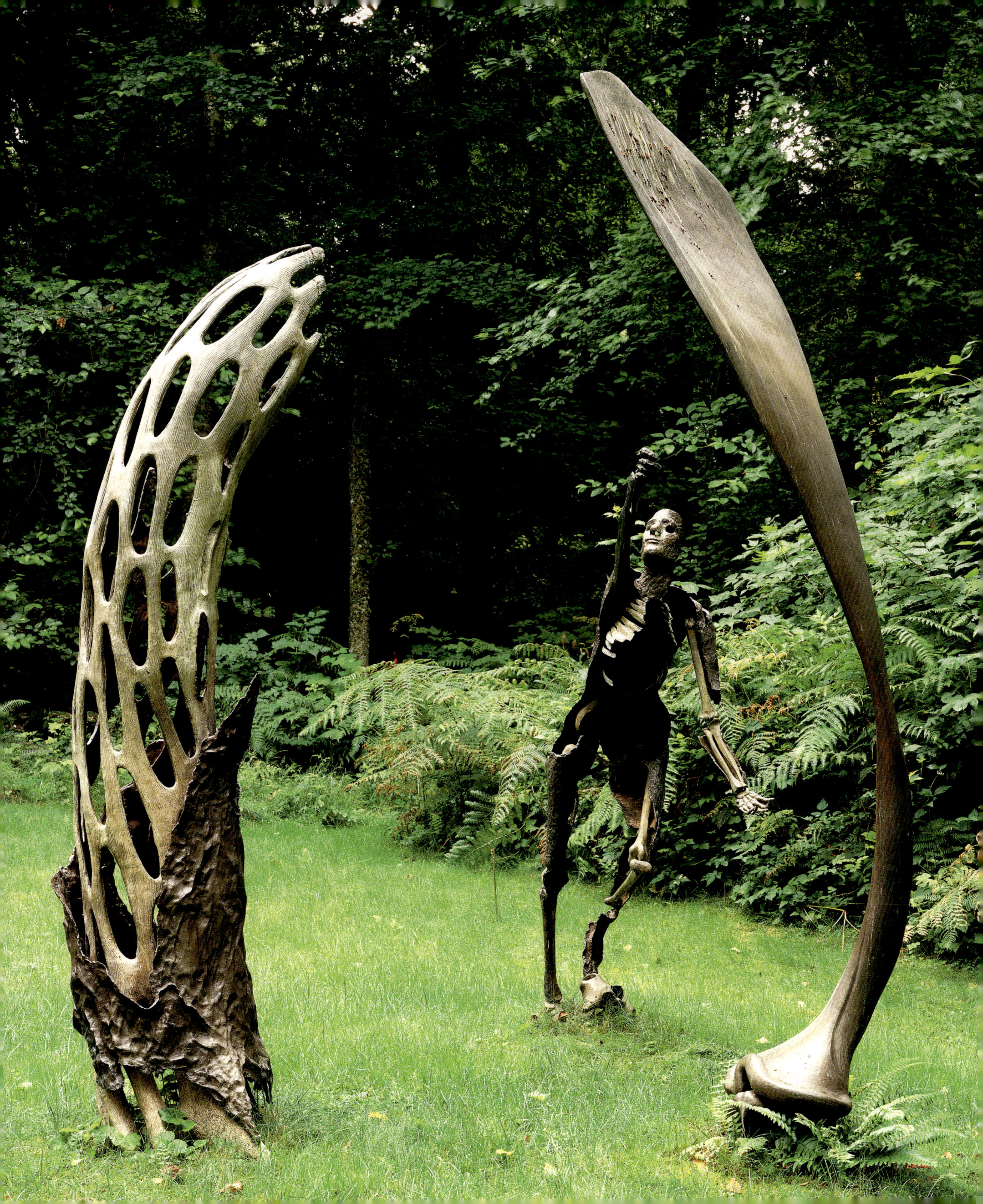

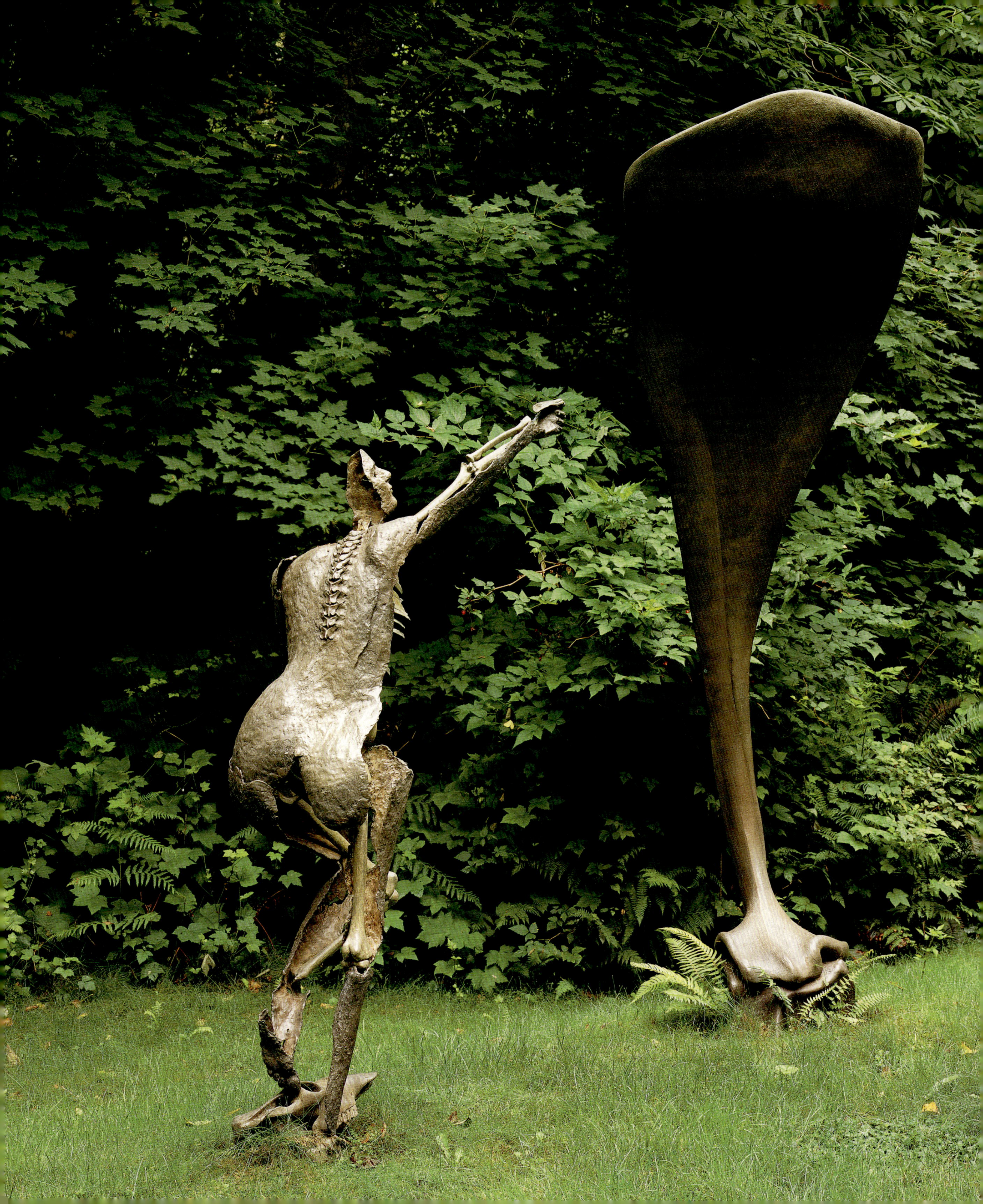

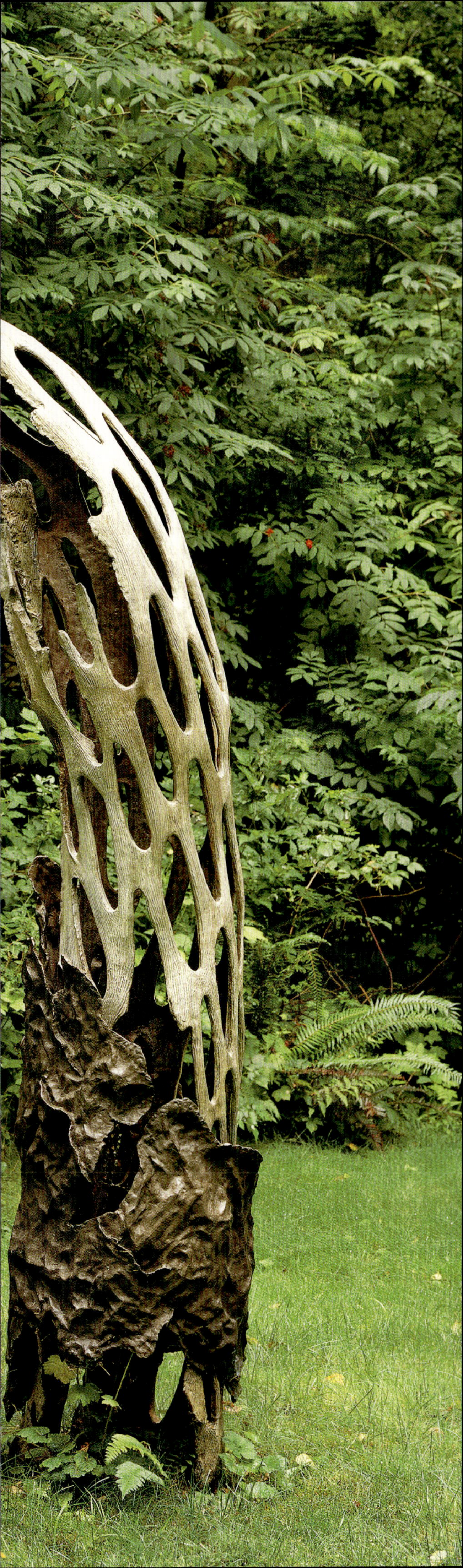

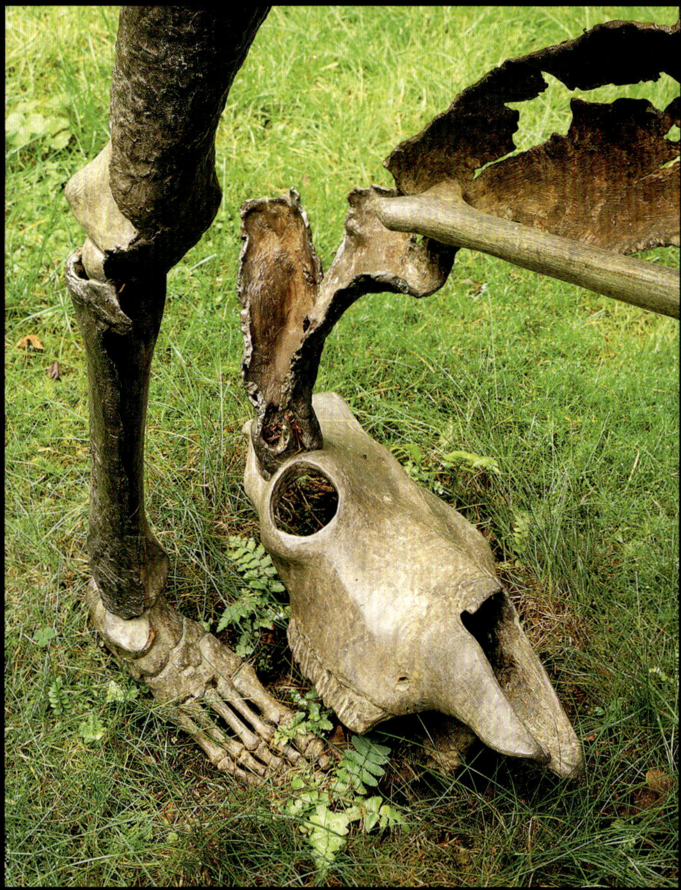

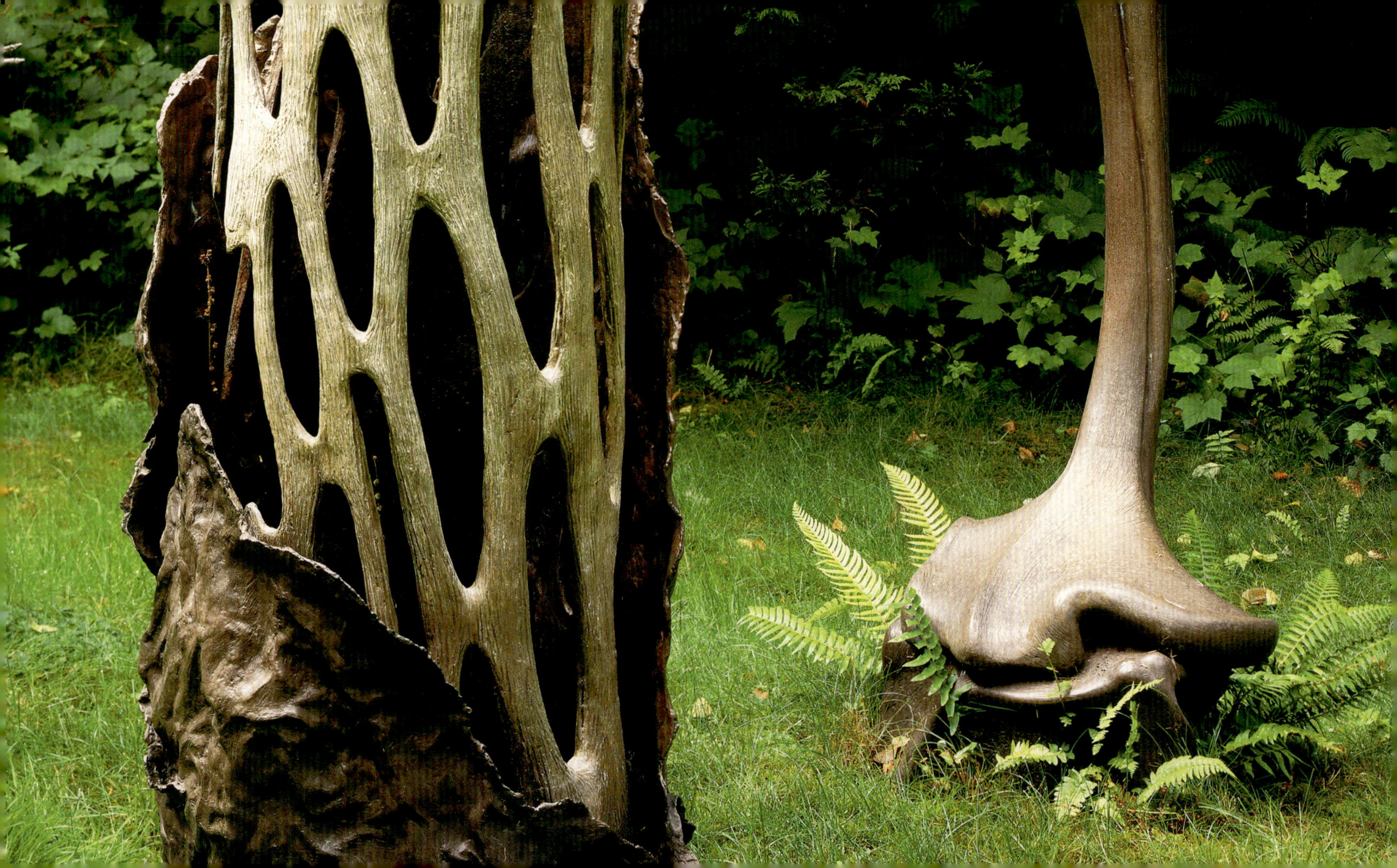

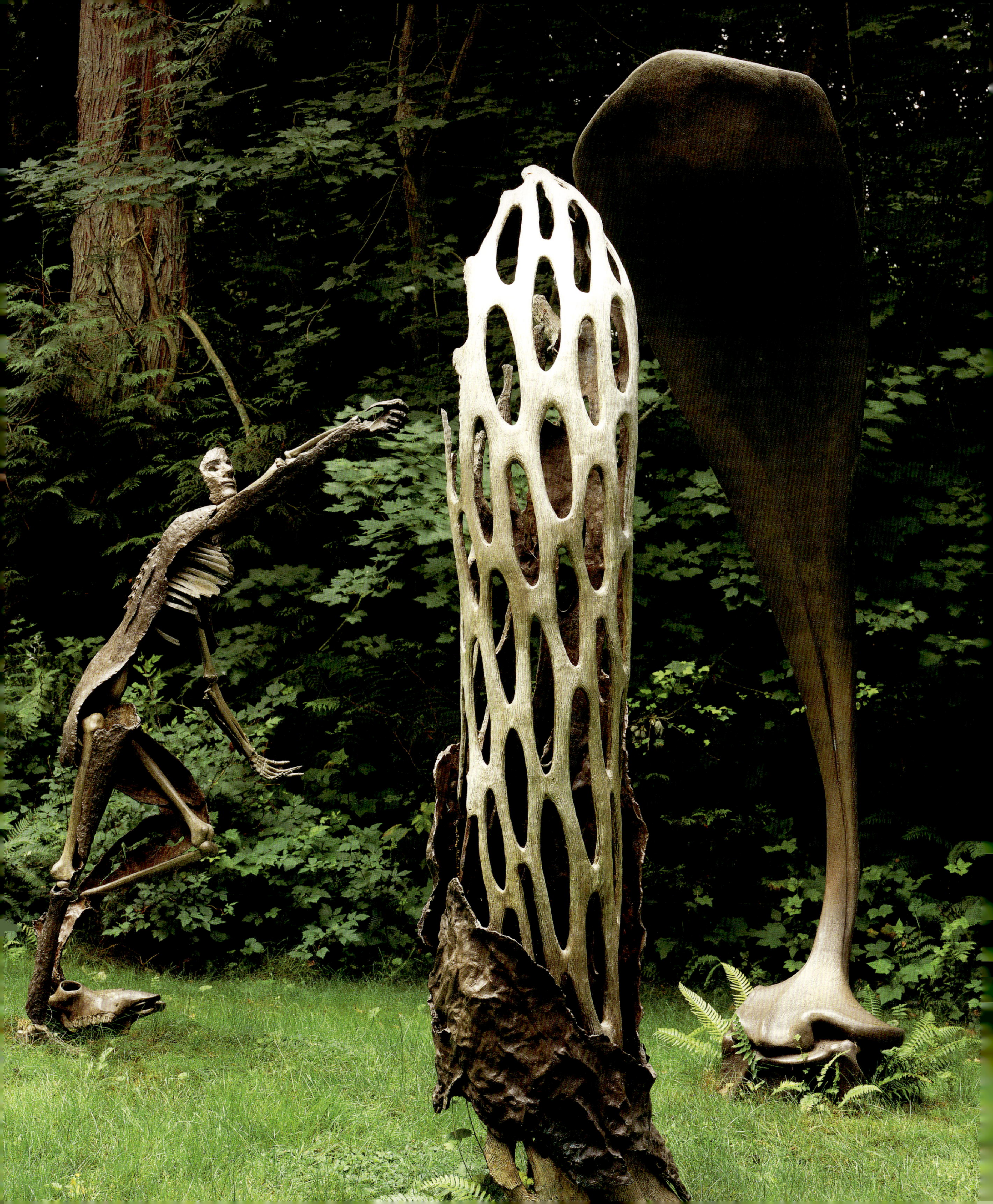

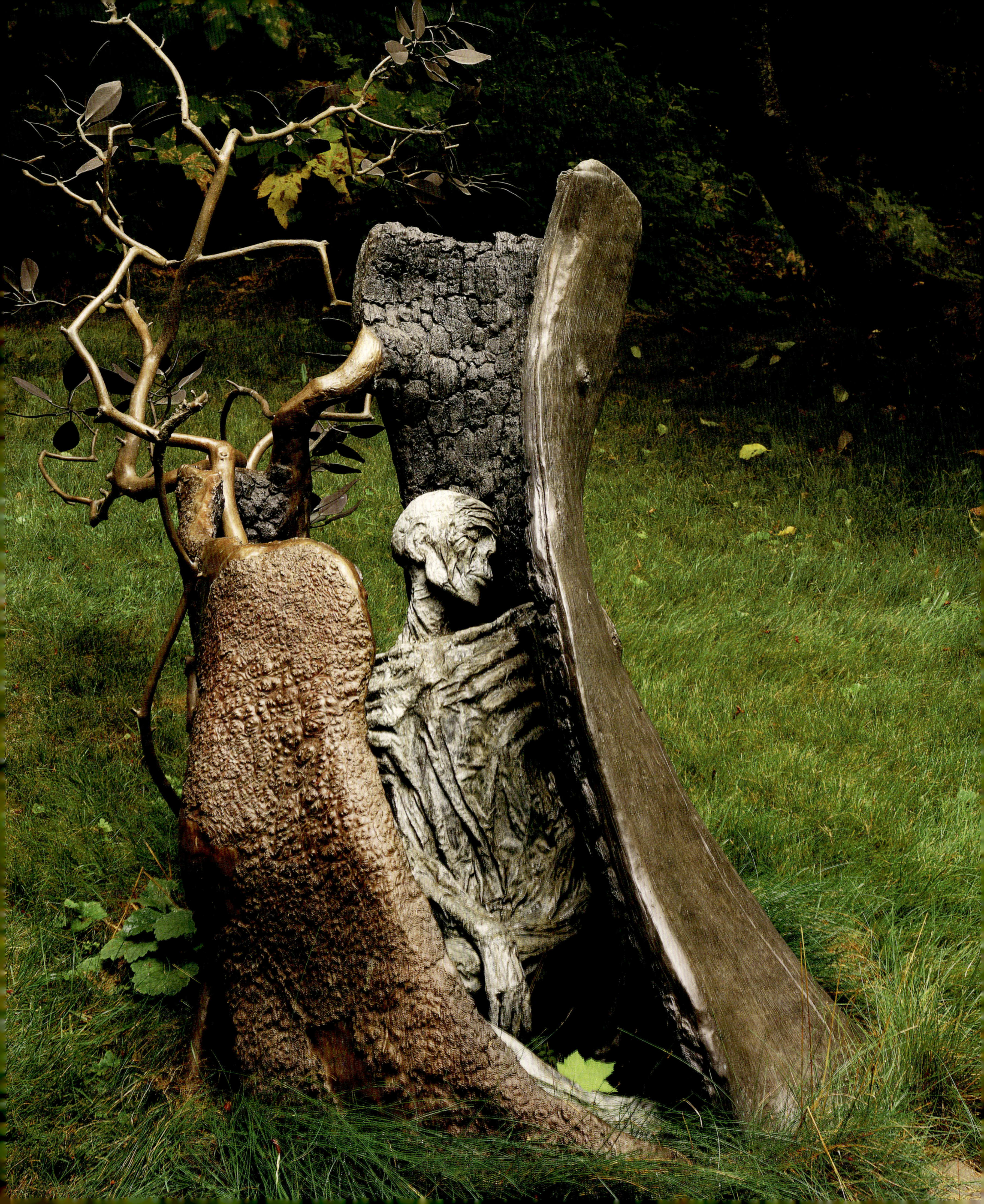

Death's Sister

The stump has burned. From one side a living branch is growing.
Life and Death are joined. Within and protected, the figure rests.
She is content. Within her the opposites are joined.
Death's Sister is Life.

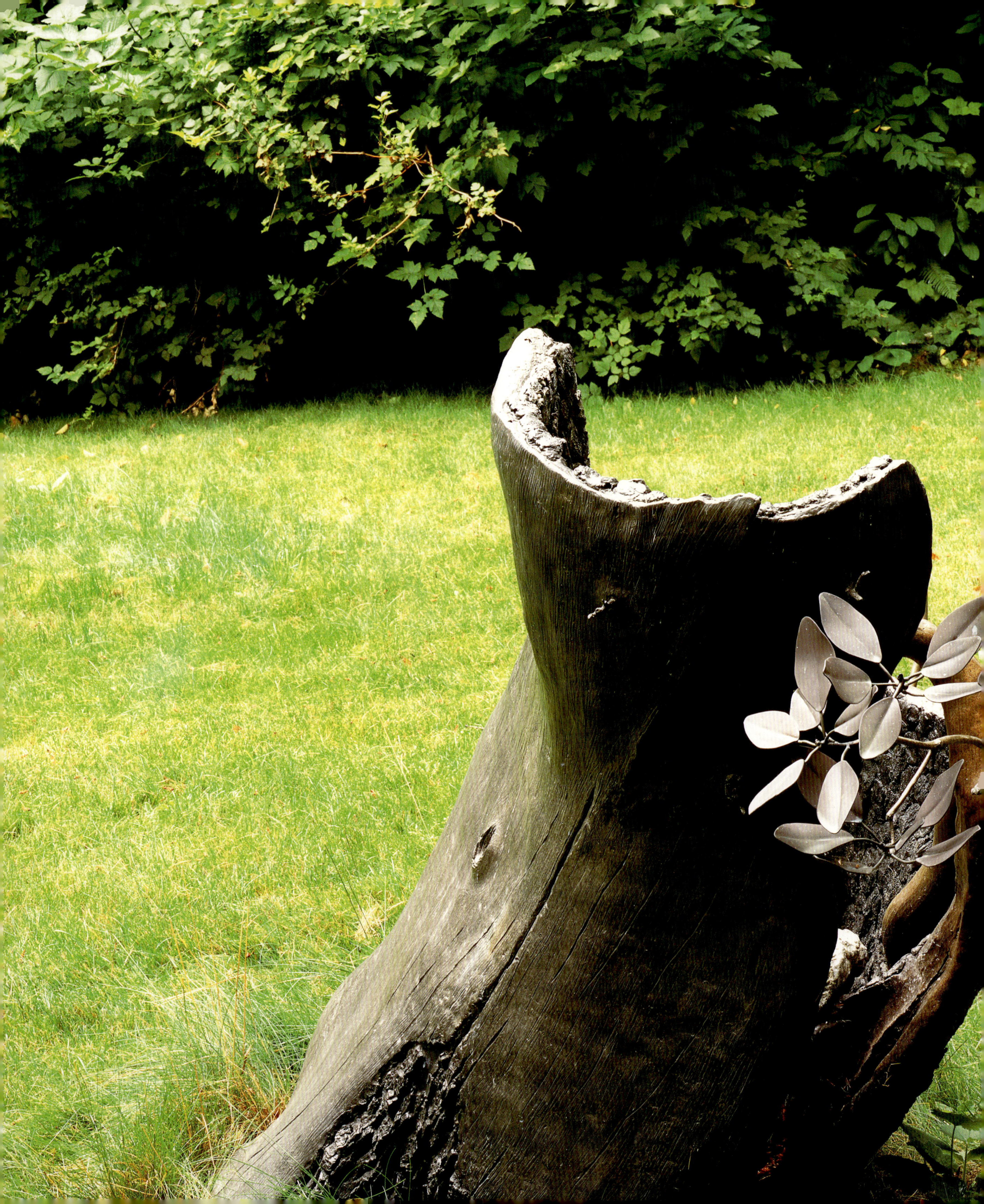

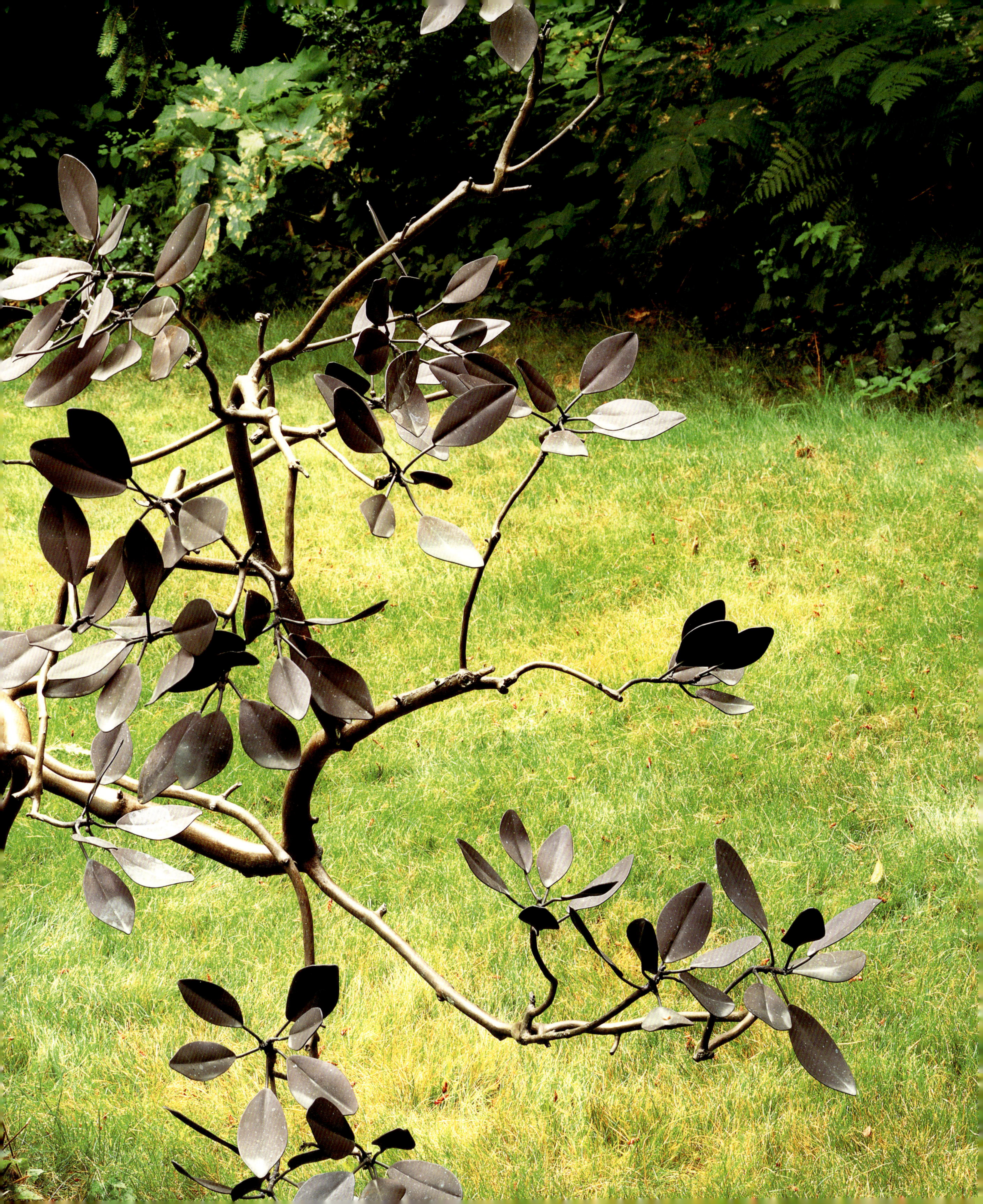

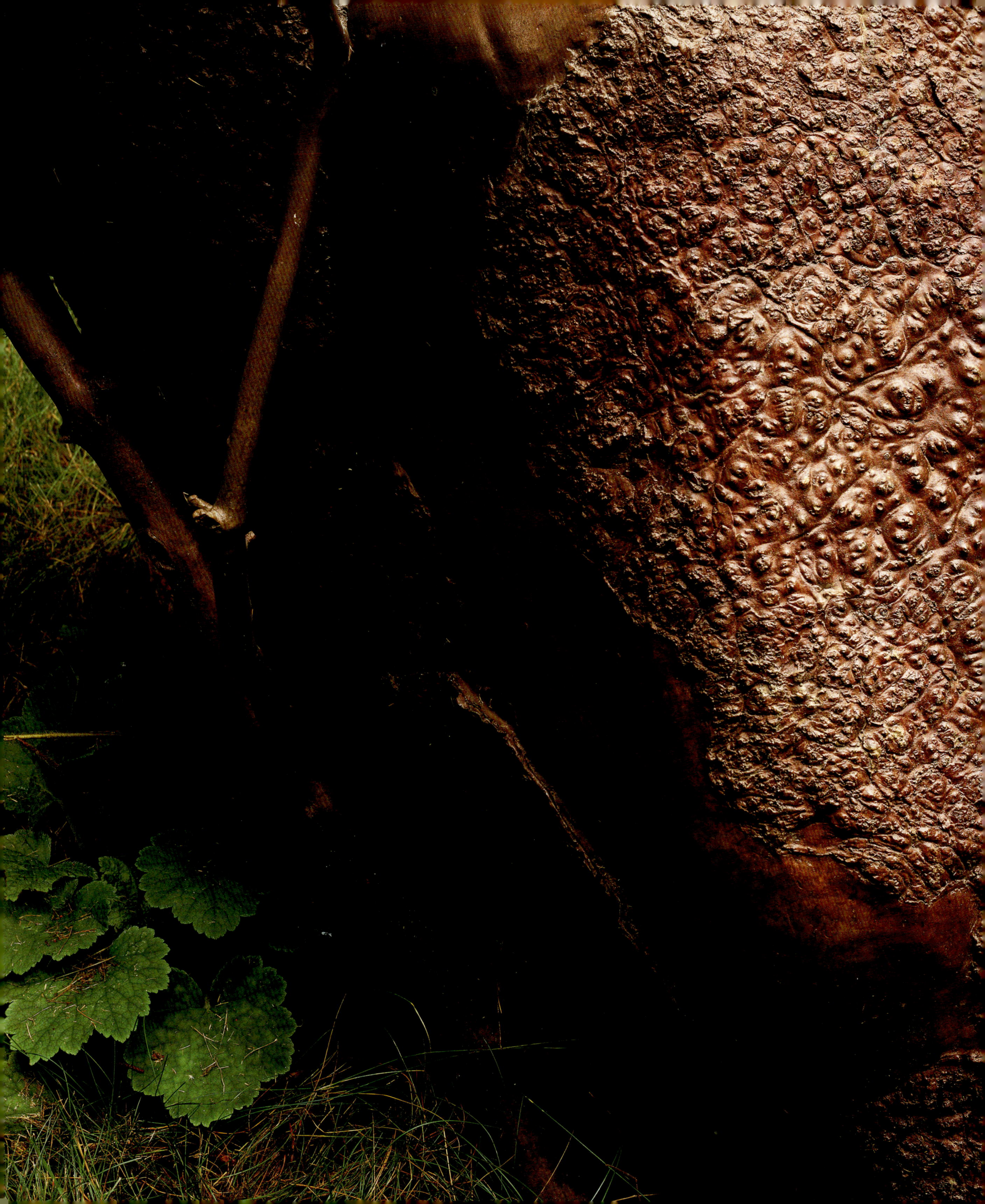

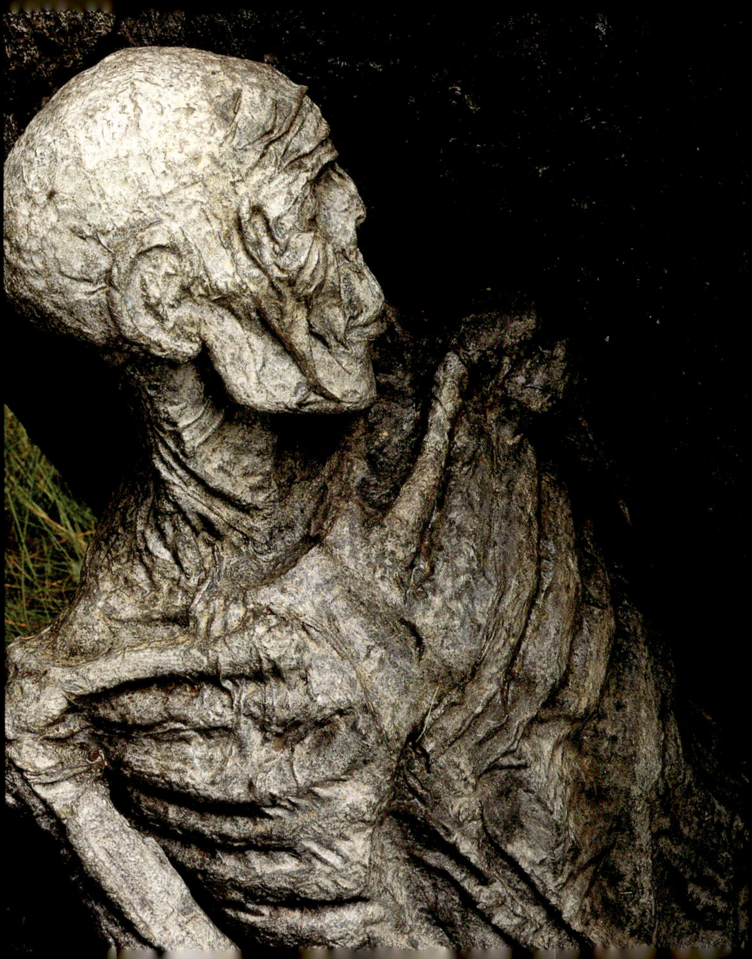

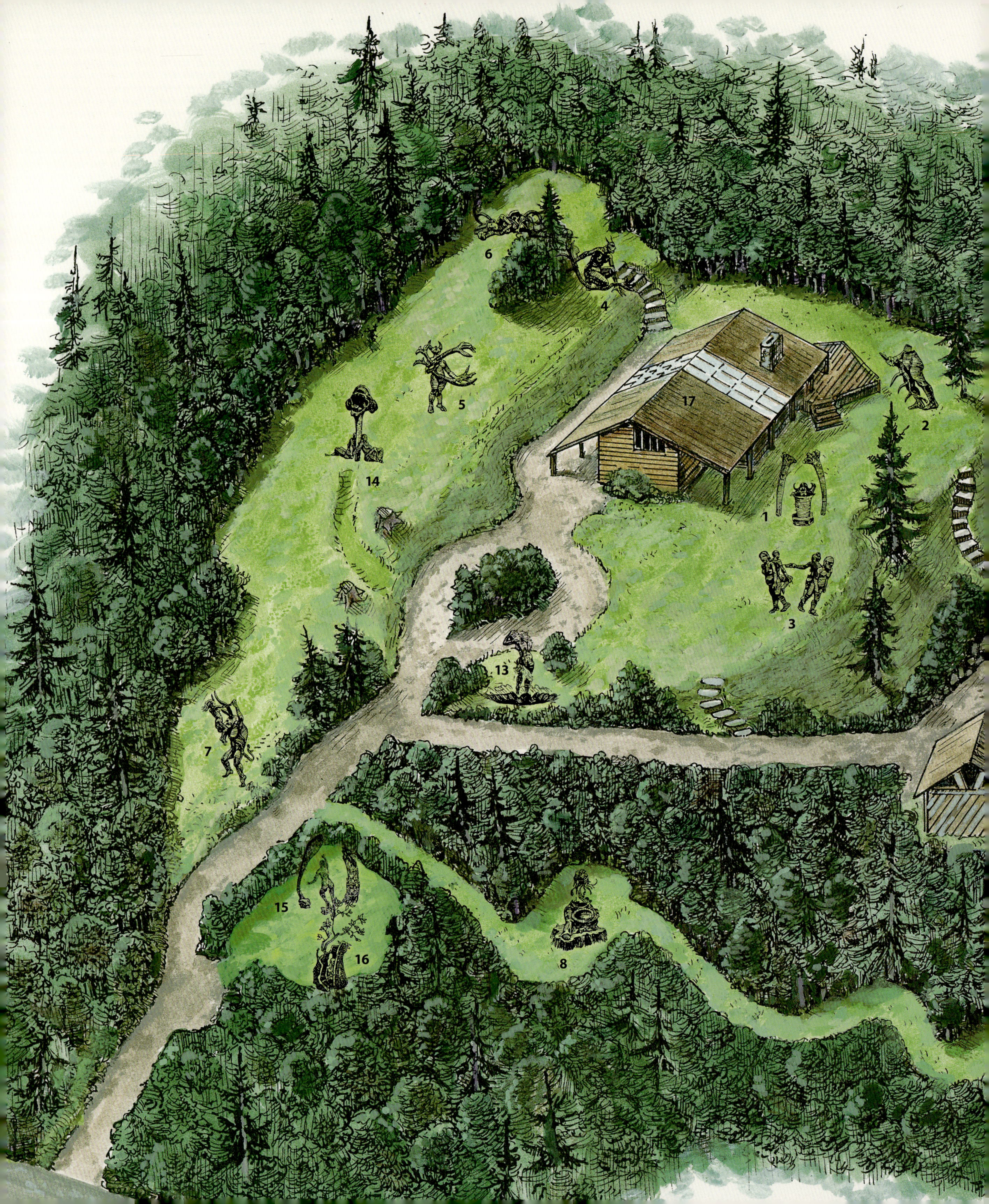

6
4
17
5
2
14
1
3
13
7
15
16
8

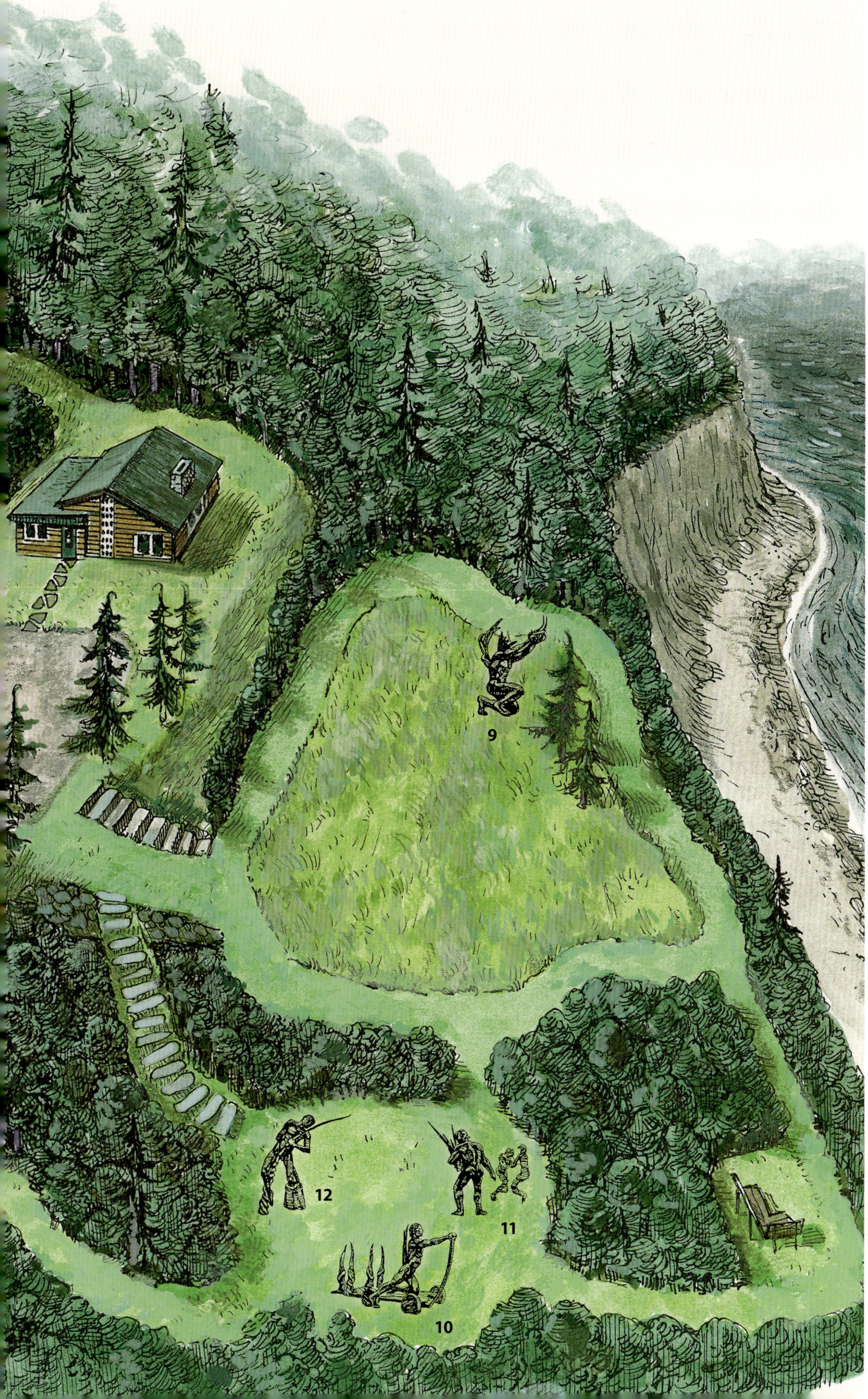

1. She of the Piece, 1992
2. Newsbringer, 1992
3. Double Dream, 1993
4. Will There Be a Place for Me?, 1994
5. Her Cry, 1993
6. Life/Death/Life, 1994
7. Dance of Life, 1995
8. Ask Gaia, 1996
9. Gifting the Giver, 1997
10. Becoming Merlin, 1998
11. Not Merlin, 1998
12. Merlin Wakes?, 1997
13. Acceptance of Sorrow, 1999
14. Backbone of the Universe, 1999
15. Trinity, 2000
16. Death's Sister, 2001
17. Bone Journey, 2001–present (in studio gallery)

Map

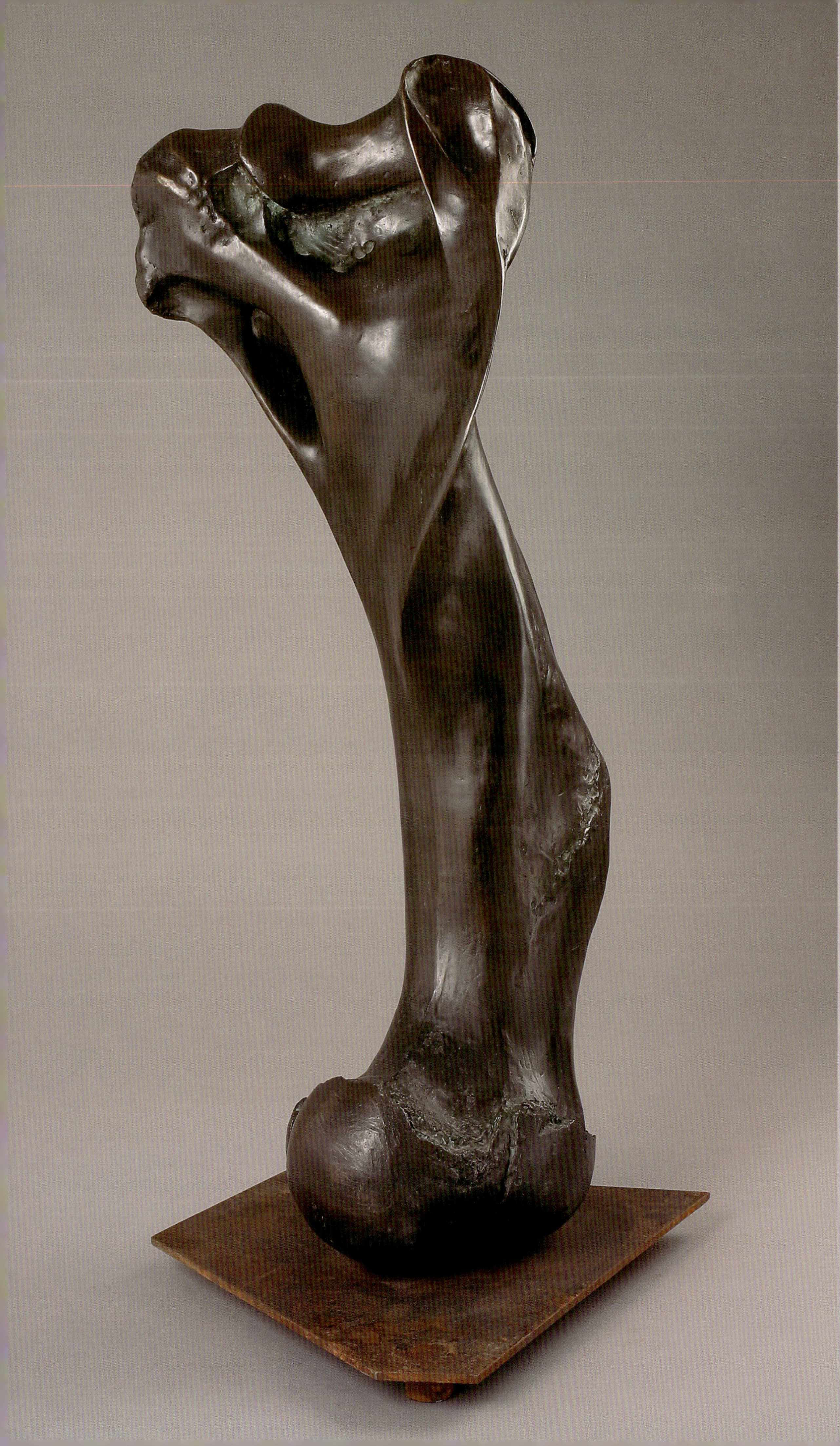

Withered Winter

Vessels

BY ANN MORRIS

THESE PIECES COME FROM THE FORESTED LAND OF mist and rain, where ravens rule and bones wash up on beaches. Here bones and plant forms come to me and from them I am given inspiration.

I have always been fascinated with bones. They are forms, that grow. Bones are given form by the forces of each individual life and support it, but their beauty is invisible until after death. They are the synthesis of life's function and form, death's architectural remains.

Vessels or boats are expressive of journey. Their forms are podlike, suggesting nature's verdant growth. They float. They shape and are shaped by water—life's principal ingredient. Plants are one of life's most abundant forms and provide us with the nourishment to continue life. Combining bones and vessels becomes for me a *Bone Journey,* a symbol of our own journey through Nature and Time. Each of our journeys is one of life and death. These vessels are its echo.

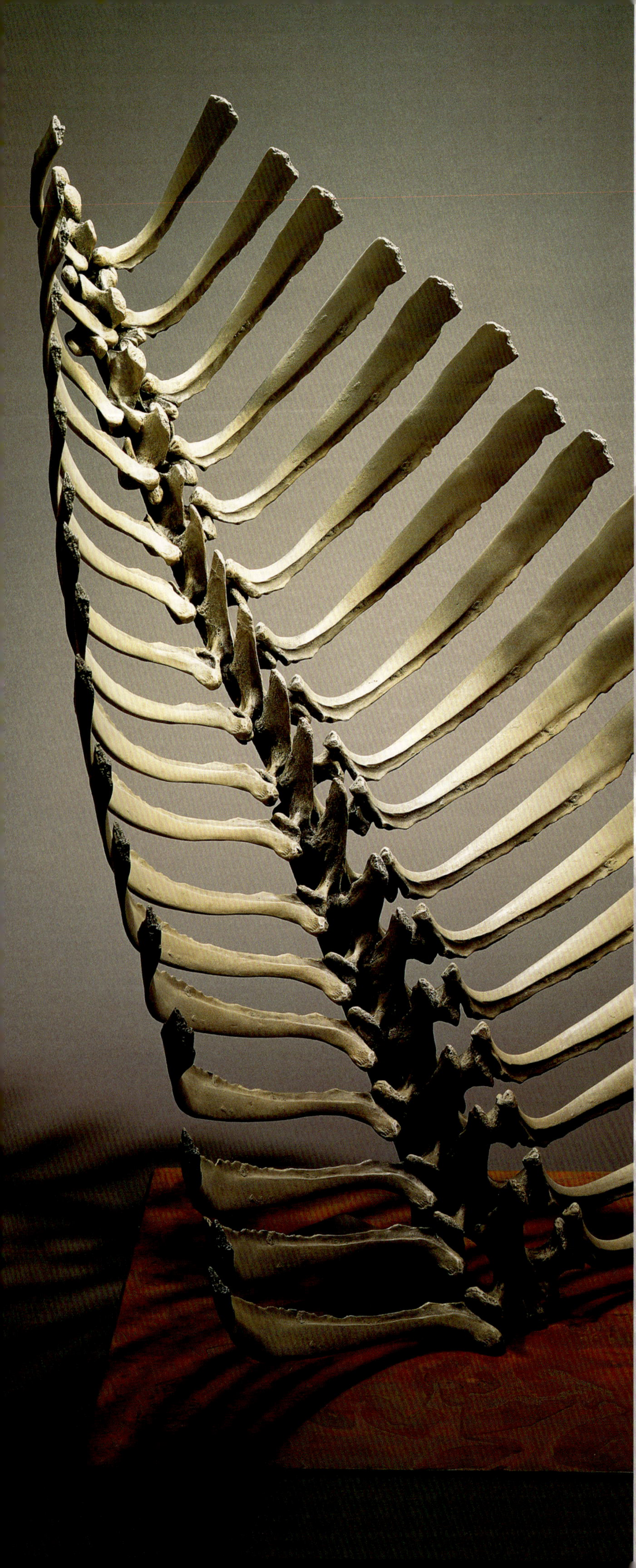

ON ANN MORRIS'S TENTH BIRTHDAY HER grandmother surprised her with a turtle shell and a pair of preserved grouse wings. The image of young Ann cherishing these memento mori as some of the most wonderful gifts she had ever received is a flashback in Morris's biography that's not hard to imagine. There is a whiff of sepulchral air in the sculptor's spacious and light-filled Lummi Island studio. It's not an aura heavy with the gravitas of graveyards, however, but rather one that celebrates mortality as the vehicle for the unbroken continuity of life.

There are bones everywhere, both natural and artful. The clean sheetrock walls of her log atelier are host to still-life ensembles of horse patellae, sheep skulls, cow ribs, heron wishbones, mummified fish, and so forth. The purposefulness of the presentation of these mortal relics and the minimalist austerity of their ossified forms make them rife objects for contemplation. In her post-child-rearing years, Morris has engaged in her artmaking with a single-minded devotion that revolves around the ongoing contemplative relationship that these bones demand of inhabitants and visitors alike.

Rising from plinths on worktables, some of the skeletal components are repeated as parts of wax figures that will be used to make molds for new bronzes, to be cast later at the Walla Walla Foundry, in Walla Walla, Washington. Morris has taken her waxes there since 2003, when her long-standing fabricator, Riverdog Foundry, in Chimacum, Washington, closed its doors.

Displayed, as well, are the creations of other bone artists that Morris admires, such as Allen Moe, whose low-fire ceramic pots are adorned with road-kill bones and viscera. Morris and Moe are of a school of independent-minded artists who have chosen rural home bases in the Puget Sound archipelago. A closeness to nature, which is inescapable in these lingering oases from

With the intimately scaled bronzes that comprise her Bone Journey, *sculptor Ann Morris has moved from mythological themes to a kind of talismanic naturalism.*

development, is tangible in the creations of many of the artists of the Cascadian/Olympic Arcadia. The Skagit and Nooksack valleys in particular—where pastoral and lush delta lands sprawl between a glaciated conifer jungle and an island-pocked inland arm of the Pacific—are regions that have spawned a strong animist aesthetic, drawing heartily from East Asian and aboriginal sensibilities.

On pedestals and shelves in a detached gallery, some of the small- and medium-size pieces, most of which Morris has cast in the last six years, await with poised equanimity their foray before the public in an upcoming exhibition. Many incorporate in their imagery references to boats or bowls, vessels that form a small armada for these journeying bones. Bones, beaks, and skulls complement, inhabit, propel, and even become vessels and, in visionary juxtapositions that recall the Surrealists' provocative trips to subconscious realms, Morris frames her sculptures in Jungian mytho-psychological symbolism.

The bone tour continues outdoors, where on a grassy berm the dismembered skeleton of a beached whale bleaches in the crystalline sunshine, slowly soaking up inspiration for a future series of bronzes. The immense creature washed up on the windward side of the island, and Morris, recognizing a once-in-a-lifetime opportunity for a bone collector such as she, had the behemoth towed to a friend's beach, where she has been slowly allowing the elements to uncover the massive skeleton.

As one wanders farther afield through what she calls the Sculpture Woods—her fifteen-acre sanctuary of stately forest and high-bank waterfront on this townless isle north of Bellingham—one encounters a series of startling bronzes framed in niches and small clearings among the greenery. Depending on which direction you head, you might come upon *Double Dream* or *Ask Gaia* or *Trinity* or any of the other sixteen monumental works that this surprisingly diminutive sculptress created between 1992 and 2001.

Bringing a neo-Mediterranean spirit of Classicism to the cedars and the firs, these are civic-scale works that the artist collectively titles *Figuration of the Human Spirit*. Perambulating the paths that pull you through the maze of salal and fern understory, one has the sense of progressing through a kind of Stations of the Cross that beads together scenes from a psychic odyssey. Mythological figures engage in heroic tableaux of interpenetrating dualities—masculine/feminine, animal/human, nature/artifice, decay/regeneration—all seeking to unite the inner world of myth/mind/spirit with the outer world of matter/nature/the garden.

Now rejoined with her brood, Morris's *Ask Gaia*—the larger-than-life representation of the ancient Grecian mother of all matter—for five years sat contemplatively on a bronze counterfeit tree stump in Webster's Woods Art Park at Port Angeles (Washington) Fine Arts Center. Her body only partially formed with sketchy anatomical detail, Morris's primal goddess was an all-encompassing presence that embraced the living forest, whose fragmented vignettes filled her many peek-a-boo voids. The bronze-on-bronze fusion of the two trunks—deity and arbor—welded together a state of being/perfection with a state of becoming/variation.

In 2001, following her exhibition at the Museum of Northwest Art in La Conner, Washington, Morris—who is not given to frequent epiphanies—felt overwhelmingly that she had completed her work with monumental figures and overtly mythological subjects. Finding herself beset by a crisis of scale, driven by economy and practicality as well as a thirst for new subjects, she began to uncover the flesh of her figures in search of the underlying structure.

Hot Bronze, Cool Bones

BY JAKE SENIUK

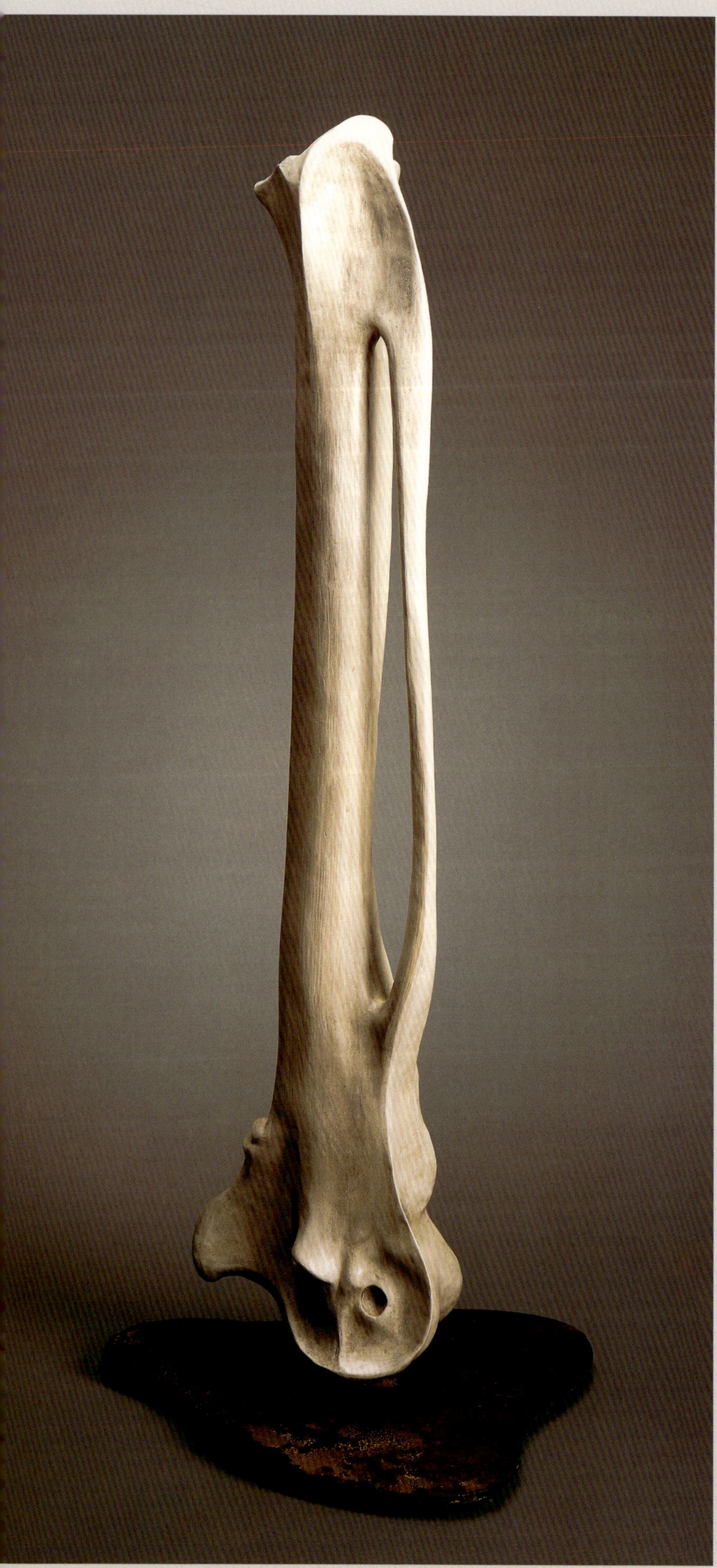

Eagle Arm

Her last two large-scale works, *Trinity* and *Death's Sister,* led the transition toward a new formal language that introduced a refreshing feeling of intimacy to her creations. The former is composed of a life-size female figure flanked by the monolithic jawbone of a cabezon and the orphaned branch of a desiccated cholla cactus. The gesticulating nude has been rent asunder to reveal the underlying bones cradled in the now-hollowed flesh, like in a cutaway anatomical chart. The fish bone and the perforated cactus trunk are enlarged to full human scale, giving the figures equal weight and the kind of parity one might expect from a grouping of the Three Graces.

In Morris's waning mythological mode the ensemble invokes several cosmic triads: human/fauna/flora; life/death/decay; past/present/future. The emergence of the bones from the flesh, and the aggrandizement of a single bone to monumentality, harbingers the reductivism in form and theme that was to follow. Morris was preparing to simplify her muse, to hone her practice, and to meditate directly upon the mortal remains that fueled her fascination, rather than through the filter of the stories associated with them.

Death's Sister brings Morris's mythological period to a close with a self-reflexive flourish. A mummified female is cradled in her final sleep within the hollow of a fire-blasted tree trunk. Absent now are all references to some ideal pantheon. This withered goddess is all too human, a bag of bones left behind by a flash of lightning that charcoaled this stump.

Despite the fragility of her subjects—melting flesh and scorched wood—the permanence of bronze suspends the moment for an eternity. And like the body double of bundled sheets and towels left sleeping on the prison cot, it is a proxy self offered up to the comptrollers of repentance, who now outwitted permit the soul to slip past the gates of Death and set wing. Morris began her monumental oeuvre a decade and a half ago with *She of the Piece,* her midlife self-portrait as a robust nude regally enshrined in a cauldron. She ends the series by transcending the body's vanity and desires, an aging artist surrendering to her muse with renewed awareness of mortality, tempered by the accruing wisdom of experience.

The mortal coil has held Ann Morris's attention from an early age. Although she saw first light in New York City, she spent most of her formative years on farms in Ohio and Iowa. Her inventor father and watercolorist mother inspired Ann to express her creative urges through her hands and to find aesthetic, as well as practical, solutions to the things she made.

The periodic signs of mortality that she experienced in the abundant nature of mid-century midwestern Americana inspired her awakening philosophical sensibilities toward budding flirtations with shamanism, long before that word ever crossed her lips. The life and death cycles she witnessed in the woods and fields impressed her with their karmic theater and soul-plumbing beauty, and in her childish reveries she imagined herself a priestess with domain over the living and the dead.

At mid-century the family moved to Southern California, where Ann studied philosophy at Pomona College. Plato's notion of the Ideal Forms, archetypal designs that can be apprehended by the mind but not the eye and which constitute the eternal and unchanging nature of reality, intrigued Morris then. Decades later her classical renderings of the figure and references to the Greek and Celtic pantheons flow naturally from a wellspring of her immersion in Platonism.

Studies in printmaking at the Pasadena Art Museum led her to seek physical expression for her ideas. However, the twin beacons of that moment—the nascent women's movement and the burgeoning West Coast arts and crafts revival—led her to a more kinesthetic paradigm. Soon, moving off the page, she began taking castings from her own body. From here grew an awareness of the skin that separates ideas from substance and the beauty and justice of expressing that dynamic through the actions of a mold.

The bronze process, which she undertook in earnest in 1990, suited her temperament and her plastic skills. Not naturally given to drawing, Morris felt comfort in the forgiveness of wax, where mass can be added or subtracted, mistakes can be easily melted and repaired, and new directions can be undertaken midstream. At the same time the malleability of the wax is countered by the ensuing bronze's rigidity, which can sustain weighty forms in fine-tuned and sometimes precarious balance. That it is also capable of holding subtly detailed textures, such as the fluked surface of her whale *Baleen Platter,* makes it an ideal medium for replicating nature's organic infrastructure. The fluidity of the medium appealed to this island dweller's amphibious predilections and gave her freedom to experiment with confidence.

After the skeletons had found their way to the light by pushing outside the body, Morris realized that these foundation forms allowed for a clearer expression of eternal ideals. To Morris bones represent the natural order, the genetic code that unwinds these miraculous flesh-and-blood machines, which house consciousness—human and other.

"I have always been fascinated with bones," she writes in her artist's statement. "Bones are given form by the forces of each individual life and support it, but their beauty is invisible until after death. They are the synthesis of life's function and form, death's architectural remains."

Morris's fascination flares brightest in the monolithic presentation of single bones such as *Eagle Arm*, a striking facsimile of the raptor's major wing bone. Flirting with the simulacrum by using a pigmented white finish, she makes the cool touch of the ivorian bronze a surprise to the fingertips. To the eye this artful body double is only given away by its hyperbolic size. Morris's choice of a confrontational scale emphasizes the ideal beauty of the form. Thus the trompe l'oeil veracity of the pedestaled piece declares itself as sculpture rather than specimen.

In *Beak Shelter* the swoop and hollowed planes of an arching predatory beak are smoothly enlarged and touch down to a baseline at three points. Driven toward abstraction by hard surfaces and naked lines, the beak's inherent sculptural form takes on an architectural presence. This could be the breezy maquette for an air terminal or some futuristic orchestra shell expressed in the vocabulary of an Eero Saarinen.

With *Heron Wish* Morris surrenders to the artful symmetry of a wishbone and finishes the graceful arch with a classic verdigris patina that, in its ancient familiarity, pays tribute to the long, long legacy of bronze work. Suggesting both a passage and a vessel, its mandorla shape is archetypally feminine. With subtlety and masterful restraint, Morris revisits her own coming-of-artistic-age, during the Judy Chicago era when feminism and self-discovery flowered in the art world.

Tantric art reduces all the shapes of the universe to two essentials: the *lingam* and the *yoni*, the round peg in the round hole, the fundamental expression of union. Morris's discovery of the portal to the feminine in the wishbone's shape is a testament to both Tantric and Platonic ideals, which are repeatedly expressed in the universal consistency of natural design.

In 1994 Morris embarked on what would become the first of eleven annual summer cruises up the inside passages of British Columbia and Alaska on the *Snow Goose,* a sixty-foot motor launch owned by her friends Burt and Sue Weber. Accompanied by other artists, including master carver Scott Jensen, she participated in collaborative sculptural projects on each excursion. The growth she garnered from these floating calisthenics was multiplied by opportunities to visit remote and historic native settlements and pristine wild lands. Shore excursions brought her in close contact with the cycles of creation and decay: avian rookeries, breaching whales, washed-up carcasses, chalky skeletons, driftwood gargoyles, sagging totems, rotting canoes.

These cocooned voyages effected a further distillation of Morris's insular sensibilities (an island is not unlike a boat at anchor in a friendly harbor) and reaffirmed her predilection for metaphoric journeys as the substance of her art. "Vessels or boats

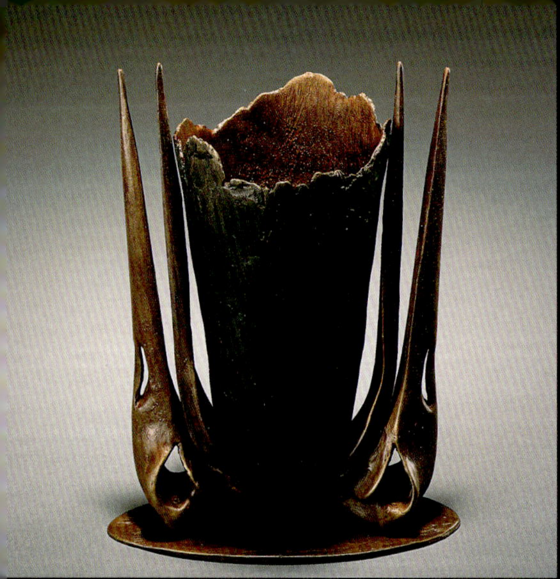

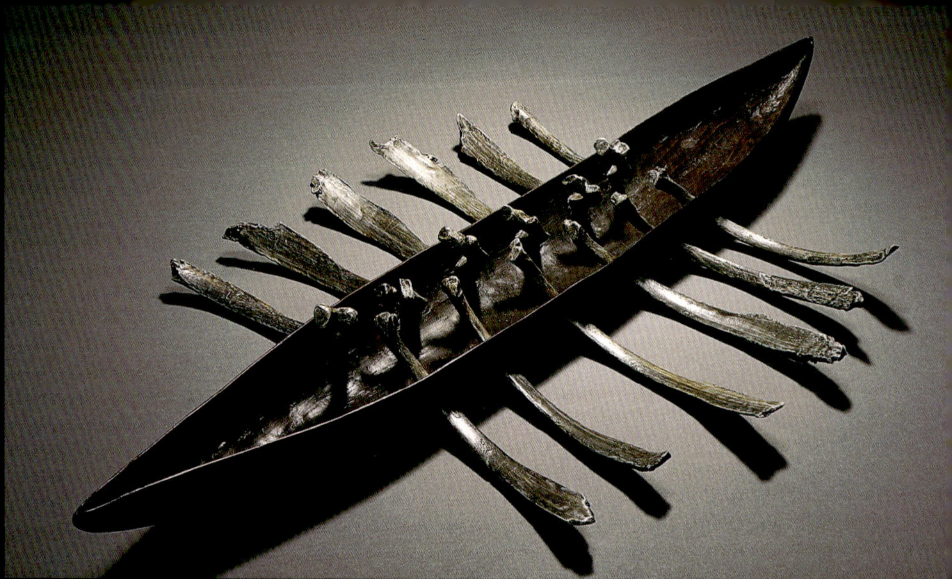

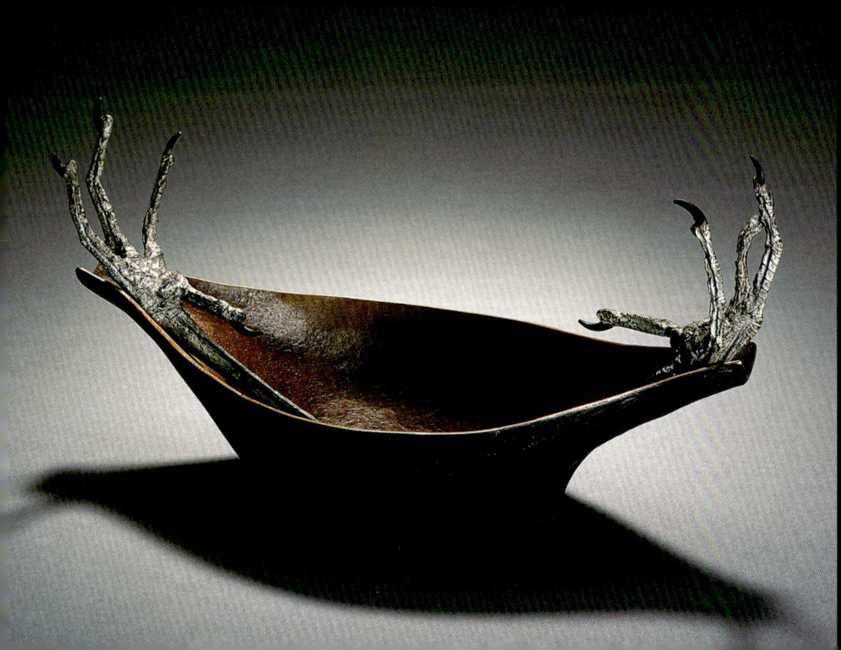

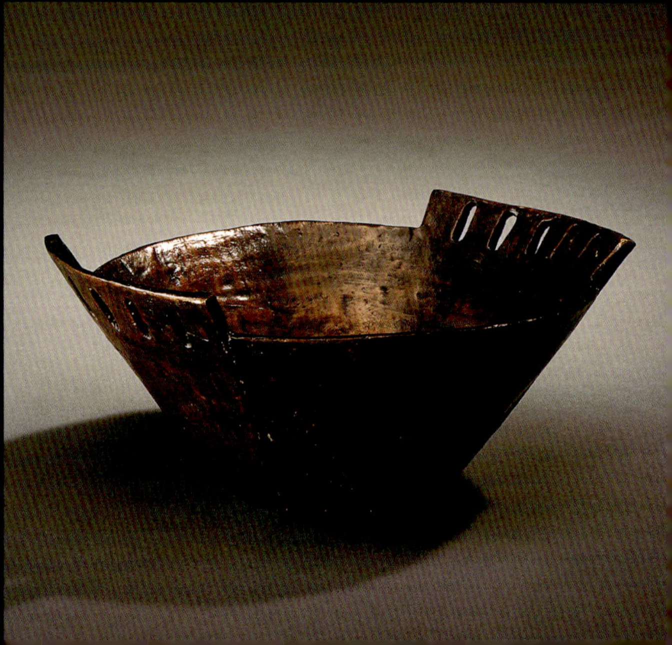

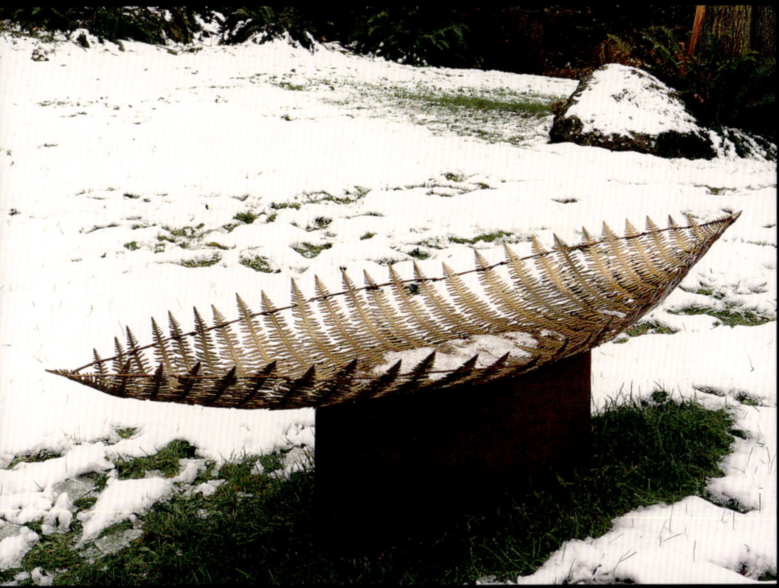

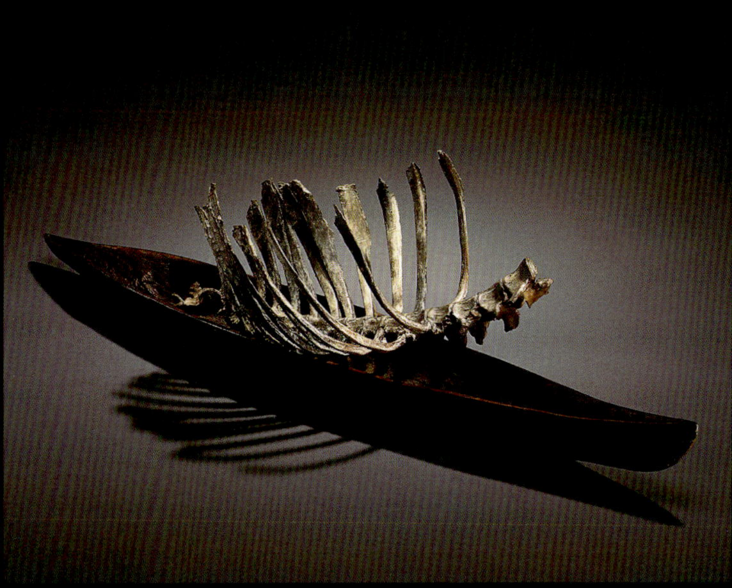

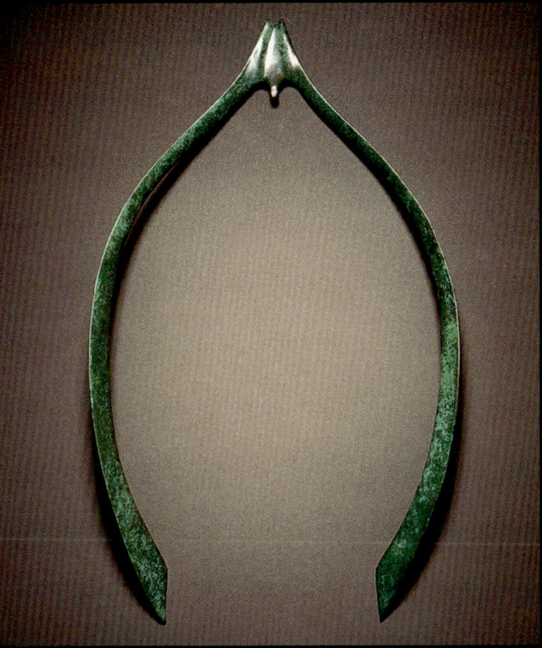

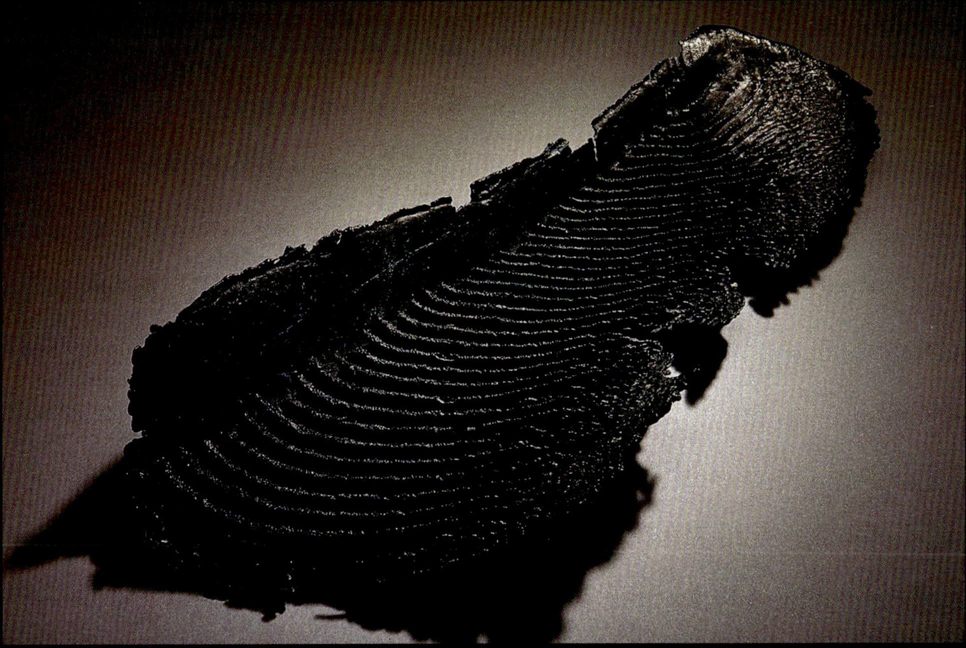

Fern Boat **Life Dugout** **Heron Wish** **Baleen Platter**

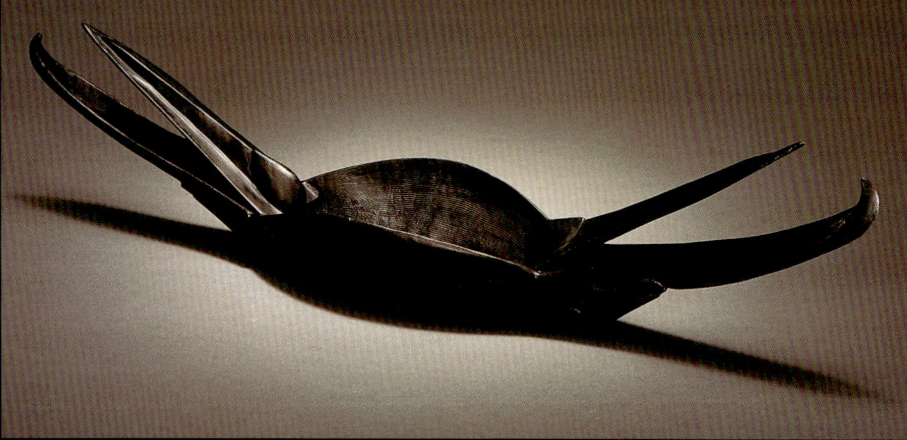

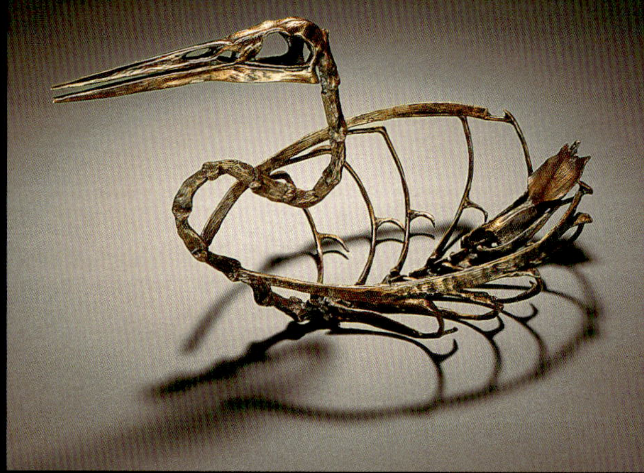

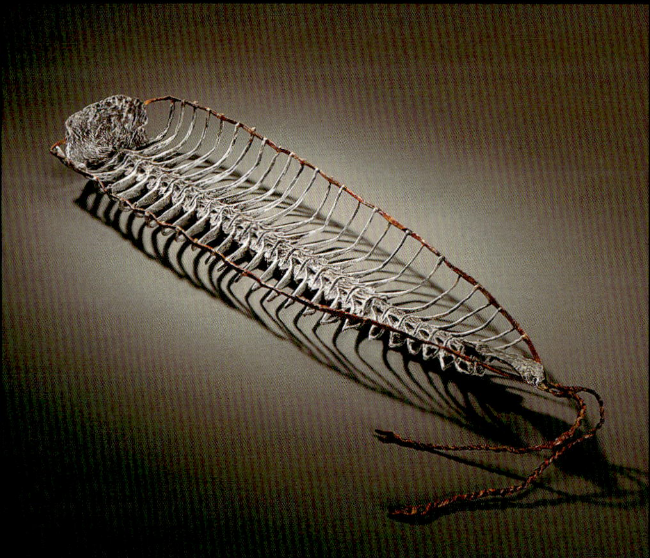

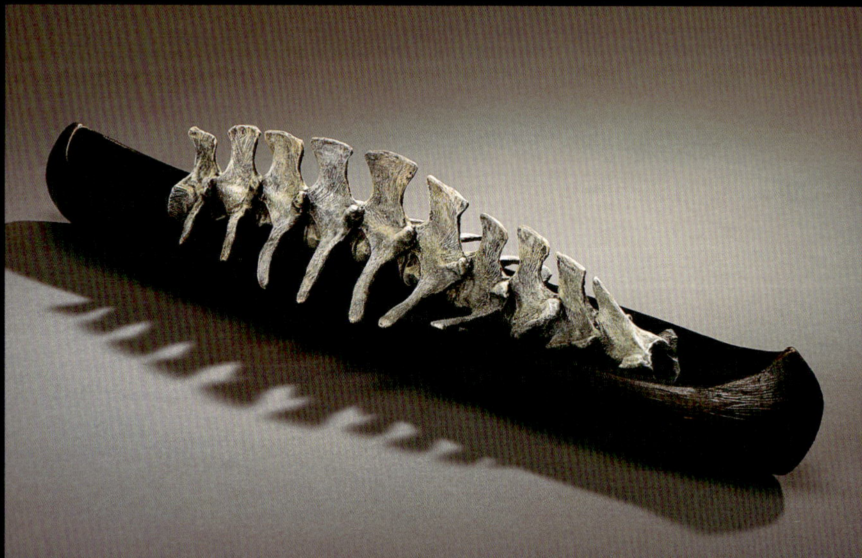

RAVEN BOWL

HERON BOWL

GHOST BOAT

BACK BOAT

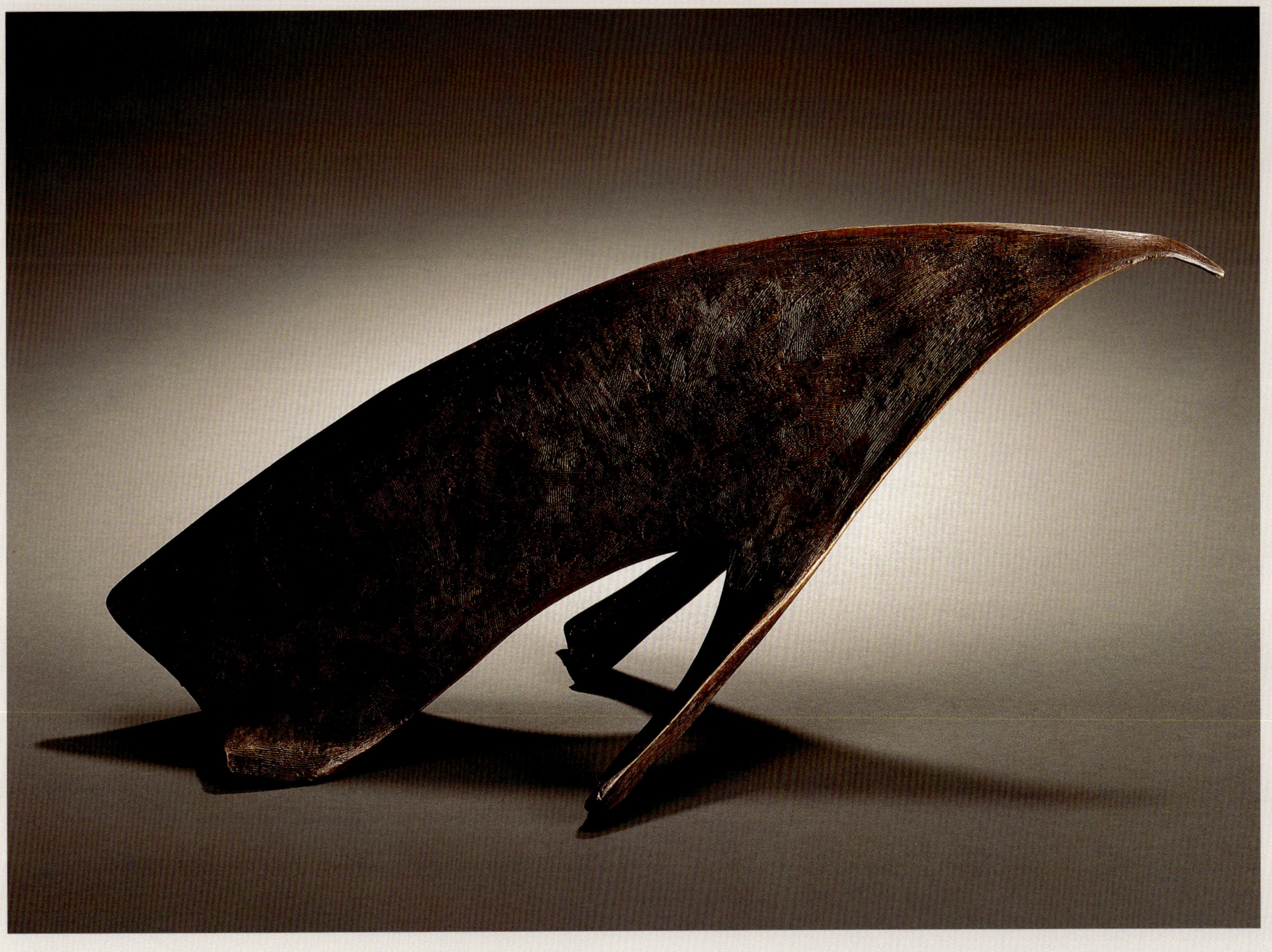

are expressive of journey," Morris writes. "Their forms are pod-like, suggesting nature's verdant growth. They float. They shape and are shaped by water—life's principal ingredient."

Drawing from the kitchen legacy of bowls, her *Snowgoose Bowl* of 1999 brought the idea of a container into the foreground of her practice. While a few of her bowls might be suitable for display on the dinner table, most are definitely more of the conversation-piece variety. Her *Knuckle Bowl,* for example, is formed in the hollow of a horse's magnified hip joint, its deep cup grooved to guide the travel of the ball joint in this socket. The beauty and durability of bone have made it a utilitarian as well as a ceremonial material in many preindustrial cultures. Like the femur trumpets of Tibetan Buddhists that give the dead a voice, Morris's bone relics goad us with their lingering personality to imagine that there is an afterlife.

It is the recurrent and inventive presence of the elliptical vessel form that brings the *journey*ing to Morris's *Bone Journey* equation. Most of the works in the series transcend the bowl-as-vessel with an evolving vocabulary of boat forms. In *Steerage* a rib protrudes through the side of an open skiff, serving as both helmsman and rudder in a single swoosh. Could this be Adam's missing rib, with Eve, herself, at the tiller? The vulvar shape and the penetration of the rib through the vessel wall is itself a kind of impregnation, a concoction that is as much Freudian as it is Tantric.

The cognate shapes—boat and seed pod—link voyage with fecundity, passage with regeneration. This is stated most succinctly in empty vessels such as *Pod Drift,* where the split husk is transformed into a canoe. In *Crab Claw* the crustacean's pincer floats high on the water, itself a curving gondola. Most of Morris's vessels, however, are inhabited with anatomical fragments that exert a talismanic presence.

In *Crow Boat* a pair of talons is the cargo of a flat-bottomed dugout. Still coiled with the energy of take-off, they are an

BEAK SHELTER

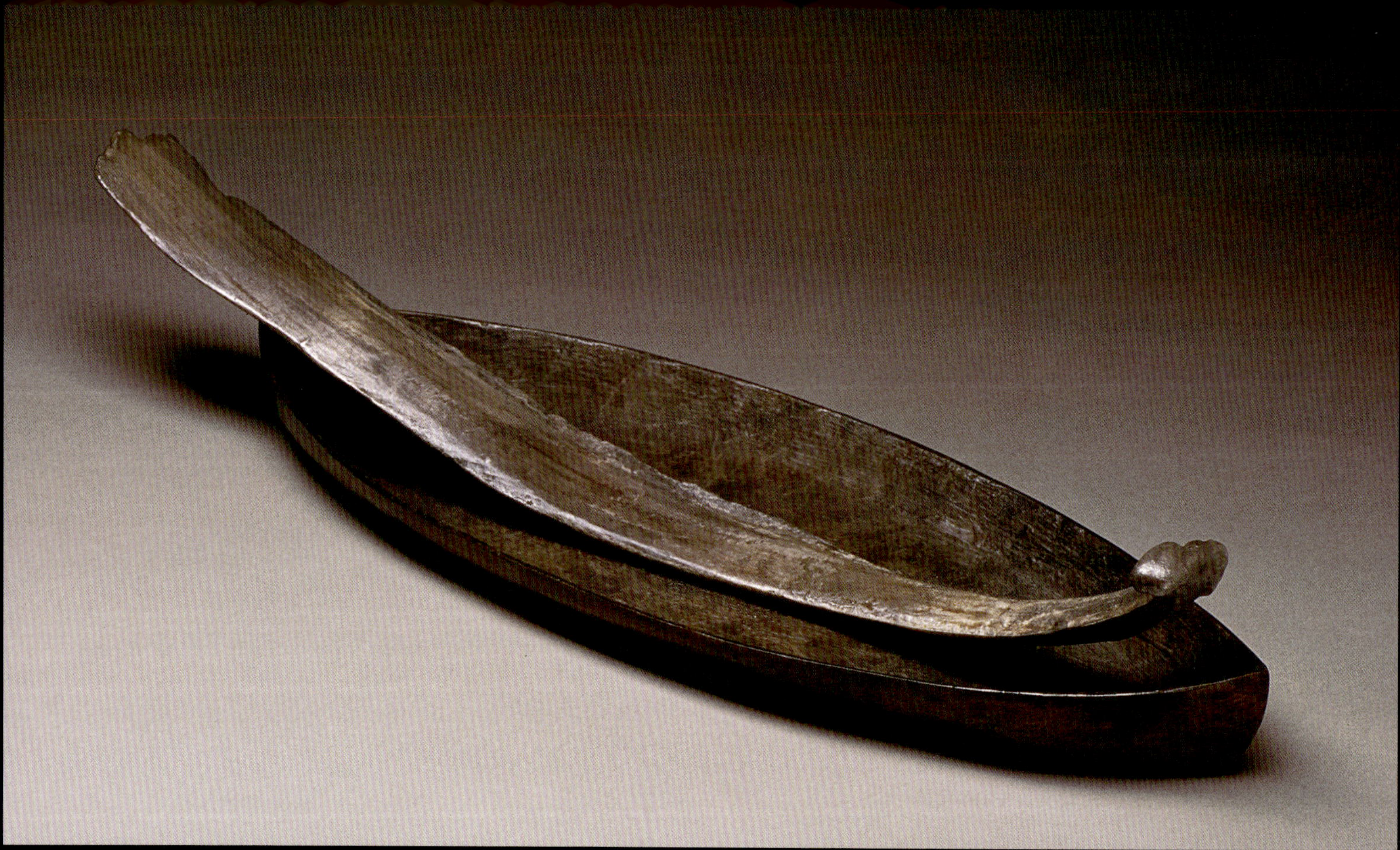

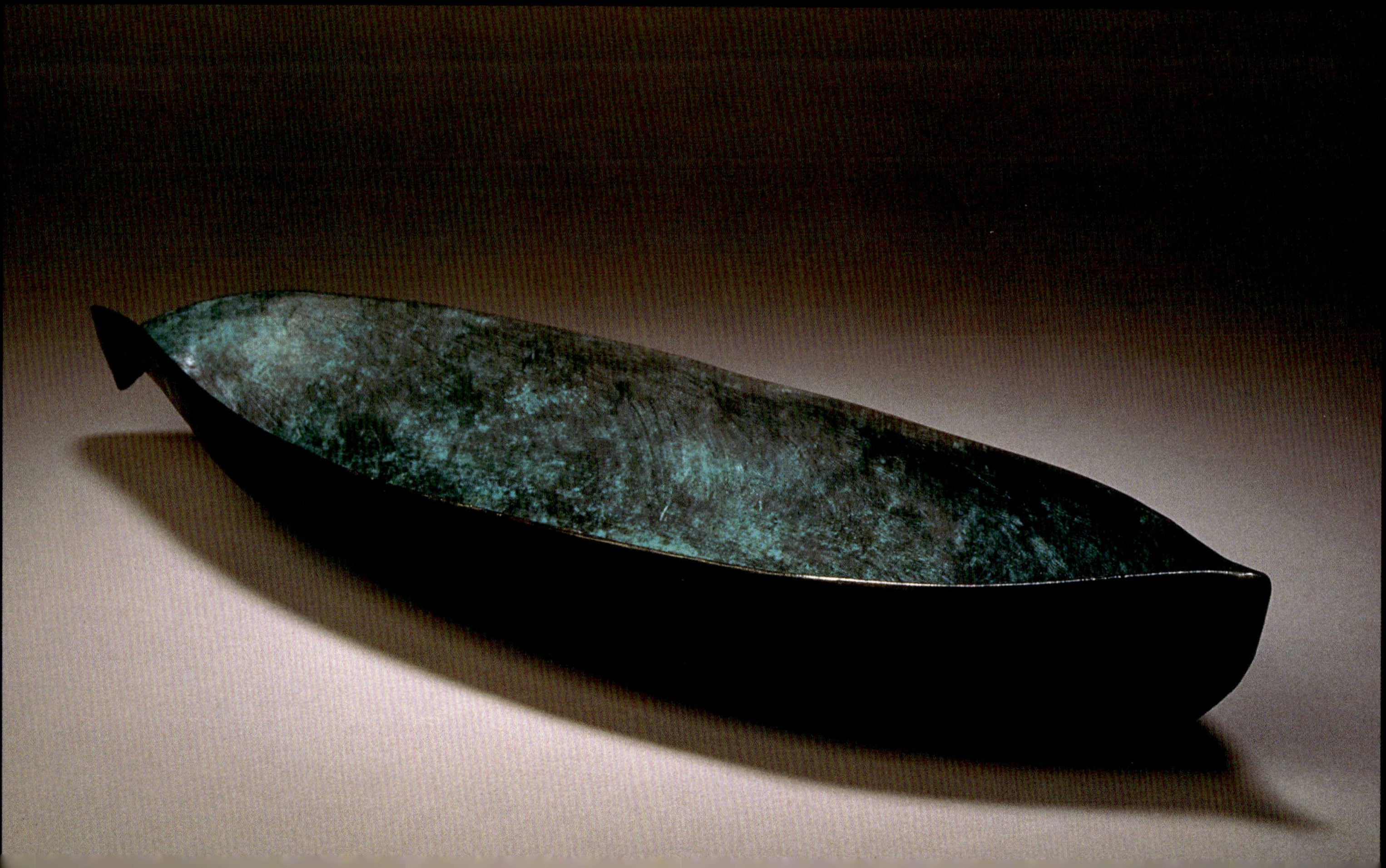

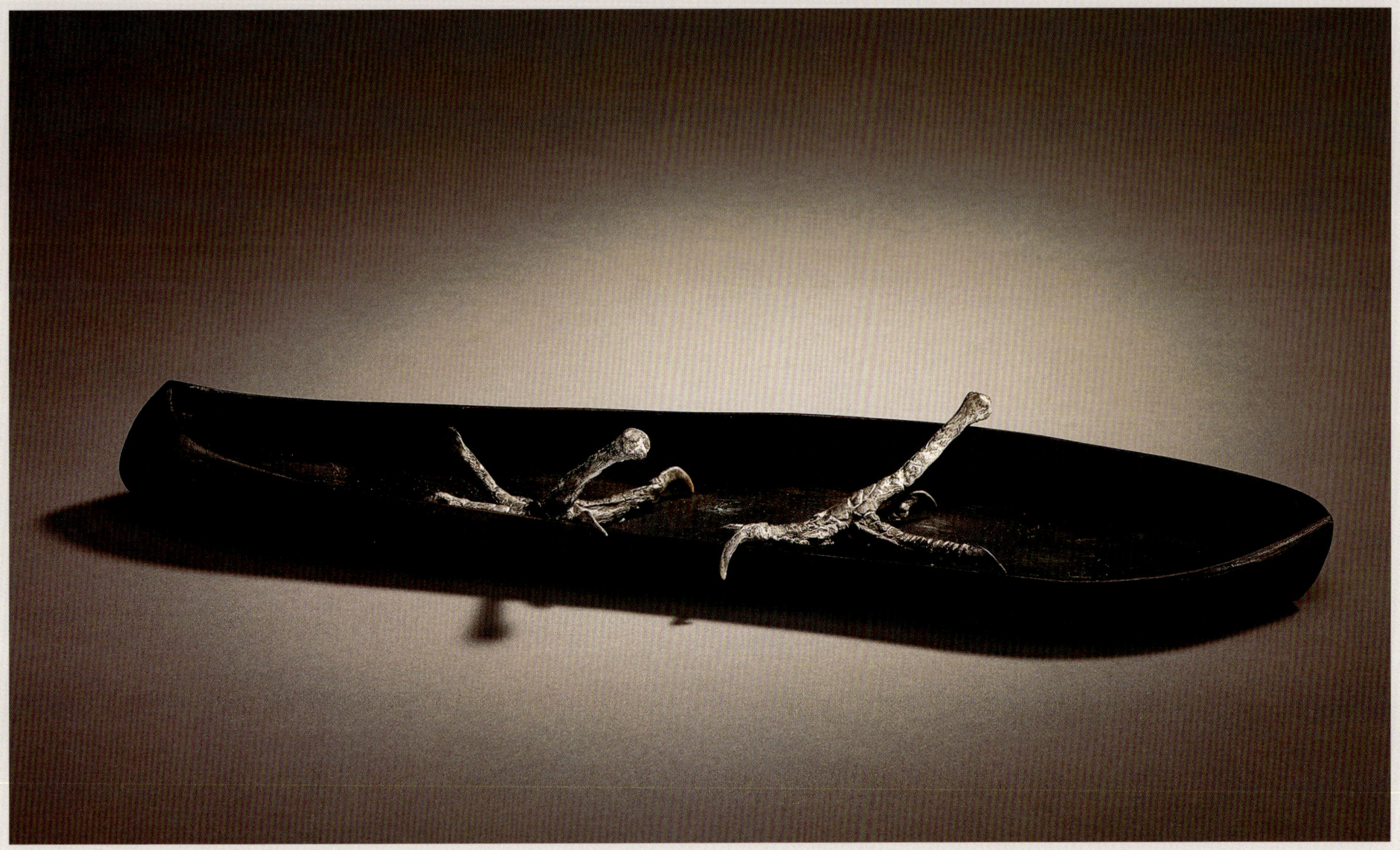

afterimage of when the midnight-black bird spread its wings and disappeared. In *Heron Drift* the narrow bark is bookended by Janus-like twin long-beaked figureheads mounted on the symmetrical prows. Here the vessel has become the body, and the body has become the passage.

While the catalogue of natural history that Morris draws on is much the same as that for indigenous Northwest carvers, she resists the highly stylized formline language that so many Anglo sculptors, smitten with the Northwest totem cultures, have embraced. Figures with a direct hand-shaped look appeal most to Morris, and her works are the testament of an artist who has achieved a language of her own.

A focal piece of the exhibition is Morris's *Fern Boat,* an eight-foot-long suspended canoe formed from dozens of overlapping fern fronds, hydro-cut from sheet bronze, welded into a lattice, and contoured to form the gently curving hull. The airiness of the uninhabited vessel sets the boat afloat in gravitationless space. Its regenerative imagery of identical repeating fronds lifts the funerary tone of the missing passenger to one of transcendence instead of loss. Ann Morris's ghosts are friendly ones who keep her good company as she molds her legacy in hot bronze.

Crow Boat

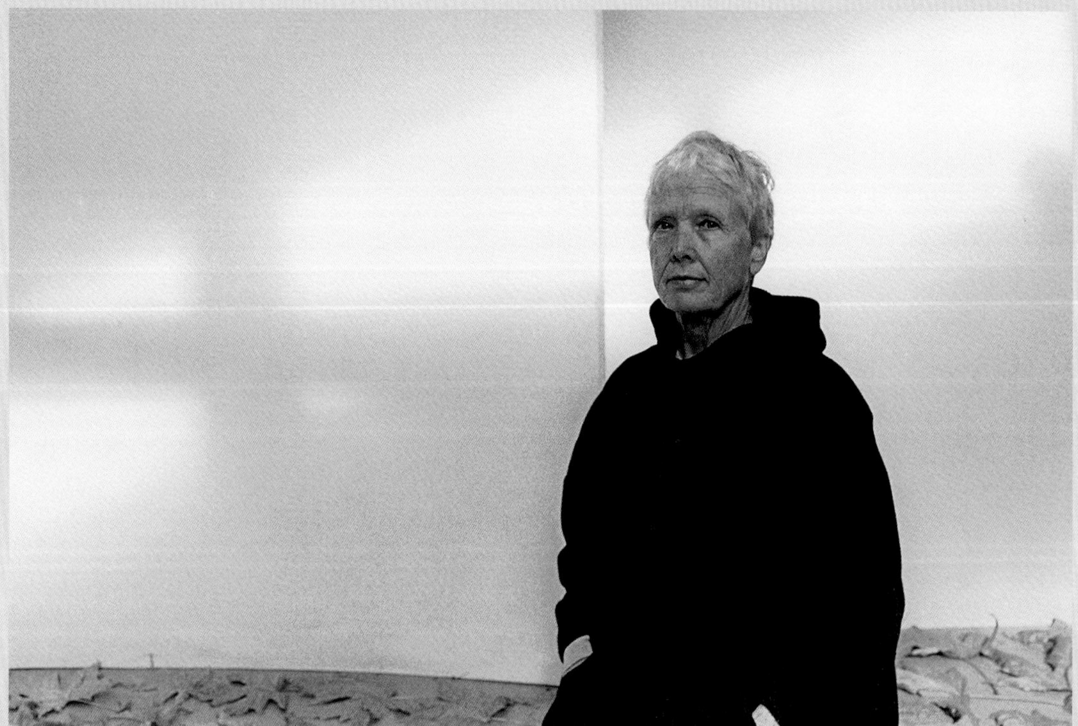

BIOGRAPHY

Born: New York, New York, 1934
Resides: Lummi Island, Washington

Education

1956 Pomona College, cum laude, B.A. Philosophy
1965 Pasadena Art Museum, Calif. Silkscreen/printmaking study with Guy Williams
1982 Women's Building, Los Angeles. Letterpress study with Susan King
1992 Riverdog Fine Arts Foundry, Chimacum, Wash. Bronze study with Tom Jay
1999 Bellingham, Wash. Anatomy study with Tom Sherwood

Teaching

1968–72 Pasadena Art Museum, Calif.

Awards & Accomplishments

2005 Award of Distinction/Grand Prize, Art Addiction Medial Museum, London
1999 Best of Show Jurors' Award, Big Rock Garden, Bellingham, Wash.
1985 Founding member of the Flintridge Foundation, Pasadena, Calif.
1973 Purchase Award, Dulin Gallery of Art, Knoxville, Tenn.
1969 Small Image Award, Santa Barbara Museum of Art, Calif.

Solo Exhibitions

2007 *Bronzes,* Lisa Harris Gallery, Seattle
Bone Journey, Island Museum of Art, Friday Harbor, Wash.
Ideal Forms, Foundry Gallery, Walla Walla, Wash.

2006 *Bone Journey,* Port Angeles Fine Arts Center, Port Angeles, Wash., and Gage Academy of Art, Seattle

2004 *Bone Journey,* Lucia Douglas Gallery, Bellingham, Wash.

2003 *Mindport,* Contemporary Arts and Crafts Gallery, Bellingham, Wash.

2001 *Bowls Full,* Lucia Douglas Gallery, Bellingham, Wash.

1987 *Arrangement of Twos,* Installation for Raw Space, ARC Gallery, Chicago

1986 Chrysalis Gallery, Western Washington University, Bellingham, Wash.

1982 *Self-Portraits,* Los Angeles Museum of Art

1981 *Shadow Waters,* Palos Verdes Art Center, Palos Verdes, Calif.

Duo Exhibitions

2006 Jeffrey Moose Gallery, Seattle; with paintings by Gerry Lonning

2005 *Vessels in Bronze,* Lucia Douglas Gallery, Bellingham, Wash.; with nature photographs by Mary Randlett
Miniatures/Monuments, Northwind Arts Center, Port Townsend, Wash.; with David Eisenhour

2004 *Bone Journey,* Stonington Gallery, Seattle; with works on paper by Rick Bartow
Bone Journey, Bronze Sculptures, Marghitta Feldman Gallery, Portland; with paintings by Jed Thomas

2001 *In the Garden of Myth and Logic,* Museum of Northwest Art, La Conner, Wash.; with paintings by Mary Henry

Group Exhibitions

Sculpture

2007 *Midsummer's Eve Art Walk,* Dunn Gardens, Seattle
Earth + Fire + Imagination, Gage Academy of Art: Steele Gallery, Seattle
Puget Soundscape, Stonington Gallery, Seattle
West Edge Sculpture Invitational, Seattle

2006 *5 from 56,* Pomona College Museum of Art, Claremont, Calif.
Winter Celebration, Stonington Gallery, Seattle
West Edge Sculpture Invitational, Seattle
Annual International Sculpture Exhibit, Big Rock Garden, Bellingham, Wash.
Inaugural Group Exhibition, The Art Mine, Port Hadlock, Wash.
La Conner Outdoor Sculpture Exhibition, La Conner, Wash.
Group Show, Foundry Gallery, Walla Walla, Wash.

2005 Annual International Sculpture Exhibit, Big Rock Garden, Bellingham, Wash. (invitational featured artist)
Create 2 Conserve, Jefferson Land Trust Invitational, Port Townsend, Wash.
Invitational, Department of Ecology, Olympia, Wash.
Art's Alive Invitational, La Conner, Wash.
Through the Eyes of the Northwest Coast Woman, Stonington Gallery, Seattle
West Edge Sculpture Invitational, Seattle

2004 On the Edge Sculpture Invitational, Seattle
7th Celebration of the Goddess, Jeffrey Moose Gallery, Seattle
Bellevue Sculpture Exhibition, Bellevue City Park, Bellevue, Wash.

2003 Outdoor Sculpture Garden, Redmond, Wash.
Viselaya Sculpture Competition, Carlisle, Mass.
Contemporary Sculpture at Chesterwood, Stockbridge, Mass.
3rd Invitational, Westcott Bay Institute, Friday Harbor, Wash.

2002 *Shadows and Reflections,* Edison Eye Gallery, Edison, Wash.
Group Sculpture Show, Bainbridge Arts & Crafts, Bainbridge Island, Wash.
2nd Invitational, Westcott Bay Institute, Friday Harbor, Wash.

2001 1st Invitational, Westcott Bay Institute, Friday Harbor, Wash.
Northwest Coast Sculpture, Stonington Gallery, Seattle

2000 *Small Works,* Lucia Douglas Gallery, Bellingham, Wash.
Art Outside, Port Angeles Fine Arts Center, Port Angeles, Wash.
New Work by Gallery Artists, Sylvia White Gallery, Santa Monica, Calif.; New York

1999 *Sculpture of the Spirit,* Forest Lawn Cemetery, Buffalo, New York
Beauty in the Beast, Maryhill Museum, Goldendale, Wash.
Annual International Sculpture Exhibit, Big Rock Garden, Bellingham, Wash. (Jurors' Award "Best of Show")
Western Michigan University Tour, Kalamazoo, Mich.

1998 Retrospective Group Show, Lucia Douglas Gallery, Bellingham, Wash.
Art of the Spirit, Forest Hills Cemetery, Boston
Bellevue Sculpture Exhibition, Bellevue City Park, Bellevue, Wash.
The Totally Sculpture Show, Port Townsend, Wash.

1997 *Contemporary Sculpture at Chesterwood,* Stockbridge, Mass.
Opening Exhibition, The Bronze Works, Shelton, Wash.

1996 Bellevue Sculpture Exhibition, Bellevue City Park, Bellevue, Wash.
16th Annual Northwest International Art Competition, Whatcom Museum of History and Art, Bellingham, Wash.

1995 *Cast at Riverdog,* Port Angeles Fine Arts Center, Port Angeles, Wash.
Northwest Sculpture Exhibition, Kirkland Library, Kirkland, Wash.

1988 Montgomery Art Gallery, Pomona College, Claremont, Calif.

1984 *From History to Action,* The Women's Building, Los Angeles

1983 *Globe Tire Building Show,* Gallery "8", Los Angeles

1981 *On Site,* water sculpture installation, Art Space, Los Angeles

1980 Water Sculpture Installation, Four Oaks Gallery, San Marino, Calif.
17 Contemporaries, Security Pacific Plaza, Los Angeles

1977 Water Sculpture Installation, Art Space, Los Angeles

1975 *Landscape '75,* Triad Gallery, North Hollywood, Calif.
Water Sculpture Installation, Baxter Art Gallery, California Institute of Technology, Pasadena, Calif.

1973 *An Exploration of Two Dimensions Coming Off the Wall,* Triad Gallery, North Hollywood, Calif.

Works on Paper

1991 *Cross Currents: Pacific Rim Book Show,* traveling exhibition

1987 *Artist's Books/Künstler-Bücher 1985–87,* San Francisco State University

1983 Katherine E. Nash Gallery, University of Minnesota, Minneapolis

1980 *Artists' Books and Drawings,* Art Works, Venice, Calif.
Friskets, Font, & Females: Contemporary Women Printers and Bookmakers, Denison Library, Scripps College, Claremont, Calif.

1978 *Perspectives,* Four Oaks Gallery, South Pasadena, Calif.

1969–79 Los Angeles Printmakers Society Juried National Exhibitions

1977 *'77 West Coast Experience,* Asahi Gallery, Tokyo

1974 *Works on Paper,* Los Angeles County Museum of Art
International Traveling Exhibition, Utah State University, Logan
California/Hawaii Regional 1974, Fine Arts Gallery of San Diego

1973 8th Dulin National Print & Drawing Show, Dulin Gallery of Art, Knoxville, Tenn. (purchase award)

1972–73 National Exhibition of Prints and Drawings, Oklahoma City, Okla.

1971 *Graphics '71,* West Los Angeles College, Los Angeles
Sky Show, University of California Art Gallery, Hayward, Calif.
Ninth Southern California Exhibition, Long Beach Museum of Art, Long Beach, Calif.

1970 Purchase Prize Competition, Laguna Beach Art Gallery, Laguna Beach, Calif.
California South Seven, Fine Arts Gallery at San Diego
All California Printmakers Show, Otis Art Institute, Los Angeles

1969 Small Image Show, Santa Barbara Museum of Art, Santa Barbara, Calif. (small image award)
All California Printmakers Show, Laguna Beach Museum of Art, Laguna Beach, Calif.
Dulin Print and Drawing Competition, Dulin Gallery of Art, Knoxville, Tenn.

Public and Corporate Collections: Sculpture

Big Rock Garden, Bellingham, Wash.
Hallie Ford Museum of Art, from the Collection of Bill Rhoades, Salem, Ore.
Museum of Northwest Art, La Conner, Wash.
The Whale Museum, Friday Harbor, Wash.

Public and Corporate Collections: Works on Paper

Aerojet General Corporation, La Jolla, Calif.
Bonaventure Hotel, Los Angeles
Coldwell Banker, Los Angeles
Collins Food International, Los Angeles
Commonwealth National Bank, Harrisburg, Pa.
Cushman & Wakefield, New York
Dulin Gallery of Art, Knoxville, Tenn.
Latham & Watkins, Atlantic Richfield Plaza, Los Angeles
Saks Fifth Avenue, Houston

Book Projects in Collections

J.F.K. Memorial Library, California State University, Los Angeles
Los Angeles Public Library
New York Public Library
Philosophy Department Library, Pomona College, Pomona, Calif.
Special Collections, Scripps College Library, Pomona, Calif.
Special Collections, University of California, Santa Barbara
University of Iowa, Iowa City
William Clark Memorial Library, University of California, Los Angeles

Bibliography

2007 "PAFAC at Twenty: Part II," *On Center* 19, no. 1 (January–March 2007), p. 7.
Russu, Petru, ed. *Famous* (World of Art Books), pp. 56–57.

2006 *Gage Academy of Art Summer Catalog 2006*, p. 5, Guest Artist.
"Hot Bronze, Cool Bones," *On Center* 18, no. 3 (August–October 2006), pp. 1–2.

2005 "Fine Lines: Drawing the Connection Between Bellingham's Beauty and Its Arts Community," *Whatcom Magazine*, Winter 2005, pp. 28–29.
Pucci, Carol. "Laid Back on Lummi," *Seattle Times*, April 24.
"Visual Arts Pick: Northwest Cast Women's Art," *Seattle Weekly*, November 16–22, 2005.

2004 Kangas, Matthew. "Visions of the Beauty, Power of the Female Form," *Seattle Times*, May 21.
McCaughan, Justin. "Big Rock Garden Park and Sculpting Success," *Whatcom Independent*.

2003 Bonenti, Charles. "Two Outdoor Juried Shows Emphasize Physicality Over Narrative," *Berkshire Eagle*.

2002 Adams, Evelyn. "Wild Talk," *Anacortes American*, July 17.
Cantor, Allyn, and Robert Peterson. "Sculpture Woods," *The Bear Deluxe Magazine*, no. 19 (Summer/Fall).

2001 "Bellingham Outdoor Art Next Tour Destination," *On Center*, April–June.
Seniuk, Jake. *In the Garden of Myth and Logic* (La Conner, Wash.).

2000 Seniuk, Jake. "A Place to See," *On Center*, May–June.

1998 Collins, Joan T. "Testament to the Spirit," *Boston Herald*, June 13.

1995 Mathews, Caitlin. "The Great Goddess: A Portrait of Presence," *Orion Magazine*, Summer.

1994 "Out of the Mold," *On Center*, Spring.

1988 Beebe, Marjorie Harth. *Art at Pomona 1887–1987: A Centennial Celebration*. Claremont, Calif.: Galleries of Claremont College.
Claremont Courier, March 5.
Pomona Today, Spring.

1987 McCracken, David. "Offbeat Arsarium Means Creepy-Crawly Art." *Chicago Tribune*, July 24.

1984 Moore, Louise. "Celebrating Women's Art," *Artweek*, June 9.

1981 Muchnic, Suzanne. Review of "On Site," *Los Angeles Times*.
Review of "Word Dreams," *Fine Print*, no. 7.

1980 Muchnic, Suzanne. "Los Angeles Contemporaries," *Los Angeles Times*.
Rosenthal, A. "Los Angeles Contemporaries," *Artweek*.

1977 "'77 West Coast Experience,
" *Asatti Gallery Publication*, no. 29 (Spring).

Library of Congress Cataloging-in-Publication Data
Lindberg, E. Theodore.
Sculpture woods : studio grounds of Ann Morris / Ted Lindberg, Jake Seniuk.
p. cm.
ISBN 978-0-295-98827-6 (hardcover : alk. paper)
1. Morris, Ann, 1934– —Themes, motives. 2. Art and mythology. 3. Symbolism in art. 4. Nature in art. 5. Outdoor sculpture—Washington (State)—Lummi Island (Island). I. Morris, Ann, 1934–. II. Seniuk, Jake. III. Title.
NB237.M6146L56 2006
730.92—dc22 2008002261

Published by
Museum of Northwest Art
P.O. Box 969
121 South First Street
La Conner, WA 98257
www.museumofnwart.org

Distributed by
University of Washington Press
P.O. Box 50096
Seattle, WA 98145-5096
www.washington.edu/uwpress

All photos by Robert Vinnedge unless otherwise noted.
Page 25: Gary Braasch
Jacket spine, endsheets, pages 3, 128–29 (background): John W. Hubbard
Pages 12–13 (all): Kevin Jones
Pages 14 (all), 16 (center), 18 (left), 26, 35–36, 73, 134 (bottom right): Dana Kershner
Pages 22–23, 37, 39: Mary Randlett
Page 128: Frank Ross

Map and icons by David Miller

Edited by Katherine Koberg and Marie Weiler
Proofread by Sharon Vonasch
Designed by John Hubbard
Separations by iocolor, Seattle
Produced by Marquand Books, Inc., Seattle
www.marquand.com
Printed and bound in China by 1010 Printing International, Ltd.